Burning with Love for God

Burning with Love for God

A Guide to the Spiritual Exercises of St. Ignatius

by

Paul C. DeCelles and M.F. Sparrow

Greenlawn Press

To Tom Noe, with sincere thanks for his invaluable help in the editing and production of *Burning with Love for God*.

ISBN: 978-0-937779-36-1

Second edition.

Copyright © 2017 by People of Praise, Inc. All rights reserved. Except for brief quotations in critical articles and reviews, no part of this book may be reproduced in any manner without prior written permission from the publisher. Write to Greenlawn Press, 107 South Greenlawn Ave., South Bend, IN 46617. Copies of this book can be ordered from the same address.

The Letter to Sister Teresa Rejadell is excerpted from *Letters of St. Ignatius of Loyola*, translated by William J. Young, S.J., (Loyola Press, 1959). Used with permission by Loyola Press. www.loyolapress.com.

Printed in the United States of America.

CONTENTS

Introduction		7
PART 1	AN OVERVIEW	
1.	Love, the Context of the Spiritual Exercises	11
2.	A Strategy for Decision-Making	23
3.	The History and Structure of the Exercises	39
PART 2	THE FIRST WEEK	
4.	Preliminaries	65
5.	Making Meditations	89
6.	Five Meditations	111
7.	Discernment of Spirits, First Week	135
PART 3	MEDITATIONS ON THE LIFE OF JESUS	
8.	Three Key Meditations	161
9.	The Graces of the Second, Third and Fourth Weeks	193
10.	Discernment of Spirits, Second Week	221
PART 4	DECISION-MAKING	
11.	Dispositions for Decision-Making	243
12.	Three Times To Make a Decision	271
13.	A Tool for Love	299
Appendix	Letter to Sister Teresa Rejadell	313
Notes		319
Index		333

INTRODUCTION

This is a book about Ignatius of Loyola's Spiritual Exercises. We are writing it for those who want to live and move and have their being as God's friend. While we are writing it for the sake of all of those who want to love their Creator and Father more, we are writing it specifically to directors. Our intended audience are those men and women who have the privilege and the responsibility of leading their brothers and sisters in Christ through the Spiritual Exercises. We are writing to Christ's servants and friends who have heard Him "recommending to them to seek to help all" by attracting them to the highest spiritual poverty, to actual poverty and to a desire for insults and contempt.[1]

This book is meant to be read with a copy of the *Spiritual Exercises* in hand. The *Spiritual Exercises* is itself a manual, a set of notes for people who are giving the retreat. Writing about the *Spiritual Exercises* is like trying to describe a piece of music using the written word. The written word is discursive; music is not. One doesn't experience the music of the *Spiritual Exercises* by reading the text. In fact, Ignatius never meant it to be given to the retreatant to read.[2] Similarly, we don't want to spoil the Exercises for people by giving them this book before they have experienced the Exercises for themselves. We have, however, found it useful to make this manual available to those who have successfully completed the Exercises.

We are aware of the irony of our present situation—writing a manual on a manual—but we need such a document. Why? In order to direct the retreat, a person needs to understand its inner workings. Ignatius, however, does not explain what he wrote or why it works so well. That it works is beyond doubt. The work of more than four centuries of Jesuits testifies to its efficacy. The Church is certainly indebted to the Spirit of God at work in Ignatius.

We believe this gem can be best understood and used by placing it in a suitable setting, namely, that of love. Set in the context of love of God and one another, the true brilliance of the Exercises shines forth in our day.

How did this book come about? We are members of the People of Praise, a charismatic, ecumenical, covenant community. Our life together has been profoundly shaped by the Exercises, as well as by the *Cursillo* and the charismatic movements. Over the years many of our young people have made the Exercises to discern their vocations. We wrote this book in order to train our directors more effectively. We often give a version of the Exercises in a four-day retreat, with each exercitant having his or her own director, sometimes followed by a Nineteenth Annotation retreat, but we have found that understanding the full 30-day retreat is foundational. This book is, therefore, about the 30-day retreat.

I

AN OVERVIEW

CHAPTER 1

LOVE, THE CONTEXT OF THE SPIRITUAL EXERCISES

In the *Spiritual Exercises* Ignatius does not often mention the love of God. In fact, in his Principle and Foundation he declares that "Man is created to praise, reverence, and serve God our Lord" (23), seemingly excluding the love of God and of one another from the fundamental purpose of human beings. Nevertheless, most people who have made the Exercises would probably say that the heart of the Exercises is love. They lead to union with God and with one another.

    By setting the Exercises in the context of love, we are changing them, but not substantially. Some might say we are subverting them, but we believe love is the fulfillment of the Exercises. Service and the obedience it entails are transformed through love. The imitation of Christ becomes participation in the life of Christ. Consolations are a movement of love which arise out of an encounter with God. The three kinds of humility become three kinds of love. Discerning the will of God becomes making a free choice out of love for God. The Spiritual Exercises are all about love. We want them to be read and studied and used in light of this context.

    So many people have written about love: poets, philosophers, theologians, novelists, songwriters, playwrights and so on. It's a difficult subject to write about because the one word "love" seems to have an incredible variety of meanings, perhaps as many meanings as there are people. We have, however, found one book in particular to be especially helpful in articulating and describing the experience of love. It's called *Love and Friendship* and it was written by a Jesuit, Jules Toner.[3] Here in this chapter and throughout the book our discussion of love will rely on and echo Toner's analysis of love.

In order to understand the Exercises, it's important to realize that there are different types of love. A person's love for another person—be it another human being or one of the three Persons of the Trinity—can be what we are calling "implemental love," "semipersonal love" or "personal love." Personal love is love in its most fundamental or radical sense. When a person experiences personal love for God, that love can, given the right conditions, develop into a friendship with God. Often, a person's love is actually a mixture of these three types of love, although usually one type or another predominates.

When I love another implementally, I am loving that person as someone who fulfills my own need. I can, for example, have implemental love for someone because he is useful in some way to me. I might love a leader as useful to the success of my cause, or I might love a business partner as necessary for the success of my business. I might love someone as a remedy to my loneliness or as a source of my own emotional fulfillment. I can also have implemental love for someone because of the pleasure his delightful qualities bring me. I might love someone because he makes me laugh and he's fun to be with. I might love someone because of his good looks or because he knows a lot about politics—and I love talking politics. This kind of implemental love is not very personal. It resembles the love someone might have for a favorite tool or treasured book.

Sometimes implemental love is easy to recognize, but sometimes it's not so easily discernible. For example, I might put a very high value on being a person who is very loving. I make every effort to treat people in a universally kind, encouraging and empathetic manner. However, if I really examine what is going on, I might discover that my encounters with other people are not about the other people; rather, they are all about me and my efforts to be a loving person. In fact, if I become really self-aware, I might discover that actually the people in my life exist at the periphery of my consciousness. They are like dim images on the horizon and they simply serve as things which prompt love to arise in me. It doesn't matter who I love; all that matters is that I love.

It's very common for a person's love of God to be primarily implemental. After all, no one can fulfill my needs as He can. He is the supreme collaborator; I love Him because

He is such a help to me. He helps me be righteous. He helps me seek justice. He gives my life meaning. He saves me from my sin. He guides my feet along the right path. Loving Him is good for my family. Because He is God, loving Him or at least showing Him due honor and respect is to my advantage. Worshipping Him brings me pleasure, and, given the right music and the right environment, it can be a genuine aesthetic experience. It's fun to delve into Scripture, and it's pleasing to make a good meditation. Besides, it's a pleasure to love Him: He's omnipotent, omniscient, all-wise and all-loving. He has so many admirable qualities. It's delightful and even exciting for me to be associated with someone so powerful; it's a privilege to love someone so perfect. It is, in fact, very difficult to move past implemental love for God precisely because He is so useful and pleasing to us. He is constantly fulfilling our needs, faithfully, without asking for anything in return.

Sometimes it's difficult to recognize the implemental nature of our love for God. I may generously devote much of my time and personal resources to serving Him, but if I stop and examine what I am doing I might realize that He is fulfilling my need to do something worthwhile and good with my life. I want to live a good life or a happy life, and loving God is the way to do so. I may be unaware of it, but I am relating to Him as the means to my ethical or psychological well-being. I might even declare that I want to be a saint, but again, if I become self-aware I might realize that my desire to love God and become holy is a way to fulfill my own desires. My effort to become a saint may be about me, and God is my helper in this enterprise. I'm not so intent on accomplishing my Father's purposes: rescuing this world from sin and filling it with His glory, His word, His wisdom, His Son. In fact, I hardly know Him; mostly I've heard about Him and read about Him. I have had few, if any, personal encounters with Him.

To say that implemental love is not very personal immediately casts a shadow over it. We naturally recoil at the thought of our love for someone being like the love we have for a tool or a favorite book. It is, however, a mistake to criticize all implemental love. It's not love in the radical sense of the word, but it is not unimportant. It greases the wheels of society, so to speak. Without it, our political, economic, social and religious life together would surely suffer. For example, implemental love is the basis of a lot of married love. It's the reason why many people get married—because it's so good for them. I want a family, a fuller life, the fulfillment and pleasure of the marriage relationship, a home and children. My spouse makes so much possible for me and does so much for me. Being married is such an advantage. Although it's not personal love, implemental love is not evil. Normally, we take very good care of those we love implementally and do them great good.

It appears that God is very willing to be loved implementally. We are in great need, and our God reveals Himself as the fulfillment of our needs. For example, on account of our sin we are in need of salvation, and God sends His Son into the world to be our Savior. We desire Him because we are in great need, and He takes that desire and works with it. He capitalizes on our implemental love and is willing to be loved as useful. We should never try to become indifferent to all the good our Father does for us just because implemental love is not love in its most radical aspect. In fact, even those who love God with personal love are not indifferent to all the pleasures and benefits that come from God. They love Him. It's unthinkable that they wouldn't delight in, take pleasure in and enjoy all the things He does for them and is for them. Great lovers of God aren't stoics, unmoved by all the good things in this world that come from God. Great lovers of God know that it brings Him joy to be useful to us, so they love Him as useful.

There is another type of love which we are calling "semipersonal love." When I love you with a semipersonal love, I am loving you as a person apart from any benefit you bring me. For example, I might love you because of your qualities, that is, because you are witty and wise, but not on account of the pleasure I get from your wit and the usefulness of your wisdom. Semipersonal love is born in me after I encounter you, experience you acting, speaking and doing things. I get an idea of the kind of person you are, and I begin to love you because of the kind of person you are. I love you as a generous, courageous and dependable person. I'm not loving you as a means to my well-being, as an implement or a tool. I am loving you as a person, in yourself, for yourself. This type of love is very common; we love many of the people around us with semipersonal love. Often, when a person talks about his affection for his classmates or co-workers or neighbors, he will talk about their good qualities.

Compared to implemental love, this second type of love is personal, but it's not the fullness of personal love. When I love you with semipersonal love, I am still relating to you as a spectator. There isn't much intimate sharing or mutual self-revelation going on. In fact, I can love you with semipersonal love without even having a genuine personal encounter with you. For example, imagine someone is your hero. You've observed him and studied him. Perhaps you've even met him. You are very aware of all his good qualities. Then one day you spend time with your hero and end up saying, "I didn't know you were a real person." Semipersonal love is real love, but personal love in its fullest or most radical sense involves more than loving someone on account of his or her good qualities.

Our love for God is often semipersonal. We love Him because of the kind of person He is: merciful, wise, faithful. We admire His qualities and love Him because of them. We might admire how hardworking Jesus was or how poor He was or how He constantly endured being insulted and criticized. We might love God our Father because He is all-knowing and all-powerful. This love for Him is real and even generative. At the same time, it might be the case that we haven't had a genuine personal encounter with Him yet. In some ways our semipersonal love for God is like a young person's love for his parents. His love isn't solely implemental. He loves his parents because of the kind of people they are, but the love isn't fully personal yet. In a certain sense he doesn't have the capacity to experience his parents as real people. After all, he knows next to nothing about their inward lives. He experiences their lives from his own perspective, but not from his parents' unique perspectives.

Although personal love is difficult to describe, most people have an instinct and a desire for it. We're not satisfied with being known and loved as a kind person or a generous person or a courageous person. After all, lots of people are kind, generous and courageous. We want to be loved on account of who we are. We want to be loved personally. We certainly aren't satisfied with being loved because we are useful or pleasant to be around. We aren't even satisfied with being loved on account of the kind of person we are. We long to hear the words, "*You* are the reason I love you." So, when we love someone with personal love, we aren't loving him for ourselves or for his good qualities. We are loving *him*—the full splendor of his personal reality. This is love in its most radical or fundamental sense.

Personal love arises in an encounter or a meeting with another person. In that encounter I experience that person acting: his words and deeds. I also experience the kind of person he or she is—his or her qualities—but sometimes I catch a glimpse of something more. I encounter a person who is revealed in his or her acts and qualities, but who is more than that, and I love that person.[4] It's relatively easy to talk about how useful someone is to me, and with some effort I can describe a person's qualities, but it is impossible to define a person. When I encounter someone personally I am encountering something indefinable. We can talk ceaselessly about someone, but everyone knows that words can't substitute for meeting the person.

We can love God, not on account of what He does for us and not on account of the kind of person He is, but simply because He is who He is. Our love for Him can become personal. When we love Him personally we aren't simply responding to His acts and gestures, nor to His wonderful qualities which are revealed in everything He does and has done. We are responding to Him. Such moments of personal love are profoundly intimate and difficult to talk about, but very real. Many people, although certainly not all, long for genuine personal encounters with God and want to love Him more and more personally. It's certainly true that God wants to be loved personally by us, not because it would be satisfying and fulfilling for Him, but because it's really good for us to love Him personally. He knows that we'll become alive in a way we didn't know was possible by loving Him in this way.

Ignatius of Loyola's Spiritual Exercises are an extremely effective tool for enkindling love of God. Some may embark on the Exercises and in the process see for the first time how useful God is and then begin to love Him that way—as useful. They begin to love Him as their Savior and their Lord. This love can be life-changing and may be the difference between heaven and hell for a person. Such people leave the retreat intent on obeying the laws of God and participating well in the Church. Others may embark on Ignatius's retreat, experience implemental love for God and then experience something more. They begin to see and relate to God as someone who is really admirable. They love Him for His traits and they want to imitate Him. They leave the retreat pursuing a life of virtue. Others experience even more. Somewhere in the retreat, God does something, and they catch a glimpse of Him, and they begin to love Him for His own sake. They leave the retreat identifying with their Savior's life and eager to participate in it. The other graces of the retreat pale in comparison to this one.

A person must of course cooperate in order to get something out of the Exercises, but their effectiveness is remarkable. People who are engaged in serious sin can embark upon the Exercises and come out of them with a new life centered around their personal love for God. People who want, sometimes desperately, to think of themselves as loving God but who aren't at all attracted to Jesus' personal life of insults and contempt, poverty and humility as portrayed in the Gospel can come out of the Exercises changed. They end up wanting to share their Lord's life in every way and even asking to share His poverty and humiliations. They find themselves accepting and admiring God's revelation of Himself in Jesus and beginning to love both Jesus and His Father personally. Some people who do the Exercises take small steps toward personal love of God. Others come out of the Exercises ablaze with love on account of one or several personal encounters with their Lord.

As desirable as it is, in and of itself, personal love for God can also be the building block for something more. When a person experiences personal love for God, that love can, given the right conditions, develop into a friendship with God. "Friendship" is another one of those words, like "love," which can mean different things to different people. When we say "friendship" we aren't referring to acquaintances hanging out together, no matter how much they love each other with some mixture of implemental, personal and semipersonal love. We aren't even referring to people who experience many moments of personal love, but whose lives run, so to speak, on parallel tracks. Rather, we have in mind a relationship where two people have "one life lived wholly by each and wholly by both together" (Toner, p. 255). We are thinking of a relationship in which two people have each other's life in common.[5]

The unity that is present in friendship is very difficult to talk about. Sometimes, when people do talk about it, it sounds as if one person becomes larger than life, and the other fades into the background. As wonderful as it is, poetic language sometimes gives this impression. "He is everything," a poet or songwriter might say. The unity that friends experience doesn't come about because one person becomes everything, be it by domination or by self-abnegation. Friends become one, yet remain distinct persons. One thinks, of course, of the Trinity: three persons, but they are one.

One of the best or at least most useful descriptions of friendship we've found is by the philosopher Michel de Montaigne (1533-1592):

> In the friendship I speak of, the souls mix and work themselves into one piece with so perfect a mixture that there is no more sign of a seam by which they were first conjoined. . . . The union of such friends, being really perfect, deprives them of all acknowledgment of mutual duties, and makes them loathe and banish from their conversation words of separation and distinction, benefit, obligation, acknowledgment, entreaty, thanks, and the like; all things—wills, thoughts, opinions, goods, wives, children, honors and lives—being in effect common between them; and that absolute concurrence of affections being no other than one soul in two bodies (according to that very proper definition of Aristotle), they can neither lend nor give anything to one another.[6]

Friends who "hate and banish from their conversation words of separation and distinction" don't speak of "my life" and "your life." They speak of "our life." It's not "my success" and "your success." It's "our success." They have the life of one another in common. They share everything: all they possess, all they think, all they feel, all they do and all they are. They are one.

The Spiritual Exercises can take a person to the place where the exercitant and his Lord have the life of one another in common. They are a tool not only for enkindling personal love but also for building friendship with God. If a person continues to do the Exercises even after he has finished the retreat, he can within a year or two begin to experience a measure of true friendship with his Lord and God. Friendship isn't, of course, a goal to be achieved; it's a way of life that becomes deeper and richer as time passes.

At this point it's tempting to expound more on friendship, especially friendship with God. We hope to do so in a future work, but for now the topic is the Exercises. It is, however, very important to realize that the Exercises are ultimately all about personal love for God and even friendship with God. The Exercises are like a path. It's important to know where this path is headed; otherwise, the director and the exercitant might stop along the way, mistakenly thinking they have reached the final destination. For example, for some exercitants the move from implemental love to semipersonal love for God can be very labor-intensive. Since implemental love is rooted in a radical love for self, their experience of the Exercises involves a radical turning from self toward God. They can then mistakenly conclude that the Exercises are all about overcoming and conquering one's self. They mistake a step along the way as the final destination. Likewise, many exercitants are dazzled by their Lord's many good qualities and want to imitate Him. This is a wonderful fruit of the Exercises, but it's a mistake to conclude that the Exercises are only about imitating the Lord and growing in virtue. After all, imitation implies words of separation and distinction. The Exercises are ultimately all about shared life. Likewise, exercitants who are consoled with an experience of personal love for their Lord need to know that even more is possible. They can be one with their Lord habitually, as friends are with each other. The Spiritual Exercises are a tool. In order to use this tool well, it's imperative for the director to be aware of everything it can do.

Is friendship with God really possible? Can a human being be friends with God? Is it really possible for two such radically different beings to live one life? Can two people be friends, one of whom is submitted to the other? It looks like Jesus lived one life with His Father, all the while acknowledging and submitting to His Father's authority. It's not too hard to imagine Him saying to His Father, "Your ways are my ways. All that you have and possess, all that you are, all that you think and do—it's all mine in you." And one can imagine God the Father saying the same to Jesus. It would appear, then, that friendship can exist between two persons, one of whom has authority over the other, but the more fundamental question remains: Can a human being be friends with God?

The short answer is yes. In Christ, as Christ, friendship with God our Father is a real possibility. We are something more than mere mortals. For "if anyone is in Christ, he is a new creation."[7] Or, as the *Catechism of the Catholic Church* points out, quoting Pius XII, "To this Spirit of Christ, as an invisible principle, is to be ascribed the fact that all the parts of the body are joined one with the other and with their exalted head; for the whole Spirit of Christ is in the head, the whole Spirit is in the body and the whole Spirit is in each of the members" (797). With Jesus and on account of Jesus, reality has changed. We are a new creation, as St. Paul said, and we have the whole Spirit of God. In the centuries following Paul, the great Fathers of the Church elaborated on this revelation. The Catholic Church offers us some of their reflections in the *Liturgy of the Hours*:

> Our nature is transformed so that we are no longer merely men, but also sons of God, spiritual men, by reason of the share we have received in the divine nature.[8]

> Through the Spirit we acquire a likeness to God; indeed, we attain what is beyond our most sublime aspirations—we become God.[9]

> My dear brethren, there is no doubt that the Son of God took our human nature into so close a union with himself that one and the same Christ is present, not only in the firstborn of all creation, but in all his saints as well. The head cannot be separated from the members, nor the members from the head.[10]

> Just as the trunk of the vine gives its own natural properties to each of its branches, so, by bestowing on them the Holy Spirit, the Word of God, the only-

> begotten Son of the Father, gives Christians a certain kinship with himself and with God the Father...."[11]

Is it possible for a person to be a friend of God? Yes. After all, as the author of 2 Peter boldly proclaims, we "share the divine nature" (1:4, NJB). Not only is friendship with God possible, it looks like it is our baptismal birthright. Perhaps it is more accurate to say that friendship with God is the conscious realization of our baptismal identity. Of course, these passages from our forefathers in the faith beg for theological reflection, but at the very least they proclaim a hope: a hope of glory, "Christ in you" (Col. 1:27).

CHAPTER 2

A STRATEGY FOR DECISION-MAKING

Since the Spiritual Exercises are a tool for enkindling love for God, it's not surprising that the exercitant spends the majority of his time meditating on events in the life of Jesus. What is perhaps surprising is the role decision-making plays in the Exercises. Quite a few of the exercises are aimed at preparing the exercitant for making good decisions, teaching him how to make good decisions and giving him the opportunity to make some decisions during the Exercises, if he so desires. For Ignatius, making decisions is a way to build a relationship with God. This is one of his greatest insights—a stroke of spiritual genius, so to speak. Love grows, and friendships develop, because friends are constantly making decisions, large and small, for the other and for the relationship. Ignatius knew that people can be united with Christ in and through their meditations, but he also thought that people can be united with Christ in and through their decision-making.

The bulk of Ignatius's teaching on decision-making is located in the *Spiritual Exercises* under the rubric of "making an election." It's common to refer to Ignatius's materials as his teaching on discerning God's will; however, we prefer to think of this material as Ignatius's teaching on making decisions or choices. The phrase "discerning God's will" has too many connotations which open the door to serious misunderstanding.

Although decision-making is only a part of the Exercises, misunderstanding what Ignatius has to say about this area can, in fact, color one's whole understanding of the Exercises. Because it is so easy to misunderstand what Ignatius is saying, we need to spend some time describing his theory of decision-making before doing anything else. We'll save the particulars about how to make a good decision for later chapters.

For Ignatius, every decision, every choice, is an opportunity for love. The exercitant can use his decisions and his actions which flow from his decisions to build friendship with God. Throughout his life the exercitant will have to make decisions: about what he does or doesn't do for a living, about where he lives, about his standard of living, about how much to give in alms, about his state in life, and so on. Ignatius wants to teach the Christian to make each of these decisions—indeed, all of his decisions—on account of love for God. The Christian should never have to ask what the love of God has to do with his work, his family, his studies or his spending money. Quite literally the love of God can guide everything he does. The Christian can eventually love and serve God *in* all things, which is the grace the exercitant asks for in the last and crowning exercise, the Contemplation To Attain Love (233).

How can a person be sure he is deciding to do something out of love for God? For example, how can he be sure that he is choosing, say, going to dental school out of love for God? How can he be sure that moving to a bigger house is for the honor and glory of God and not merely for his own ease and comfort? After all, if a person really wants something, it's not all that hard to come up with reasons why it will serve God. It's easy to fool oneself.

The experienced director knows how easily people can fool themselves into thinking they are doing something for God. It's common for people to choose what they want and then try to find a way to serve and love God in what they have chosen. So, to continue with the dentistry example, a person might first decide to pursue dentistry and afterward find ways to serve God in his chosen career. When making a decision, these people want God "to come to what they desire, and they do not decide to give up the sum of money in order to go to God" (154). They want to involve God in their decision by trying to convince themselves that what they want is the best thing they can do to love God. As we'll see later, Ignatius says that people like this belong to "the second class of men" (154).

So how can a person be sure that love of God is inspiring his decision? Ignatius has a very effective strategy, but it isn't easily understood on account of the language he uses. In order to choose something out of love for God, a person must, says Ignatius, make himself "indifferent to all created things" (23). What does this mean? It means that, when faced with a choice, say, to go to dental school or to accept a certain job offer, a person strives for a state of mind in which he prefers neither dental school nor the job offer. It means getting himself to a state of mind in which he prefers neither x nor y. In Ignatius's words, "I neither desire nor am I inclined to have riches rather than poverty, to seek honor rather than dishonor, to desire a long life rather than a short life" (166, see also 23). Often in the Ignatian literature people who are indifferent are described as being "detached."

When Ignatius recommends that people become indifferent, he isn't recommending that they become apathetic and convince themselves not to care about anything. Quite the contrary. Indifferent people in the Ignatian sense are full of desire. They care passionately. It's just that they care passionately about one thing only—whatever will serve, honor and glorify God. Indifferent people make efforts—huge efforts, in fact—to want neither x nor y "unless the service of God our Lord alone move them to do so" (155). One student of the Spiritual Exercises compared the indifferent man to a coiled spring: "Psychologically, indifference is not a static attitude. It is a state of dynamic equilibrium or balance between conflicting tensions. Like a coiled spring, the will retains all its energy and awaits only an orientation to spring into action."[12] The indifferent person isn't desireless; he is full of desire. He wants whatever will help his Lord be louder, brighter and firmer in this world. Ignatius puts it this way: his "one desire and choice should be what is more conducive to the end for which we are created" (23).

It's very important for the director and the exercitant to know and understand that indifference isn't about being unfeeling. It's about being in a place before the Lord where nothing is out of the question. "I have learned, in whatever state I am, to be content. I know how to be abased, and I know how to abound; in any and all circumstances I have learned the secret of facing plenty and hunger, abundance and want. I can do all things in Him who strengthens me" (Phil. 4:11-13).

The indifferent man experiences great freedom on account of his "one desire and choice." When someone gets to the point of indifference, he's then in a good place to choose something that will build his friendship with God. He can discern what will be more conducive to the honor and glory of God. Love for God will determine his choice.

Most people don't embark upon the Spiritual Exercises in a state of detachment. The typical exercitant doesn't come to the Exercises indifferent. On some occasions, perhaps, his love for God inspires a choice, but most of the time other loves determine his choices. Love for music or beauty or sports may inspire his choices. Or he chooses on account of his love for adventure and the thrill of being on the front lines. Or he makes the decisions he does because the success of his children is his number one priority. He may order his life around his love for recreation or fine food or even good health. Or money determines many of the choices he makes.

The typical exercitant doesn't usually regard all things—money, sports, success, beauty, art, and so on—in such a way that he prefers only what will enable him to love and serve God the most. Usually he's inclined, sometimes strongly, in one particular direction. He has an attachment which prevents him from being indifferent. Ignatius calls such attachments "inordinate." When something other than God inspires people's choices—when they are living for money or music or computers and ordering their lives around these loves—their lives are out of order. God created them for friendship with himself, not for money, music or knowledge.

Often, when talking about inordinate attachments and becoming indifferent by ridding oneself of them, people will begin to argue for the morality of the thing they desire inordinately. They might ask, for instance, what's wrong with music or beauty or sports? The answer is that nothing is wrong with them. They are all legitimate and good things. If I'm inordinately attached, the problem isn't with the things I desire. The problem is with me. My loves are out of order. I've got some attachment that is competing with my attachment to God or has even displaced it. I'm taking something God intended as a tool for loving Him and making it my end.

The Exercises were designed to help people deal with their inordinate attachments and put their lives in order. They "have as their purpose the conquest of self and the regulation of one's life in such a way that no decision is made under the influence of any inordinate attachment" (21). In other words, they are designed to help people make every decision in such a way that it is made out of love for their Lord and eventually in union with their Lord.

Ignatius has a twofold strategy for helping someone overcome his inordinate attachments and experience the freedom of indifference. The first prong of his strategy involves helping him become detached. The second prong consists of providing many opportunities for the love between the exercitant and his Lord to be enkindled and grow. Ignatius wants to help the exercitant become more and more attached to the Lord. In the Exercises he pursues these two goals simultaneously.

In order to overcome the exercitant's inordinate attachments and reach a place of indifference, Ignatius offers an aggressive tactic commonly referred to in the literature as *agere contra*, to act against. If someone perceives he is inclined to one thing over another, Ignatius recommends that he stir up feelings for the very thing he is not inclined to choose. The introductory notes to the *Spiritual Exercises* contain a good description of this strategy. Ignatius has just commented on how important it is for the director to allow the Creator to deal directly with the creature, and then he says:

> For this—namely, that the Creator and Lord may work more surely in His creature—it is very expedient, if it happens that the soul is attached or inclined to a thing inordinately, that one should move himself, putting forth all his strength, to come to the contrary of what he is wrongly drawn to. Thus if he inclines to seeking and possessing an office or benefice, not for the honor and glory of God our Lord, nor for the spiritual well-being of souls, but for his own temporal advantage and interests, he ought to excite his feelings to the contrary, being instant in prayers and other spiritual exercises, and asking God our Lord for the contrary, namely, not to want such office or benefice, or any other thing, unless His Divine Majesty, putting his desires in order, change his first inclination for him, so that the motive for desiring or having one thing or

another be only the service, honor, and glory of His Divine Majesty.[13]

So, the core of Ignatius's *agere contra* strategy involves the exercitant perceiving that he is inclined to one thing over another and then proceeding "to excite his feelings to the contrary." This is a way to battle his inordinate attachments.

Let's take some modern examples. Say that I'm trying to decide whether to join a missionary company or to go to graduate school. I want to make my decision out of love for God, but I can't yet say that I am in a place, psychologically, where all things are equally possible. I can't say that I neither desire nor am inclined to seek graduate school rather than working in the mission field, to live close to my family rather than far from them, to seek a private school education for my children rather than a public school education. If I am trying to get to a place of indifference, balanced between two choices, not inclining one way or another, wanting only to love and be friends with my King, and I perceive that I have some inordinate attachments, what do I do? Excite feelings to the contrary by praying for the contrary thing. "Lord, ever since I was in high school I wanted to work in the mission field, but choose me to go to graduate school. O what an honor to labor ingloriously for you." Or I might pray, "Lord, choose me to go on mission even if I have to send my children to public schools. O Lord, what a grace, to place my children totally in your hands." If the exercitant perceives that he is very much inclined to live near his family, he could pray, "Lord, choose me to leave behind father and mother, brothers and sisters, for the sake of your kingdom, just as you did."

Such prayers are a leap of faith for the exercitant. They are a way for him to place himself entirely in his Lord's hands. This strategy of *agere contra* is an exercise in stretching the imagination. It's an opportunity to envision oneself in a totally different kind of life. By praying for the opportunity to go to graduate school or to send his children to public school or to move away from family, the exercitant is psychologically putting himself in those situations, so that he can go there if that's what love calls for.

The strategy of *agere contra* appears in several important meditations in the Exercises. At one point, about a quarter of the way into the Exercises, the exercitant considers a man who responds with great love to the call of Christ the King. Such a man hears the call of Christ the King to labor with Him and even suffer with Him. He wants to be with his King. He finds Him very attractive. He even wants to labor in the dirtiest, foulest trenches, if that is where his King is. Of course, such people answer the call of their King and offer themselves for the work, but they do more. They also act "against their own sensuality and against their carnal and worldly love" (97, Mullan). They want to tame any excessive loves: of ease and comfort, of good food, rest and relaxation, of good movies and beautiful things, etc. In other words, they want to act against anything in themselves that might get in the way of hearing and responding to the call of their King. They are, after all, inflamed with love for Him.

The *agere contra* strategy also appears at other points in the Exercises. In the meditation on the Two Standards, Ignatius paints a picture of two camps: Satan's camp and the Lord's camp. Satan recruits people to his camp by offering them riches and the empty honors of the world and then ensnares them with pride. Christ Jesus offers His recruits poverty, insults and contempt, and humility. In Chapter 8 we'll discuss this quite astonishing picture of Christ's strategy for saving the world. For now, however, it's enough to note that Ignatius has the exercitant pray three times at the end of the meditation for the grace to be received under the Lord's standard,

> first in the highest spiritual poverty, and—if His Divine Majesty would be served and would want to choose and receive me—not less in actual poverty; second, in suffering contumely and injuries, to imitate Him more in them, if only I can suffer them without the sin of any person, or displeasure of His Divine Majesty (147, Mullan).

As we'll see more clearly later, the exercitant is praying to be with the one he loves and to join Him in His life.

If someone finds himself feeling a repugnance to poverty, so that he is not in fact indifferent to poverty or riches, Ignatius has him pray and plead and beg the Lord for poverty. He lays this strategy out very clearly in a note: "When we feel a tendency or repugnance against actual poverty, when we are not indifferent to poverty and riches, it is very helpful, in order to crush such disordered tendency, even though corrupt nature rebel against it, to beg our Lord in the colloquies to choose us to serve Him in actual poverty. We should insist that we desire it, beg for it, plead for it, provided, of course, that it be for the service and praise of His Divine Goodness" (157; this translation is a combination of Mullan and Puhl). Ignatius is saying to the exercitant, if the thought of poverty is difficult, ask for poverty. If he finds the thought of insults and contempt unbearable, ask for insults and contempt—*agere contra*.

Often, when people unfamiliar with the Exercises discover that Ignatius directs a person to pray for poverty, insults and contempt, they think this exercise is simply insane or even masochistic. Ignatius's strategy isn't crazy or sick. He's trying to lead the exercitant to a place where all things are possible. He wants the exercitant to be able to stand before his Lord and say, "I'm not ruling anything out, Lord. Whatever will serve you, I'm willing to do." "All things are possible to him who believes" (Mk. 9:23).

The goal in decision-making is to be in a balance before one's choices, indifferent about one's options, because the thing that one desires, the only thing that one really desires, is to make a decision inspired by love for one's Lord. The person doesn't desire poverty more than wealth, insults more than honor, etc. In fact, sometimes people can fall into the trap of becoming inordinately attached to poverty and dishonor. Actually, what's usually going on is that they are inordinately attached to being the best at whatever they do. They want to seem to be the best Christian. So, for example, they think that being poor with Jesus, or being celibate, is the best form of the Christian life. Then they choose to be poor or celibate. One time we met a woman who was inordinately attached to poverty. She chose to go to a third world country to be with the poor, but it wasn't a decision in the Lord. She was driven by her inordinate attachment, not by her Lord.

The exercitant should be attached to the Lord, not to poverty and humiliations. He should get to a place where he can say, "I can live either way: rich or poor, honored or dishonored." Then he can use his decision-making and his actions to build friendship with God. He also becomes a good soldier, able to make decisions in the fray, so to speak. For example, when Francis Xavier first went to Japan he wore a worn-out cassock, but when he appeared before the Japanese nobility they scorned him and laughed at him, so the next time he appeared in court he came dressed in finery. He wasn't attached to his poverty and was able to see that changing his clothes would further God's work. In the late 1800s Hudson Taylor, the founder of the China Inland Mission, also faced a decision about how he was going to dress. He had been living in China for several years trying to evangelize the Chinese. He was not very successful until he abandoned his Western clothes and adopted the hairstyle and clothing of a Chinese peasant. All the other missionaries ostracized him for this move, but it turned out to be the key to successful evangelization.

Hudson Taylor was like the man in the meditation on the Kingdom of Christ, the one who, inflamed with love, acts against anything in himself that might get in the way of being detached. In preparation for responding to his King's call, the man in the meditation acts against his sensuality and his carnal and worldly love. For years before going to China, Hudson Taylor lived in poverty, fasted, slept on the floor and accepted insults and contempt gladly so that he would be ready to go to China. His *agere contra* paid off, because when he got to China he was able to see what the other missionaries were unable to see—the importance of dressing like a native—and he was able to embrace the humiliation entailed in his change of costume and hairstyle.

Because it is sometimes such a big effort to identify and act against one's inordinate attachments, people can mistakenly think that this is what the Spiritual Exercises are all about. They begin the Exercises and are quickly consumed with conquering and subduing the flesh. In other words, they take the battle against inordinate attachments as an end in itself instead of a means to an end. There is a very real danger of turning the Exercises into a program for one's own perfection: I've got to be perfectly in order, perfectly detached, etc.[14] Overcoming one's inordinate attachments is an essential subplot in the Exercises, but not the main story. The Exercises are all about building and maintaining a relationship of love.

Overcoming inordinate attachments is, then, just one component of Ignatius's strategy for decision-making. The second component involves strengthening the bonds of love and affection between the exercitant and his Lord. That's one of the reasons Ignatius has a person spend so much time meditating on the Gospels. The meditations are designed to help a person know the Lord more so that he can love Him more, follow Him more closely and respond to His sorrows and His joy as a friend would. In fact, decisions are the fruit of the love between the exercitant and the Lord. Pedro Arrupe, S.J., expresses this well in the following poem:

> Nothing is more practical than finding God.
> That is,
> Than falling in love in a quite absolute, final way.
> What you are in love with, what seizes your
> imagination, will affect everything.
> It will decide what will get you out of bed in the
> morning,
> What you will do with your evenings,
> How you spend your weekends,
> What you read,
> Who you know,
> What breaks your heart,
> and
> What amazes you with joy and gratitude.
> Fall in Love, stay in Love and it will decide everything.[15]

This is really an extraordinary vision of decision-making. The most important questions for the exercitant aren't what is the right thing to do or what is the best thing to do or what is the most reasonable thing to do or even what do you want me to do. The fundamental questions for the exercitant are: What can I do out of love for my Lord, how can I build our (embryonic) friendship, and what do you, Lord, want to do? The exercitant can't answer these questions by himself. They presuppose another person. Being in and acting out of a living relationship of love is the cornerstone of Ignatius's decision-making method.

In order to grasp the length and breadth and depth of Ignatius's vision, it's important to realize there are other good ways to make decisions, ways that avoid some of the risks that come with making decisions in the context of a living relationship of love. One common method for making decisions involves taking a universal principle such as "do good," "seek justice" or "love your neighbor" and then figuring out what to do in a particular circumstance. In other words, making decisions involves applying universal principles to particular circumstances. The universal principles can come from a variety of sources: Christian tradition, family tradition, popular culture or Scripture. For example, a person might read the Gospels and then abstract lessons from them. His reasoning might go something like this: Jesus was born in a stable. He humbled Himself. Therefore humility has to be a part of my life, and in this instance I should humble myself by turning the other cheek. Wherever the ethical norms come from, the person uses them, often balancing them against each other, to arrive at a decision about what to do in a particular instance.

It's worth taking note that this method of decision-making can give a person a certain independence from God. A person receives or develops a set of principles for acting. He can then sit back and run his life according to the principles. He's got a manual for acting and doesn't usually need to consult the author. Instead of relating to God in an ongoing and personal way, he just follows the principles. He may relate to God about all sorts of things—especially his emotional life—but not about the choices and decisions he is making.

If this person does relate to God at all in his decision-making, it's as an occasional help when he can't figure out what to do by himself. For example, someone might turn to God and ask, should I be humble and accept this injustice or should I speak out against it? It's hard to decide because sometimes Jesus speaks out very strongly, and other times he chooses to be silent. In such a case the logic required to apply general principles to the particular instance is especially complex, so the person turns to God and asks for help. Normally the person can figure out what to do, but occasionally he needs help. He's relating to God as a means—as his helper—and he's glad for the help.

Ignatius's method of decision-making does not revolve around reasoning from general principles. When the exercitant makes a decision, he isn't following a set of principles, he's relating to a person. Following a set of principles might be very attractive for some people because it involves more autonomy and less risk than relating to and following a person, but Ignatius would say that what a person needs to know to make a decision can't be written in an ethics manual or captured by a set of general principles. It comes from being in a living relationship with the Lord.

Decision-making turns out to be very personal. Decisions arise out of a relationship of love, and in each relationship of love the love is as unique as the persons loving. For example, what God and Joe decide to do in a particular situation will be different from what God and Sam decide to do in a similar situation, because Joe and Sam are different people with different histories, temperaments, characters, gifts and limitations.

Not all decision-making methods are so personal. Sometimes when people talk about decision-making they have in mind a method which involves a deliberation about what is better or best in a particular situation. For example, a recent college graduate might try to decide whether being in the mission field is better than going to graduate school. Or a college student might try to decide where he is going to live for the summer by figuring out whether it is more for the glory of God for a person—any person—to live in a household with other adults rather than with one's nuclear family. If he decides it is better to live in a household and then meets someone in similar circumstances who decided it was better to live with his family, he may legitimately wonder who is right. Other people's decisions become confusing or even threatening for him. Or if he decides that one course of action is better than the other, he is then faced with a potentially difficult and even morally troublesome decision: is he going to do the best thing or not?

Ignatius's method of decision-making does not, however, involve desiring and choosing what is more for the glory of God in the abstract. He doesn't lead a person to make a decision which has to be applicable to many people. In fact, the kind of decision Ignatius envisions is a very personal one. The best becomes what is best for the Lord and the person—given who each of them is and given the particular circumstances surrounding the decision.

So far, we've seen that Ignatius's strategy for decision-making involves overcoming one's inordinate attachments and stirring up love for God. Ideally, decisions are the fruit of love between the exercitant and his Lord. It's not surprising that the process of decision-making is very personal. What is perhaps more surprising is that the process is also collaborative. Ignatius doesn't lose sight of the fact that God is in authority, and the exercitant is under His authority, but he also envisions the Christian as a free and responsible decision-maker. The Spiritual Exercises provide the opportunity for a person to exercise his decision-making capacity with and in and for Christ Jesus.

Obedience to God's commandments is a sine qua non for Ignatius. It's the doorway to the Christian life and Christian decision-making. Nevertheless, Ignatius's method of decision-making doesn't revolve around the Christian receiving God's directions for each and every detail of his life and then obeying them. Although he does teach the exercitant how to recognize the voice of his Lord, Ignatius isn't teaching the exercitant how to get better and better at hearing directions for what he is to do in the concrete circumstances of his life. He's actually providing the occasion and the teaching necessary for the exercitant to become more of an acting person in this world, capable of being a friend to his Lord and Master.

When some people talk about Christian decision-making, they frequently speak in terms of "discerning God's will." They have in mind a process whereby they discover or God reveals what He has in mind for their particular situation.[16] "Lord, do you want me to go to Notre Dame or Indiana University? Please tell me." The process of finding out what He has in mind is daunting, to say the least. They wonder, Will the Lord tell me what He wants me to do? Will I be able to hear Him? Will it be something I want to do? This particular model of Christian decision-making seems to presuppose that God has something particular in mind for a person's decision. It assumes that He has a plan, and that the decision-maker is supposed to find out what that plan is. A good decision becomes one where the decision-maker correctly discerns God's plan, and a bad decision becomes one where the decision-maker is mistaken about God's plan. This way of thinking about decision-making can also make it seem as if drawing closer to God increases one's chances of "having to do" what one is loath to do. For the lucky ones, God's will is the same as their will, but the unlucky ones have to deny themselves and submit their wills to His will. We like to call this the "command and obey" model of decision-making.

Those who subscribe to a command-and-obey model of decision-making frequently face certain quandaries and temptations. For example, it's difficult to figure out how often and in what kind of circumstances they should attempt to discover God's will. Should they try to find out what He has in mind for where they go to school? For what they major in? For what classes they take? For whether they do their calculus homework tonight or their chemistry homework? One has to wonder, do Jesus' disciples really look for and receive marching orders for every detail of their lives? And if so, what about personal responsibility?

It's tempting, especially for people overwhelmed or terrified by a difficult decision, to relate to God in order to escape personal responsibility for their decision-making. Those who subscribe to a command-and-obey model of decision-making are in danger of becoming servile—never taking any initiative and never taking responsibility for their actions and intentions. For example, when faced with a difficult decision they might beg God, "Just tell me what to do, and I'll do it. Just tell me whether I should ask Suzanne to marry me, and I'll do whatever you say." Whatever one says about decision-making, and however one tries to relate to God, no one can escape the fact that each of us is personally accountable to God for his decisions.

The command-and-obey model of decision-making certainly takes into account God's authority, but it hardly describes the decision-making that happens in a friendship, nor the decision-making that happens in a relationship which is on the road to friendship. Does a friend make decisions about his beloved's life—where he goes to school, what he studies, etc.—without his beloved's input and participation? When one person has a way he wants things to go, and another person's role is to implement that plan, we don't normally call that relationship a friendship. In fact, when one person relates to another person as a tool for carrying out his will, we normally call that domination, not love. Normally, people don't aspire to relationships in which they are used by another person for his plans and purposes. When they do, we say they have a problem—they are servile, and they are abdicating their God-given personal responsibility.

The command-and-obey model not only fails to describe friends making decisions together, it also seems inadequate to describe Jesus and His Father acting together. Even though Jesus said, "The Son can do nothing of His own accord, but only what He sees the Father doing" (Jn. 5:19), we don't think of Him as simply carrying out the Father's orders. Likewise, even though Jesus said, "The word which you hear is not mine, but the Father's" (Jn. 14:24), we don't think of Him as a mere conduit for His Father's words. It doesn't ring true to us to say God our Father is the divine puppeteer, and Jesus is His puppet. We naturally recoil at a picture of the Father orchestrating Jesus' every move and dictating to Him His every word. We don't think of God the Father as being wholly in control of Jesus, nor do we think of Jesus as being wholly under His Father's control. Jesus wasn't simply a tool in His Father's hands, as if He were an extension of His Father, ruled by His Father's will. We recoil at such a thought because it doesn't seem to describe the heights and depths and glory of personal love and friendship. Although Jesus was always under His Father's authority, always subject to Him, and was always doing His will, He wasn't moved by His Father like a puppet. He was moved by His Father because He loved His Father.

It's an extraordinary reality. God is Lord. He has all authority. He gives us the Ten Commandments, but beyond that He doesn't usually tell us what to do or not do. He is Lord, and He certainly can tell us what to do, but He doesn't. He doesn't take over our lives and run them for us. He certainly could do what we are doing better than we, but He asks us to do it ourselves. He is, however, totally for us. He's pouring Himself out for us, laboring for us in everything that is. He helps us and gives us gifts to enable us to live and work. He encourages us, establishes limits for our choices, forgives us, and picks us up when we fall, but the actual task of running our lives is ours. We are free and responsible, and He's pouring Himself out for us. We'll return to this reality when we discuss Ignatius's last exercise, the Contemplation to Attain the Love of God (230).

So what does it mean for a Christian to make decisions? If he's not reasoning from general principles, pursuing the best, or receiving his superior's directions, what is the Christian doing when he is making an Ignatian election? Quite simply, he's loving his Lord. In the last meditation of the Exercises Ignatius points out that love—and we would add decision-making—"consists in mutual communication. That is to say, the lover gives and communicates to the loved one what they have or something of what they have, or are able to give; and in turn the one loved does the same for the lover."[17] Ignatius's strategy for decision-making boils down to this: be one with your Lord in whatever way you can, and then act out of that union. The Spiritual Exercises create an environment where this becomes possible.

CHAPTER 3

THE HISTORY AND STRUCTURE OF THE EXERCISES

The Exercises are a tool for building love and friendship, and decision-making is integral to love and friendship. So in one sense it's relatively easy to say that the Exercises are all about love, but in another sense it's very difficult to say what this retreat is about. The Exercises create circumstances in which a meeting and a communication between God and the individual person can take place. Ultimately, the Exercises are about whatever the individual and God decide they are about. They are so highly personal that it's difficult to say they are about any one particular thing.

We can, however, ask why Ignatius created this retreat. What was he trying to accomplish? Ignatius, one with his Lord, knew that He didn't merely want to save individuals; He also wanted to enlist them in His struggle to save the world.[18] Ignatius wanted to produce men like Francis Xavier, who left his home never to return, or Jean de Brébeuf, who was willing to die rather than deny his Lord. He wanted to create people like Antonio Ruiz de Montoya, who was willing to venture into the Amazon rainforest and endure unspeakable hardships to bring salvation to the people there. He wanted to create men like the unnamed botanist who worked 20 years in a South American reduction trying to find a way to grow their cash crop, yerba maté trees, nearer to the reductions. He wanted to create men like the Jesuit Benedict Goës, who sacrificed his life trying to find an overland route to China.

Ignatius wanted to create men who would go anywhere and do anything for their Lord. He wanted men who were just as willing to work patiently in logistics as to fight valiantly on the front lines. He wanted to create good soldiers for the army of the Lord. Ignatius knew that the salvation of the world depends on people volunteering unreservedly like this.

Of course, Ignatius was very aware that Christ the King's army is different from any other army. Soldiers in the army of the Lord are united in love with their general. Ignatius was trying to recruit soldiers to live one life with their Lord. He knew it was possible for a man to love his Lord so much that they could have "one life, lived wholly by each and wholly by both together."[19] It's an astonishing plan. Ignatius wanted men who could, by virtue of their union with the Lord, say, "it is no longer I who live, but Christ who lives in me," (Gal. 2:20) and "I'm being sent by my Father into the world to save it."[20]

Although it's very difficult to describe the purpose of the Spiritual Exercises in a way that does them justice, it is possible to describe the structure of the retreat. For example, what happens on the first day of the retreat? The second day, etc.? Readers who would prefer to have an overview of the retreat before delving into the more technical elements of the retreat's structure can go immediately to the following chapter and return to these essential details later.

To understand the structure of the retreat, it seems logical to turn to the text, to the retreat manual itself. One of the first things a person might notice about the text is that it isn't a recipe book. At first glance it seems to be a rather confusing medley of instructions, notes, meditations, contemplations, rules, etc., organized into "weeks," some that are four days long, and some that can be as many as 12 days long. It doesn't initially appear to be systematic or orderly. If someone comes to the text somewhat familiar with the form of an Ignatian meditation, such as the Two Standards meditation, he may be surprised to find that a typical Ignatian meditation doesn't appear until paragraph 45. In fact, paragraph 45 is entitled "First Exercise" but it isn't at all the first thing the exercitant is assigned to do. What's going on? In order to answer this question, it's helpful to know at least a little history.

Early Jesuit sources often referred to the Exercises, but they meant several different things when they referred to "giving the Exercises." Sometimes they meant giving a 30-day retreat. Of course, not everyone could make a 30-day retreat, so the Jesuits adapted the 30-day retreat for the sake of those "engaged in public affairs or necessary business" (19). This form of the Exercises required that a person be able to devote an hour and a half daily to the Exercises for a period of approximately nine months. Sometimes, when the early Jesuits referred to giving the Exercises, they were referring to this extended form of the 30-day retreat. Of course, there were many people who could not even do this extended retreat, so the Jesuits took the first part of the Exercises (the First Week), presented them to people and spoke of giving the First Week as "giving the Exercises." Even then, they gave the First Week in different ways to different people. They did it one way for those who were illiterate and another way for those who had more education. Ignatius's manual was designed to be a guide to giving the Spiritual Exercises in a wide variety of circumstances. It was written for the director, equipping him to give the Exercises to many different kinds of people in many different circumstances. There is no one formula. Ultimately, the form of the Exercises depends upon the judgment of the director.

Historically, it looks like the early Jesuits most often gave the exercises of the First Week. This is one of the places where the Roman Catholic context of the Exercises comes to the forefront. Giving the Exercises to illiterate people meant teaching them how to examine their conscience, teaching them a method of prayer and recommending frequent Confession and frequent reception of Holy Communion. The prayer method taught by the early Jesuits to illiterate people wasn't much more than an examination of conscience which began with asking God for grace to do the examination well and ended with what Ignatius calls a colloquy—speaking to God as one friend to another. To the modern student of the Exercises, these few exercises may not sound like much, but they were apparently experienced as life-changing and life-giving.

If the early Jesuits were giving the exercises of the First Week to someone of "more ability," they would add several things: an explanation of the Principle and Foundation and some of the meditations of the First Week. Usually they added the first meditation (45-53), which was a meditation on the three sins (Lucifer's, Adam and Eve's, and that of someone who went to hell on account of one mortal sin). They also added the second meditation on personal sins (55-61) and the fifth meditation on hell (65-71). Making the exercises of the First Week gave someone an experience of himself as a choice-maker—someone who actually chooses his own destiny. Going through the exercises of the First Week was a powerful experience. The accounts from early Jesuit sources read like some accounts of early American revivals.[21] They are replete with stories of feuding town factions being reconciled, convents of nuns being reformed, people reforming their lives, etc.

From our 21st-century vantage point, it's difficult to know exactly why the exercises of the First Week were so powerful, but it does help to know a few things about the historical context. Most historians say that Ignatius invented the institution known as the "retreat." Although the Desert Fathers often spoke of one monk giving spiritual guidance to another, the experience of having a personal guide even for a few days was new to the Catholics of the 16th century. Ignatius also propagated a little-known devotional practice called a "general confession," which usually ended the First Week. Apparently a retreat, coupled with personal direction and capped with a general confession, was a potent mix.

A general confession was something different from the confession that was obligatory for all Catholics. It was a review of one's whole life with a confessor and was preceded by a soul-searching moral inventory which often took up to three days.[22] People who undertook a general confession didn't do so on account of legal obligation or ritual duty. It was a dramatic statement that one was changing his life, turning away from sin and toward a more devout life.

What about the 30-day retreats? They were very much in demand, and the Jesuits didn't have the resources to give them to everyone who asked. How did they choose 30-day exercitants? Many factors were involved, but they seemed to prefer men who had not yet made permanent life commitments. They also wanted men who, "themselves being helped, will be able to help many others."[23] They were especially looking for people who, after making the Spiritual Exercises, could then give them, if not in their entirety, then at least the First Week.

One early Jesuit, Juan Alfonso de Vitoria, who was taught by Ignatius himself how to give the Spiritual Exercises, said this about potential candidates:

> It does not seem advisable to encourage a person to go into seclusion for making the Exercises unless he possess the following qualifications, or at least the more important of them. First, he should be someone who may be expected to bear considerable fruit in the Lord's household if he is called thereto. Second, even if he lacks this degree of developed capacity in skills or acquired knowledge and the like, he should at least possess the age and intelligence needed for making progress. Third, he would be in a position to make a decision regarding his own life, even for the state of perfection if God should deign to call him to it. Fourth, he should have a good and presentable appearance, etc. Fifth, he should not [be] so strongly attached to anything that it would be hard getting him to place himself in equilibrium before God; rather, he ought to be uneasy in some respect, with a desire to know what he ought to do with himself and an uncertainty about this.[24]

We live in a different age, but several things about these recommendations seem especially pertinent. When faced with choosing people to make the Exercises, the director should choose people who are in a position to make a decision about their lives. He should avoid people who are too young or who are too entangled in the world's affairs to make a change. The director should also be looking for people who stand a chance of reaching a point of equilibrium. There has to be at least the possibility of the exercitant getting to a point where he says, "I don't prefer graduate school to the mission field; they are both possible for me. I'll do whatever the Lord wants: riches or poverty, marriage or celibacy, etc. I hold them in a balance before the Lord." Additionally, the director should be looking for people who are restless in at least some areas of their lives. Vitoria's comment about restlessness seems especially pertinent to our day and time. The director should be on the lookout for a person who is "uneasy in some respect, with a desire to know what he ought to do with himself and an uncertainty about this."[25]

Although the Jesuits gave the Exercises to people in all circumstances of life, they were, as we've seen, especially interested in giving them to men who had not yet made what they called "a state in life decision." In Ignatius's time, people normally understood the choice of a state in life as a choice between the "way of the Commandments" and "the way of perfection." The distinction between these two ways or states of life was derived from the story of the rich young man (See Matthew 19:16-22 and Mark 10:17-22). A young man came up to Jesus and asked Him, "What must I do to inherit eternal life?" Jesus told him to "keep the commandments." Then the young man asked what more he could do and Jesus replied, "If you would be perfect, go, sell what you possess and give to the poor, and you will have treasure in heaven; and come, follow me." The way of the Commandments was understood to be obligatory for every Christian. The way of perfection was understood to be a call from God, but not at all necessary for salvation.

By Ignatius's time, choosing the way of perfection meant deciding to live a life not only of poverty but also of chastity and obedience. Together, poverty, chastity and obedience were called the "evangelical counsels" (counsels, not Commandments). If a person chose the way of perfection, he normally lived it out in a religious order such as the Franciscans or the Dominicans.

Although the way of the counsels included poverty, chastity and obedience, it seems that a decision for the counsels was often primarily a decision for poverty. In particular, clerical exercitants often had to make a choice about whether or not they were going to accept a benefice. In Ignatius's time, a benefice was a typical way of supporting the clergy. If he had a benefice, a man would, for the duration of his life, receive a fixed income from Church property in return for spiritual services such as reciting the Divine Office, celebrating mass or doing the kind of care of souls a parish priest would do. Ignatius and his followers chose not to accept benefices, so that they could give their spiritual ministries without charge. Forgoing a benefice meant forgoing a fixed income. One of the early Jesuits even described the state in life decision as a decision "whether or not he wants to follow actual poverty, which consists of being stripped of possessions."[26]

In Ignatius's time, making an election during the course of the Exercises was not limited to a choice between the way of the counsels and the way of the Commandments. Several of the early Jesuit directories mention the possibility of making an election about other important matters.[27] In his notes on how to make good choices, Ignatius himself says that a choice can be made about matters which are either "morally indifferent or good in themselves" (170, Ivens). Primarily, though, Ignatius seemed to be focused on the choice between the counsels or the Commandments. If a person was not in a position to make a choice about his state in life, either because he had already made one or because he didn't want to or because of other life circumstances, Ignatius offered some instruction on how "To Amend and Reform One's Own Life and State" (189, Mullan) or, as another translation puts it, "Directions for the Amendment and Reformation of One's Way of Living in His State of Life" (189, Puhl).

At that time, in that culture and in those particular circumstances, answering the call of Christ to join Him in His saving work was almost synonymous with making vows of poverty, chastity and obedience. Today, our situation is very different. The Holy Spirit, through a variety of developments in the Roman Catholic Church and through the sons and daughters of the Reformation—including Hudson Taylor of the China Inland Mission, John Lake, Elisabeth Elliot and their forefathers in the faith—has taught us that vows of poverty, chastity and obedience are not a necessary prerequisite for enlisting in Christ's army.

What does this mean for those who give the Exercises? We envision giving the Exercises to a person who is "uneasy in some respect, with a desire to know what he ought to do with himself and an uncertainty about this."[28] Such a person could be 22 or 65 or anywhere in-between. He could be married or single or living a life of dedicated celibacy. These people might embark on the Exercises because they have some kind of decision to make or just because they feel the stirring of the Holy Spirit and desire more. During the course of the Exercises they will end up confronting these questions and similar ones: What kind of future do I envision for myself? What role are money and status going to play in my life? How can I join Christ? As they meditate on the life of Jesus, they usually make choices about how they want to live their lives in Christ, based on what they are experiencing of the Lord.

After the death of Ignatius and the other early Jesuits, the practice of giving the Exercises began to evolve. Throughout his life, Ignatius was very conscious that there were three people involved in the Exercises: the director, the exercitant and God. He said the director of the Exercises "should permit the Creator to deal directly with the creature, and the creature directly with his Creator and Lord" (15). He also advised that, "while one is engaged in the Spiritual Exercises, it is more suitable and much better that the Creator and Lord in person communicate Himself to the devout soul in quest of the divine will, that He inflame it with His love and praise, and dispose it for the way in which it could better serve God in the future" (15). He also instructs the director, who in turn instructs the exercitant, about how to discern the workings of God (and the Enemy) in the exercitant's soul. In other words, Ignatius was extremely conscious that God was at work in the Exercises. In the years following Ignatius's death, there was less and less stress on God's activity with the exercitant. The application and activity of the exercitant and the role of the director became more prominent.

By the time of Vatican II in the Catholic Church, the Exercises were seldom given on a one-to-one basis. Most often, a director would preach the Exercises to a large group of people. He would talk about and amplify an Ignatian meditation, and the retreatants would go off to think and pray about what he said. Discerning consolations and desolations had disappeared, along with the role of the director as a personal guide through the retreat. After Vatican II, the role of the director and the rules on the discernment of spirits were rediscovered, so to speak.

We'd like to move on now and discuss what a typical 30-day retreat looked like. We want to do this to provide a baseline for our adaptations. A director can't really give the Exercises in a way Ignatius would recognize as his own without a basic understanding of the 30-day retreat. It's not immediately obvious to someone who first picks up this manual what the daily schedule of a 30-day retreat looked like. As a step towards understanding the Spiritual Exercises, we are going to lay out a typical, early, 30-day retreat schedule and make a few preliminary comments about it.

A director usually began the retreat by introducing four things: Principle and Foundation (23), Particular Examen (24-31), General Examen (32-43) and General Confession (44). The first two days were relaxed and didn't have a set schedule. They were meant to be a transition from the exercitant's busy life in the world to the quiet of a silent 30-day retreat. If the director thought it necessary or helpful, a person might take three or four days for these first exercises, or even just one day. The director would begin by explaining the Principle and Foundation and then sending the exercitant off to think about it and about his own life in light of it. Different Jesuits explained the Principle and Foundation in different ways. As the exercitant moved on to the second day of the retreat, he was to call to mind frequently the Principle and Foundation. We'll talk more about the Principle and Foundation in the next chapter.

The Particular Examen was an examination of conscience in which a person focused on a particular fault and tried to root it out of his life. During the Exercises, it was usually focused on how well the exercitant was making the Exercises and aimed at overcoming a particular obstacle he faced in making the Exercises well. In the General Examen a person examined his conscience, looking not for a particular fault but for any fault in his thoughts, words and deeds that day. Although the exercitant began preparing for a general confession on the second day of the retreat, Ignatius recommended that he make the general confession at the end of the First Week (44). A person prepared for the general confession by recollecting the sins of his whole past life.

The schedule becomes more rigorous on the third day of the retreat, with four scheduled meditations. By the fourth day of the retreat the exercitant is doing five meditations a day.

> 1.3.1: First Exercise (45-53), on the first, second and third sin, done at midnight, presented to the exercitant the night before
> 1.3.2: Second Exercise (55-61), on personal sins

1.3.3: Third Exercise (62-63), which is a repetition of the first two exercises with a new colloquy at the end
1.3.4: Fourth Exercise (64), which is a summary of the third exercise

1.4.1: First Exercise (45-53)
1.4.2: Second Exercise (55-61)
1.4.3: Third Exercise (62-63)
1.4.4: Fourth Exercise (64)
1.4.5: Fifth Exercise (65-71), which is a meditation on hell

1.5.1: First Exercise (45-53)
1.5.2: Second Exercise (55-61)
1.5.3: Third Exercise (62-63)
1.5.4: Fourth Exercise (64)
1.5.5: Fifth Exercise (65-71)

1.6.1: First Exercise (45-53)
1.6.2: Second Exercise (55-61)
1.6.3: Third Exercise (62-63)
1.6.4: Fourth Exercise (64)
1.6.5: Fifth Exercise (65-71)

Days four, five and six are repetitions of day three, with the addition of a fifth meditation on Hell. Repetition is obviously a key part of Ignatius's strategy. There is some disagreement in the sources about what Ignatius intended for days four through six. Vitoria, who claims to have been taught by Ignatius, says that after the preliminaries of the first few days the director should present the first exercise and have him repeat it four times, and on the next day the director should present the second exercise and assign four repetitions, etc.[29] Ignatius himself seems to have said things that sound like Vitoria's schema and things that sound like the schema we have presented.[30]

Ignatius makes a point of saying that the director can lengthen or shorten the number of days spent meditating on the first five exercises. He can also add other exercises, for example, "on death and other punishments of sin, on judgment, etc." (71). The practice among the early Jesuits seems to have been to substitute meditations on death and judgment for the meditation on Hell; however, exercitants always meditated on Hell at least once. A wise director would have made sure to give his exercitant the meditation on Hell on the last day of the First Week, just before moving on to the meditation on the Kingdom of Christ. The meditation on the Kingdom of Christ presupposes and builds on the meditation on Hell.

What criteria did the director use for lengthening or shortening the number of days or number of hours spent meditating on a particular topic? Ignatius says, "as age, condition of health, and the physical constitution of the exercitant permit" (72). Although it doesn't appear so at first glance, the 30-day schedule is actually very rigorous. It was also the case that a director might want someone to linger longer over a set of exercises if he wasn't getting the grace he asked for, or to move on if he did get the grace he asked for.

At the beginning of each meditation Ignatius had the exercitant pray for a particular grace, asking God for "what I want and desire" (48).

In the first meditation the exercitant asks for "shame and confusion, because I see how many have been lost on account of a single mortal sin, and how many times I have deserved eternal damnation, because of the many grievous sins that I have committed" (48).

In the second meditation he asks "for a growing and intense sorrow and tears for my sin" (55).

The third and fourth meditations are repetitions.

In the fifth meditation the exercitant asks "for a deep sense of the pain which the lost suffer, in order that, if, through my faults, I should forget the love of the Eternal Lord, at least the fear of the pains may help me not to come into sin" (65, Puhl and Mullan).

As a sort of prelude to the Second Week, Ignatius has the exercitant make the Kingdom of Christ meditation (91-98) twice, once upon rising in the morning and once either before the noonday meal or before the evening meal. Many of the early Jesuit directors said that the lighter schedule of this day helped the exercitant recover from the intense experience of the previous few days. Technically, this meditation, the Kingdom of Christ, is not part of the Second Week. According to Ignatius, the first day of the Second Week begins with the meditation on the Incarnation.

The exercitant actually makes the Kingdom of Christ meditation twice. In fact, during the Second Week, a person will sometimes make a meditation twice. Making a meditation, however, differs from what Ignatius calls "repeating" a meditation. When someone repeats a meditation he doesn't reconsider each and every point; rather, he returns to certain points that were more salient for him personally.

The Second Week resumes the five-meditations-a-day schedule.

- 2.1.1: The Incarnation (101-109)
- 2.1.2: The Nativity (110-117)
- 2.1.3: Repetition (118-119)
- 2.1.4: Repetition (120)
- 2.1.5: Application of the senses to the matter of the first and second exercises (121-126)

- 2.2.1: Presentation in the Temple (268, cf. 132)
- 2.2.2: Flight into Egypt (269, cf. 132)
- 2.2.3: Repetition (cf. 118-119)
- 2.2.4: Repetition (cf. 120)
- 2.2.5: Application of the senses to the matter of the first and second exercises (cf. 121-126)

- 2.3.1: Obedience of the Child Jesus to His Parents (271, cf. 134)
- 2.3.2: Finding of the Child Jesus in the Temple (272, cf. 134)
- 2.3.3: Repetition (cf. 118-119)
- 2.3.4: Repetition (cf. 120)
- 2.3.5: Application of the senses to the matter of the first and second exercises (cf. 121-126)

- 2.4.1: Meditation, The Two Standards (136-147)
- 2.4.2: Meditation, The Two Standards (136-147)
- 2.4.3: Repetition (cf. 148)

2.4.4: Repetition (cf. 148)
2.4.5: Three Classes of Men (149-156)

2.5.1: Baptism of Christ (273, cf. 158)
2.5.2: Baptism of Christ (273, cf. 158)
2.5.3: Repetition (cf. 118-119)
2.5.4: Repetition (cf. 120)
2.5.5: Application of the senses (cf. 121-126)

2.6.1: Temptation of Christ (274, cf. 161)
2.6.2: Temptation of Christ (274, cf. 161)
2.6.3: Repetition (cf. 118-119)
2.6.4: Repetition (cf. 120)
2.6.5: Application of the senses (cf. 121-126)

2.7.1: Vocation of the Apostles (275, cf. 161)
2.7.2: Vocation of the Apostles (275, cf. 161)
2.7.3: Repetition (cf. 118-119)
2.7.4: Repetition (cf. 120)
2.7.5: Application of the senses (cf. 121-126)

2.8.1: Sermon on the Mount (278, cf. 161)
2.8.2: Sermon on the Mount (278, cf. 161)
2.8.3: Repetition (cf. 118-119)
2.8.4: Repetition (cf. 120)
2.8.5: Application of the senses (cf. 121-126)

2.9.1: Christ Walks Upon the Waters (280, cf. 161)
2.9.2: Christ Walks Upon the Waters (280, cf. 161)
2.9.3: Repetition (cf. 118-119)
2.9.4: Repetition (cf. 120)
2.9.5: Application of the senses (cf. 121-126)

2.10.1: Jesus Preaches in the Temple (288, cf. 161)
2.10.2: Jesus Preaches in the Temple (288, cf. 161)
2.10.3: Repetition (cf. 118-119)
2.10.4: Repetition (cf. 120)
2.10.5: Application of the senses (cf. 121-126)

2.11.1: The Raising of Lazarus (285, cf. 161)
2.11.2: The Raising of Lazarus (285, cf. 161)
2.11.3: Repetition (cf. 118-119)
2.11.4: Repetition (cf. 120)
2.11.5: Application of the senses (cf. 121-126)

2.12.1: Palm Sunday (287, cf. 161)
2.12.2: Palm Sunday (287, cf. 161)
2.12.3: Repetition (cf. 118-119)
2.12.4: Repetition (cf. 120)
2.12.5: Application of the senses (cf. 121-126)

When he's speaking generally, Ignatius refers to the third and fourth meditations in a day as "repetitions." When he's giving specific instructions, he differentiates between the two repetitions. He says the third exercise of the day is "a repetition of the first and second exercises" in which "we should pay attention to and dwell upon those points in which we have experienced greater consolation or desolation or greater spiritual appreciation" (62). Ignatius calls the fourth exercise a summary, explaining, "I have called it a summary, because the intellect, without any digression, diligently thinks over and recalls the matter contemplated in the previous exercises" (64).

What is the application of the senses? Many people are accustomed to think of Ignatian meditation as a method of meditating on Scripture in which a person applies his senses to a scene in Scripture. A person sees in his imagination the people and the places, he hears what the people are saying or might have said, etc. Ignatius has the exercitant do this in the application of the senses. The first four meditations in the day are, for lack of a better term, more discursive. The exercitant considers the different people, what they say, and what they do, but it's not so imaginative. At the end of the day, he applies his senses to the scene he is meditating on. This is meant to be the culmination of the day and very sweet. Ignatius directs a person to apply his sense of sight to the scene, then his sense of hearing, but then his instructions seem to take a turn towards affectivity and devotion. He instructs the exercitant "to smell and to taste with the smell and the taste the infinite fragrance and sweetness of the

Divinity, of the soul, and of its virtues, and of all, according to the person who is being contemplated" (124, Mullan). Then he tells him, "to apply the sense of touch, for example, by embracing and kissing the place where the persons stand or are seated" (125).

Ignatius has the exercitant consider the obedience of the child Jesus before His finding in the Temple, even though the scriptural order is the reverse. He considers the "first state of life" that "of the Commandments" and says that Jesus gave an example of this when He was obedient to His parents. The second state of life, that of "the counsels," is exemplified by Jesus when "He remained in the temple and left His foster father and His Mother to devote Himself exclusively to the service of His eternal Father" (135). Hence the change of order.

Every day, five times a day, throughout this Second Week, except on the fourth day, the exercitant asks "for an intimate knowledge of our Lord, who has become man for me, that I may love Him more and follow Him more closely" (104). On the fourth day, which is the day he meditates on the Two Standards and the Three Classes of Men, the exercitant asks four times "for knowledge of the deceits of the rebel chief and help to guard myself against them" (139), and also asks "for knowledge of the true life which the supreme and true Captain shows and grace to imitate Him" (139, Mullan). At the end of the fourth day he asks "for the grace to choose what is more for the glory of His Divine Majesty and the salvation of my soul" (152).

After the meditation on the Two Standards, Ignatius introduces a colloquy in which the exercitant speaks first to "our Lady," then to Jesus, and then to the Father. The threefold nature of the colloquy emphasizes its importance. It also stirs up a person's desire. In this colloquy the exercitant begins to use the *agere contra* strategy (cf. 157). He is to ask for the grace to be received under Christ's standard, "first in the highest spiritual poverty, and should the Divine Majesty be pleased thereby, and deign to choose and accept me, even in actual poverty; secondly, in bearing insults and wrongs, thereby to imitate Him better, provided only I can suffer these without sin on the part of another, and without offense of the Divine Majesty" (147). Ignatius isn't recommending a rote prayer. The exercitant is still to speak to his Lord as one friend to another, but his prayer should involve heartfelt conversation about spiritual poverty, actual poverty, and bearing insults and wrongs. For the rest of the Second Week, Ignatius recommends (159, 161) that a person frequently make the threefold colloquy of the Two Standards.

The Second Week begins with the exercitant meditating on two incidents per day (Ignatius calls them "mysteries") from the life of Christ. On the fifth day of the week he changes that and has the exercitant meditate on one mystery. Why the change? If someone has a choice or a decision to make, he makes it during the Second Week. As we've already noted, Ignatius calls this decision-making an "election." When the exercitant begins the time of the election, Ignatius lightens his load by having him meditate on just one mystery a day, so he has the mental space to be considering his election.

If someone has a decision to make, he begins to discuss it with the director on the fifth day. From then on he is pondering the decision and keeping track of the consolations and desolations he is experiencing as he is making the meditations and as he is talking to the Lord about his decision. The director, for his part, is teaching the exercitant about making a choice (see 169-189). In other words, the election is going on concurrently with the meditations between days five and twelve. (Actually, the director briefly brings up the issue for the first time on the fourth day.)

The exercitant shouldn't be considering the election during the meditations, per se. He should be using the time between the meditations to ponder his decision and to speak to the Lord about his decision. If needed, the director may discontinue the meditations for a day or two while someone considers his election. The director could also lessen the number of daily meditations by eliminating one of the repetitions. Just before the election, the director presents the Three Kinds of Humility (165-167). Ignatius says "these should be thought over from time to time during the whole day" (164).

If someone isn't making an election, the director can still give him the Three Kinds of Humility. Also, if someone isn't making an election, normally the director would continue the schedule of the first three days—meditating on two mysteries a day.

When laying out the Second Week, Ignatius offers 14 scenes from the life of Christ for meditation and refers the director to a list of mysteries (261-312) near the back of the book. The list of mysteries contains 26 scenes from the life of Christ that could be used in the Second Week. Why so many? The director can pick and choose which mysteries he thinks would be most beneficial to the exercitant. He can also lengthen or shorten the week as he sees fit and as the Lord leads. For example, if someone is making an election, the director might have him do additional meditations, especially if he is having trouble reaching a point of indifference, where he neither desires nor is inclined "to have riches rather than poverty, to seek honor rather than dishonor" and "to desire a long life rather than a short life" (166).

The schedule of the Third Week is similar to that of the Second Week.

    3.1.1: Last Supper (289, cf. 190-198)
    3.1.2: Agony in the Garden (290, cf. 200-204)
    3.1.3: Repetition
    3.1.4: Repetition
    3.1.5: Application of the senses

    3.2.1: From the Garden to the House of Annas (291, cf. 208)
    3.2.2: From the House of Annas to the House of Caiaphas (292, cf. 208)
    3.2.3: Repetition
    3.2.4: Repetition
    3.2.5: Application of the senses

    3.3.1: From the House of Caiaphas to the House of Pilate (293, cf. 208)
    3.3.2: From the House of Pilate to the House of Herod (294, cf. 208)
    3.3.3: Repetition
    3.3.4: Repetition
    3.3.5: Application of the senses

3.4.1: From the House of Herod to that of Pilate, first half of what happened there (295, cf. 208)
3.4.2: From the House of Herod to that of Pilate, second half of what happened there (295, cf. 208)
3.4.3: Repetition
3.4.4: Repetition
3.4.5: Application of the senses

3.5.1: From the House of Pilate to the Cross (296, cf. 208)
3.5.2: Jesus Dies on the Cross (297, cf. 208)
3.5.3: Repetition
3.5.4: Repetition
3.5.5: Application of the senses

3.6.1: From the Cross to the Sepulcher (298, cf. 208)
3.6.2: From the Sepulcher "to the house to which our Lady retired after the burial of her Son" (208)
3.6.3: Repetition
3.6.4: Repetition
3.6.5: Application of the senses

3.7.1: Consider the whole passion (208)
3.7.2: Consider the whole passion (208)
3.7.3: In place of the two repetitions and the application of the Senses, the exercitant should consider "as frequently as possible" (208) Jesus in the tomb and the desolation of Mary and the disciples.

During the first meditation of the week, the exercitant asks "for sorrow, compassion, and shame because the Lord is going to His suffering for my sins" (193). In every other meditation of the week he asks "for sorrow with Christ in sorrow, anguish with Christ in anguish, tears and deep grief because of the great affliction Christ endures for me" (203).

If the director wants someone to spend more time meditating on the passion, he can use more mysteries—making the washing of the feet one mystery and the Last Supper another, for example. If he wishes someone to take less time, he can combine mysteries, but the exercitant should meditate on the whole passion. Or the director can have the exercitant meditate on five mysteries a day, without any repetitions or application of the senses.

After meditating on the mysteries of the passion, the exercitant should go over the whole passion. He can do this several ways. He can consider the whole passion twice, as noted above. He can take three days and consider half the passion on one day, the other half on the next day, and the whole passion on the third day.

Week Four has a slightly lighter schedule.

4.1.1:	The Resurrection–First Apparition (299, cf. 218-225)
4.1.2:	The Resurrection–Second Apparition (300)
4.1.3:	Repetition
4.1.4:	Application of the senses
4.2.1:	The Resurrection–Third Apparition (301)
4.2.2:	The Resurrection–Fourth Apparition (302)
4.2.3:	Repetition
4.2.4:	Application of the senses
4.3.1:	The Resurrection–Fifth Apparition (303)
4.3.2:	The Resurrection–Sixth Apparition (304)
4.3.3:	Repetition
4.3.4:	Application of the senses
4.4.1:	The Resurrection–Seventh Apparition (305)
4.4.2:	The Resurrection–Eighth Apparition (306)
4.4.3:	Repetition
4.4.4:	Application of the senses
4.5.1:	The Resurrection–Ninth Apparition (307)
4.5.2:	The Resurrection–Tenth Apparition (308)
4.5.3:	Repetition
4.5.4:	Application of the senses
4.6.1:	The Resurrection–Eleventh Apparition (309)
4.6.2:	The Ascension (312)

4.6.3:   Repetition
4.6.4:   Application of the senses

During this week, Ignatius has the exercitant meditate four times a day instead of the more rigorous five times a day. In each meditation the exercitant asks "for the grace to be glad and rejoice intensely because of the great joy and the glory of Christ our Lord" (221). There are actually 13 apparitions listed in the mysteries. The director can lengthen or shorten this week as he sees fit, along the lines of the previous week.

The retreat ends with the Contemplation to Attain Love (230-237). Ignatius does not say how many times this exercise is to be made or repeated.

It's important to have a clear picture in one's mind of the 30-day schedule, because then Ignatius's manual becomes more intelligible. When people talk about and write about the Exercises they tend to focus on a few meditations—the Kingdom of Christ, the Two Standards and the Three Classes of Men—or on the importance of being detached as the key to decision-making and becoming a better Christian. We've already spent a lot of time talking about detachment, and we will spend a great deal of time discussing these three famous meditations. Still, we hope that by going through the schedule we've made it clear that the Exercises themselves are all about Jesus.

As a person makes the Exercises, he begins to see what a life lived for God's glory looks like. The exercitant is led by means of the oft-repeated threefold colloquy of the Two Standards to look at Jesus' life in a new way. He begins to look at Jesus' life through the lens of His standard: poverty, insults, contempt and humility. The exercitant comes to admire Jesus, the way He lived and the way He saved the world. He begins to admire Jesus' total rejection of earthly means of power and the way He forged ahead in spite of insults and ignominy. He realizes the power of poverty, ignominy and humility and learns to see the glory of God in them. As his admiration grows, he gradually grows to love Jesus, so that by the end of the Spiritual Exercises there isn't anything he wouldn't do for his Lord.

Although we've already spent a lot of time describing the 30-day schedule, there's more to point out about it. Praying five one-hour meditations a day isn't the only thing the exercitant is doing. Ignatius has him doing a lot more things, many of which are described in the Additional Directions (73-90) and various other places throughout the *Spiritual Exercises.*

Before listing and discussing all the additional things the exercitant was charged to do, it's important to emphasize that Ignatius was keenly aware of God's action during the retreat. For example, he's careful to remind the director not to interfere with the Creator dealing "directly with the creature and the creature directly with his Creator and Lord" (15). He reminds the director that while someone is making the Spiritual Exercises it's much better "that the Creator and Lord in person communicate Himself to the devout soul in quest of the divine will, that He inflame it with His love and praise, and dispose it for the way in which it could better serve God in the future" (15). In each exercise the exercitant asks God for a specific grace: sorrow, joy, etc. He must ask God; the grace is at God's initiative. Also, Ignatius's Rules for Discernment of Spirits are all about coming to recognize to some degree God's action in the soul (and the Enemy's action). In other words, God's action is key to the Spiritual Exercises. Historically, this was a point of contention. Ignatius was called before the Inquisition several times on account of this point, but he didn't stop reminding directors about God's action in a person's soul.

With this as the background, we can turn to some of the directions Ignatius gives the exercitant. He wants him to do everything he can to cooperate with God. The director encourages the exercitant to begin the Exercises with "great courage and generosity toward his Creator and Lord, offering Him all his will and liberty, that His Divine Majesty may make use of his person and of all he has according to His most Holy Will" (15, Mullan).

The director also gives the exercitant instructions about his inner and outer comportment as he goes through the Exercises. He should be thinking about the meditation even when he isn't making the meditation. Ignatius recommends that the exercitant, as he is falling asleep the night before, briefly think about the exercise he is going to make in the morning.

Each day upon rising, and while he is dressing, the exercitant is to think about the meditation he is about to make, trying to think thoughts in keeping with the subject matter and trying to stir up the appropriate feelings. During the First Week, Ignatius gives the following as an example of how someone should think and feel: "I will seek to rouse myself to shame for my many sins by using examples, let us say, of a knight brought before his king and the whole court, filled with shame and confusion for having grievously offended his lord from whom he had formerly received many gifts and favors" (74). During the Second Week the exercitant is to call to mind the subject matter of the exercise "with the desire to know better the eternal Word Incarnate in order to serve and follow Him more closely" (130). During the Third Week he is to make an effort "to be sad and grieve because of the great sorrow and suffering of Christ our Lord" (206). During the Fourth Week he is to call to mind the subject matter of the exercise he is about to make and then "strive to feel joy and happiness at the great joy and happiness of Christ our Lord" (229).

Before each meditation, a person should pause momentarily a step or two from the place he is to pray, and with "mind raised on high" he should consider that "God our Lord beholds" him, and then he should make an act of reverence or humility (75). After each meditation, for about 15 minutes, he should consider "how it went with me . . . and if badly, I will look for the cause from which it proceeds, and having so seen it, will be sorry, in order to correct myself in future; and if well, I will give thanks to God our Lord, and will do in like manner another time" (77, Mullan). This brief reflection can be done either seated or walking leisurely. It is not meant to be part of the prayer time, but something done afterward (77). The exercitant should also be keeping a record of his consolations and desolations so as to better inform his director (17).

During the day, between meditations, the exercitant should not let his thoughts wander aimlessly. He should continue diligently seeking the grace of the week:

> • During the First Week, "I should not think of things that give pleasure and joy, as the glory of heaven, the Resurrection, etc., for if I wish to feel pain, sorrow, and tears for my sins, every consideration promoting

joy and happiness will impede it. I should rather keep in mind that I want to be sorry and feel pain" (78).
• During the Second Week the exercitant should "call to mind frequently the mysteries of the life of Christ our Lord from the Incarnation to the place or mystery I am contemplating" (130).
• During the Third Week, "I will rouse myself to sorrow, suffering, and anguish by frequently calling to mind the labors, fatigue, and suffering which Christ our Lord endured from the time of His birth down to the mystery of the Passion upon which I am engaged at present" (206).
• During the Fourth Week the exercitant should "call to mind and think on what causes pleasure, happiness, and spiritual joy, for instance, the glory of heaven" (229).

Such simple practices turn out to be a great help to a person making the Spiritual Exercises.

Not only does the exercitant keep his interior environment (his thoughts between meditations) in conformity with the mysteries being considered, but he also tries to do the same with his exterior environment. He should "take care to darken his room, or admit the light; to make use of pleasant or disagreeable weather, in as far as he perceives that it may be of profit, and help to find what he desires" (130). So, for example, when he is considering his sins or meditating on the passion, he darkens his room and avoids laughter. When contemplating the resurrection, he enjoys beautiful weather or the warmth of a fire.

Besides making meditations, the exercitant does several other things during the retreat. He attends mass and vespers daily. He also talks with his director daily. From the Second Week on, between meditations, he can read some passages from *The Imitation of Christ* or from the Gospels or lives of the saints. Ignatius says this is very profitable, although a person shouldn't get ahead of himself, reading about the passion when he is contemplating the Nativity, for example. The exercitant also cleans his room, sweeps and makes his bed, even if this is very humiliating for him to do because he normally would have had servants do this for him.

Twice a day for 15 minutes the exercitant makes a general and particular examination of conscience. The purpose of this is to root out any particular obstacles that are getting in the way of his making the Exercises well and more generally to uncover and uproot any negligence in making the Exercises or practicing the Additional Directions. For example, the exercitant might notice that he keeps trying to comfort himself with thoughts of Christ's resurrection while he is meditating on the passion. He would then take steps to change this behavior.

When suitable to the mystery being contemplated, the exercitant does penance (82-89). He can do penance in the area of eating by fasting.[31] He can do penance in regard to sleeping by, for example, sleeping on a rough bed. He can also do penance by chastising the body. Ignatius's discussion of penance may seem outdated to some, but actually it reveals that he is an astute student of human nature. For example, in regard to fasting he comments that, "if we do away with what is superfluous, it is not penance, but temperance" (83), yet he also counsels moderation.

Why do penance? This is perhaps a topic for another book, but there are two things we can say. First, these self-imposed austerities are a way for a person to get a grip on himself and take charge of his life. It often helps a person make the turn from being driven (by desires for ease and comfort, good food, rest and relaxation) to being the driver. Furthermore, and perhaps more to our point, one early Jesuit offered this rationale for penances. He said the exercitant "should be instructed on how necessary . . . are corporal austerities such as fasts, disciplines and hair shirts, night-watches, rough bed, etc. For the Lord gives to each one the grace of the Lord, and it would seem that a person disposes himself for this better if he strives and labors to achieve it not only with his spirit but also with his body."[32]

By now it should be clear that the exercitant should be very active in this retreat. Throughout the retreat he is told to want, to wish, to desire. In each prelude he asks for what he wants and desires. He does many things to "find more readily what he desires" (73). He is aggressively pursuing the grace and consolation of the Lord.

II
THE FIRST WEEK

CHAPTER 4

PRELIMINARIES

The First Week of the Spiritual Exercises centers around sin. It is designed to help a person turn from his sin, repudiate past sin and resolve to avoid all sin in the future. There are great graces to be had during this First Week, but it is often a difficult time for people. It's hard to meditate on sin, and the Enemy is often at work. It's also a challenging week for the director. During the First Week, the director has to get to know the exercitant, introduce him to the Exercises, teach him how to make meditations and to practice the Additional Directions, introduce him to the art of discerning the movements of his soul and begin a conversation about inordinate attachments. He must also guide the exercitant as he comes face to face with his sin and its consequences, pointing him toward "godly grief," which produces repentance and leads to God, and away from "worldly grief," which produces death (2 Cor. 7:10). Giving the First Week of the Spiritual Exercises requires flexibility and insight on the part of the director.

The retreat begins with two to four days of very important preliminaries. The director has four things he needs to do during these first few days. The order in which these things happen can vary according to the needs of the exercitant and the circumstances of the retreat, but they should happen within the first few days. The director should spend time getting to know the exercitant and inquiring about his hopes for the retreat. He should begin to teach the exercitant how to make the Exercises. He should also present and explain paragraph 23, which is a succinct statement about the goal of the Christian life and the strategy for reaching that goal. The early Jesuits called this statement "The Foundation." Finally, the director should help the exercitant begin to evaluate his life in light of the Foundation.

The exercitant's first encounters with the director help him look forward to the retreat with anticipation. These first encounters serve like the vestibule of a church. They prepare a person to enter into the retreat just as a vestibule helps a person enter into a church. The director has a lot of things he needs to tell the exercitant, but he has to be careful not to overwhelm the exercitant with a lot of details. The skilled director gives the exercitant what he needs to know at the moment he needs it.

Early on in the retreat, the director spends some time getting to know the exercitant. Some directors like to give the exercitant specific questions to think about in order to facilitate this. For example, a director might ask a person about his moment closest to Christ in the last year or the last week. Depending on the circumstances, he might ask someone whether he feels he has done anything for the Lord, or he might ask about the hardest thing he's done for the Lord, or the most important thing he's done for the Lord. Some directors actually give an exercitant questions like these and send him off for half an hour or so to think about it. Other directors prefer to let a person's story unfold in a less structured way.

The director should make sure that he asks the exercitant about his hopes for the retreat. Most people have something they want to get out of the retreat, and it's important for the director to know this. Sometimes, however, a person's hope is rather vague. For example, someone might say he wants a better relationship with the Lord. The director shouldn't assume he knows what that means. Instead, he can ask more questions in order to help the exercitant articulate his desires. For example, the director might ask what a better relationship would look like. If it were better, how would the exercitant know it was better? If you had a better relationship with the Lord, what do you think your life would look like a year from now?

As a person talks about his life and his hopes for the retreat, it's often a good time for the director to ask him about potential obstacles. Most people know themselves well enough to anticipate certain obstacles. One person might say he has trouble sitting still for an hour. Another might mention that he gives up easily when he encounters obstacles, and so on. The director should ask the exercitant what he can do to avoid the anticipated obstacle. The exercitant should make a simple and doable plan to conquer the obstacle. Besides giving the director insight into the exercitant's character—the retreat is often a microcosm of life—this conversation foreshadows an important theme of the First Week: The exercitant can do things which will help him achieve his goal. He is not a victim of his circumstances or of his character.

During these preliminary conversations, some people talk about their life and hopes in vague religious language. For example, someone might say that until recently he was struggling with his faith. Or he might talk about how he wants to serve the Lord with his whole life. The director needs to artfully change the ground of the conversation so that the exercitant begins to talk not only about his psychological states but also about what he is doing or hopes to do or has done in the past. He might ask, what does struggling with your faith look like? An exercitant might respond by saying it looks like lots of drinking and swearing. The director might ask the exercitant how his life changed when he stopped struggling with his faith. An exercitant might reveal that he began praying regularly and spending more time with brothers and sisters in Christ. Of course, the director shouldn't push someone to reveal something he doesn't want to reveal, but it's important to establish a climate of realism.

The director can instill hopeful anticipation in the exercitant by pointing out the benefits of what he has already done, namely, withdrawing from his ordinary life to make this retreat. The director can remind him that he has already spoken very persuasively to the Lord. His choice to withdraw for a time from the demands of his daily life speaks eloquently of desire. Love, after all, manifests itself in deeds, or, as the adage says, actions speak louder than words.

It's usually a good idea for the director to enumerate some of the benefits of keeping silence and of withdrawing for a time from one's brothers and sisters in Christ and from all one's various responsibilities. Normally, the exercitant's attention is divided among many important things, and rightly so. This retreat gives him an opportunity to focus all his time and attention on one thing—"to praise, reverence, and serve God our Lord, and by this means to save his soul" (23). The freedom he has on the retreat to focus his mind and heart on one thing can bear great fruit. Because he is keeping silence, the exercitant is more apt to turn to the Lord, to think about Him and talk with Him. The more he approaches the Lord, the more he's present to Him; and the more he's present to Him, the more they can accomplish together. Describing these benefits of the retreat also heightens anticipation in the exercitant.

Before getting too far into the retreat, the director takes time to explain his role and to give the exercitant some instructions on how to relate to him as director. Although he certainly doesn't say this to the exercitant, the director isn't trying to befriend the exercitant. His role is to give the exercitant exercises to do and to help him recognize the work of the Lord and the work of the Enemy during the retreat. Along the way, the director also does some teaching. For example, he'll teach the exercitant how to make a meditation and how to discern the work of the Enemy and the work of the Lord in his soul. Some directors like to compare themselves to coaches: they give athletes drills, they teach about the game, and they point out the opponent's tactics, but the athlete does all the work. The coach is on the sidelines.

At some point early on, the director mentions to the exercitant that what he gets out of the retreat will be in proportion to the effort he puts into it. One of the earliest instructions on how to give the Exercises (called a "directory"), purportedly dictated by Ignatius, put it this way: "he can also be told by way of remark or admonition to remember that the fruit he draws from the Spiritual Exercises will be proportional to how fully he abandons himself into the Lord's hands."[33] The more a person applies himself, the more he'll get out of the retreat. It's important for the exercitant to understand that it's his retreat. He doesn't just participate in the retreat; he makes the retreat.

In order to ensure good communication, the director charges the exercitant with two tasks. First, he tells him to be "ready to put a good interpretation" on what the director says, rather than "condemn it as false" (22). He encourages the exercitant to ask questions, especially if he thinks the director has said something false. If he is making an exercise and something the director said comes to mind and begins to trouble him, the exercitant should assume the best of his director and talk to him at the first available opportunity.

Second, he encourages the exercitant to be open and honest with him.

At this point in the retreat, the director shouldn't overwhelm a person by discussing consolations and desolations at length. However, he usually wants to say something that will heighten the exercitant's awareness of what he is experiencing, so that he will begin to talk to the director about the movements of his soul, even before he knows what a consolation or desolation is. The director might say something like this, "By the way, you'll experience a lot of different things on this retreat. You might be filled with zeal to do something in your life differently. At another time, you might feel hopeless or full of doubt. Both kinds of experiences are normal, and telling me about them will help me guide you. Not everything you feel is a spiritual experience, but sometimes what you are feeling is the work of the Lord and his Holy Spirit or the work of the Enemy. When the time comes, I can help you figure out what's going on." Although the director doesn't normally begin the retreat with a comprehensive teaching on consolations and desolations, he should let the exercitant's needs guide him. If, for example, someone tells him about a consolation or desolation that he experienced on the way to the retreat, the director might very well begin the retreat by briefly introducing the topic of discernment of spirits.

Many of these preliminary comments are enumerated at the beginning of the *Spiritual Exercises* in a section entitled "Introductory Observations" or, in more literal translations, "Annotations." Ignatius notes, "The purpose of these observations is to provide some understanding of the Spiritual Exercises which follow and serve as a help both for the one who is to give them and for the exercitant" (1). So far we've referred to Annotations 20 (the benefits of withdrawing from daily life) and 17 (being open about the movements of one's soul). It's a good idea for the director to study all these annotations before beginning a retreat, but he should remember that some are only for him and others are for the exercitant. It's important for the director to realize that Ignatius's manual doesn't begin the way the retreat does. The director has to figure out which annotations he's going to give to a person, how he's going to give them and when he's going to give them.

Annotation 5 gives some noteworthy advice to the director for the beginning of the retreat: "It is very helpful to him who is receiving the Spiritual Exercises to enter into them with great courage and generosity toward his Creator and Lord, offering Him all his will and liberty, that His Divine Majesty may make use of his person and of all he has according to His most Holy Will" (5, Mullan). What's the director to do with this advice? He can suggest that the exercitant offer the entire retreat and himself with it to the Lord, praying for the grace to be open and generous with the Lord, so that he can love and serve the Lord in all things. The director can make this real by suggesting a specific time—before going to bed, for example—and a specific way—on his knees, perhaps—to make this offering.

There are a few more things the director should tell the exercitant at some point early in the retreat. He's got to give the exercitant some guidance about the use of his time, especially with respect to the meditations. Although a meditation normally lasts an hour, it's fine for a person to take an hour and 15 minutes or so to finish a meditation. He's not a slave to the clock. On the other hand, he shouldn't take any longer than an hour and a half. If he spends too long at any particular exercise, he'll become fatigued and will eventually tire of prayer. The exercitant must, however, spend at least a full hour making a meditation and colloquy. Ignatius recommends, "Let him rather exceed an hour than not use the full time. For the enemy is accustomed to make every effort that the hour to be devoted to a contemplation, meditation, or prayer should be shortened" (12).

The director also prepares the exercitant for the moment when he will be tempted to cut short his hour of prayer. Sooner or later, most exercitants experience moments of desolation. Their soul is moved by the Enemy. They feel hopeless or listless, and the last thing they want to do is continue in an exercise for a full hour. In such instances, Ignatius recommends his *agere contra* strategy. "Hence in order to fight against the desolation and conquer the temptation, the exercitant must always remain in the exercise a little more than a full hour. Thus he will accustom himself not only to resist the enemy, but even to overthrow him" (13). It turns out to be very important for the exercitant to pray, say, five extra minutes when he is tempted to quit five minutes early.

After a few days of the retreat, the director should make sure he inquires about a person's physical needs. Is he getting enough sleep? Enough to eat? Is his place of prayer adequate? Is he warm enough? The director might also ask the exercitant how he is experiencing the silence. It's a new experience for many exercitants, and many find it very difficult. Some exercitants can't bear being by themselves. They are accustomed to distracting themselves with pleasure or painkillers—licit or illicit. They need encouragement from the director. If they turn the volume down and keep it down, they are more likely to hear the voice of God.

Besides learning about the life and hopes of the exercitant and teaching him a few things about making the Exercises, the director explains what Ignatius calls the Principle and Foundation (23) on the first day or two of the retreat. It's called the Foundation because the whole retreat builds on it. Each meditation begins with a prayer which echoes this Foundation. It's called the Principle, because it's the source or origin of the Spiritual Exercises. It's like the headwaters of the Exercises; the whole retreat flows from it. At first glance it looks like a rather dry, academic statement. It is, however, an all-encompassing declaration of purposeful Christian living.

Ignatius was a keen observer of human nature. He knew that human beings act for a purpose. People have all sorts of wants and desires and they act to get what they want. They are making choices all the time. In fact, they choose the shape and direction of their lives, sometimes consciously, sometimes not so consciously. He also knew that if a person has a very clear-cut purpose in mind, he is more likely to achieve it. This is a rather commonplace truth, even today. Think of the Olympic athlete who orders her whole life to get the gold medal, or the business that achieves remarkable success because it has a well-defined purpose.

In his Principle and Foundation, Ignatius takes this rather commonplace truth—that it really is possible to think straight and act decisively to achieve a purpose—and applies it to the Christian life. The first step to dynamic, effective Christianity is to get clear about our purpose as human beings. "Man is created to praise, reverence, and serve God our Lord," says Ignatius (23). People live for different things—art, money, success, food—lots of different things. They can, however, choose to live for the praise and service of their Lord and God—the purpose for which God created them. Their purpose and God's purpose for them can be the same thing, if they so choose. Ignatius goes on to point out that God has graciously given us many tools to achieve our purpose: "the other things on the face of the earth are created for man and that they may help him in prosecuting the end for which he is created" (23, Mullan). Food, clothing, jobs, education, marriage, money, recreation and, indeed, all things are potential means. God gave them to us to help us achieve our purpose.

It only makes sense to use the things that will help us achieve our end and to avoid the things that don't help us. That's what clear-thinking people do. It's the way people normally act when they set out to achieve something. They choose not only what is good and legitimate but what will most help them achieve their end. Again, the Olympic athlete comes to mind. She chooses where to live based on what will help her win the gold. She orders her education around her training and her eating and her sleeping and so on. The Christian can, according to Ignatius, act in a similar manner, "desiring and choosing only what is most conducive for us to the end for which we are created," namely, "to praise, reverence and serve God our Lord" (23, Mullan).

Here, at the beginning of the Exercises, Ignatius is challenging the exercitant. "Go ahead," Ignatius is saying, "take the steering wheel of your life and become an acting person. Don't let life just happen to you!" Of course, Ignatius is offering him the opportunity to become a certain kind of acting person, one who accepts and pursues God's purpose for humankind. It turns out that considering the Principle and Foundation is a consciousness-raising exercise.

The big question facing Christians is, how do we choose what is most conducive to our end? "Man is created to praise, reverence and serve God our Lord," and the "other things on the face of the earth" are there for us to use to achieve our purpose. But how do we choose among them? How does a person choose where he lives or how he lives or what he does? Ignatius has an answer to this question (see Chapter 2). He says, in effect, make yourself stand as a balance beam at equilibrium before all the potential means, so that you are not inclined to poverty or to riches, to sickness or to health, to honor or to dishonor, to a long life or to a short life. As we've seen, he calls this being "indifferent," not inclined one way or the other. Only then can we freely see and choose what is "most conducive for us to the end for which we are created."

Because of its central role in the Exercises, it's important that the director understand the Principle and Foundation thoroughly. It turns out that Ignatius has several different ways of describing God's purpose in creating mankind. In the Principle and Foundation he says we are created "for the praise, reverence and service of God our Lord." At other times he uses phrases such as "for the glory and service of God our Lord" or "for the glory and honor of God our Lord." In fact, he speaks of "glory," "praise" and "honor" synonymously. When he does use one of these words, it's often in close relationship to the phrase "service of God."[34]

In this context, when Ignatius refers to the praise of God, he isn't talking about praise given in words. He's talking about living and acting for the glory of God. In Scripture, the "glory" of God often refers to the manifest presence of God: on Mt. Sinai, on Moses' face, in the cloud that filled Solomon's Temple and preeminently in Jesus. When Ignatius talks about glorifying God by praising, reverencing and serving Him, he is thinking of "human persons insofar as they are alive with God's life in Christ and are manifesting that life in the world."[35]

One of the most notable things about Ignatius's description of mankind's purpose is its dynamic character. As the exercitant will discover in his meditations on the life of Jesus and in the Contemplation to Attain Love, to be alive with God's life is to be active. God is sustaining His creation at each and every moment, He's laboring for His creation (including mankind) and He's pouring himself out for us and our world. The Exercises are an invitation to participate in that life, which is a sign of personal love.

Ignatius has more to say about God's purpose in creating mankind. He says that God created us so that we could praise, reverence and serve Him and by this means save our souls. God doesn't want our praise, reverence and service for His own sake, but for our sake. It's for the salvation of our souls. When he refers to the salvation of the soul, Ignatius doesn't simply mean obeying the Commandments so that when we die we can get to heaven. He means the health of the whole person. He means a well-ordered life instead of a disordered one. He's talking about the well-being of the person and the harmonious possession of life here and now. God desires our love and service not for His own sake, but for our sakes. He knows that by loving Him we will become alive in a way we didn't know was possible.

After declaring God's purpose for man, Ignatius goes on to talk about the purpose of the rest of creation. Puhl's translation reads, "The other things on the face of the earth are created for man to help him in attaining the end for which he is created." Mullan's translation is much more accurate, "And the other things on the face of the earth are created for man and that they may help him in prosecuting the end for which he is created." The contrast is "created for man to help him" versus "created for man and that they may help him." This distinction isn't too important at the beginning of the Exercises, but it does set the stage for the Contemplation to Attain Love. It captures better the overflowing love of God. "All other things on the face of the earth are created for man." What a gift!

In this context, "man" means human beings, taken collectively. Often when the exercitant hears the Principle and Foundation he immediately applies it to himself and begins to think something like, "God created *me* for a purpose. The other things on the face of the earth are for me to use to help me attain my purpose." In other words, the exercitant takes the Principle and Foundation in a personal sense. This is a good thing, but it does open the door to potential confusion. The exercitant can mistakenly think that "the other things on the face of the earth" means everything and *everybody* besides himself. That's not what Ignatius means. He means human beings, taken collectively, are created for a purpose. Therefore, "the other things on the face of the earth" doesn't refer to other human beings. Another human being is never to be used as a means to an end.

As we've noted in the second chapter, Ignatius's concept of indifference is easily misunderstood. He's not recommending a state of apathy. Nor is he recommending that someone be indifferent to all the suffering, all the pain and all the evil in the world. He certainly isn't recommending that the exercitant be indifferent to all the good and all the truth and all the beauty of the world. In other words, he isn't trying to make Christians who are somehow "above it all." His goal is, rather, to make Christians who are fully engaged in the world, one with God in His love for the world.

Ignatius is, however, saying that being detached—without partiality, like a balance beam at equilibrium—is a necessary prerequisite to making decisions in union with the Lord. As he explains what indifference means, the director may very well also make reference to inordinate attachments or, as we sometimes say, disordered loves and unruly desires. After all, most exercitants have some attachment that prevents them from being indifferent. It's important, however, to note that indifference and inordinate attachments are not the same thing. Inordinate attachments are obstacles to indifference. The director could very well present the Principle and Foundation without talking about these obstacles to indifference.

Often exercitants are puzzled when they hear that they shouldn't prefer "health to sickness, riches to poverty, honor to dishonor, a long life to a short life." It's helpful for the director to have a variety of examples at hand. The point of the examples is to highlight the freedom that comes from indifference. So, for example, the early Jesuit Antonio Ruiz de Montoya, who labored in the reductions of South America, was able to make important decisions because of the freedom his indifference afforded him. Should he go to Spain to procure for his beloved Indians the right to bear arms, or should he stay with them? Should he stay in Spain, tangled in bureaucratic red tape, or return to his beloved Indians? In both cases, he was able to detach himself from the available options and choose what would better serve his King. Likewise, the Pentecostal preacher and healer Smith Wigglesworth was indifferent. He was poor, totally dependent on the Lord. He had no income other than free-will offerings, yet he wasn't attached to poverty. He did not choose the cheapest way to travel because he knew it was more physically draining; he knew he had to be fit for his preaching and healing sessions. He used to say, "I'm not saving the Lord's money; I'm saving the Lord's servant."[36] He was free to see what would do more for the honor and glory of God.

Sometimes exercitants can see that they don't want money—having it or not having it—to influence their decision-making. They understand at least the theoretical possibility of making a choice on the basis of what would give God the greater glory, not on the basis of money. So too with honor and dishonor. They can see how it's a good thing for one's choice to be inspired by what would give God the greater glory, not by the potential praise or criticism of others. These same exercitants stumble at not preferring sickness to health or a long life to a short life. "Isn't sickness an evil?" they ask. "Didn't Jesus want everyone healed?"

One has only to think of a 16th-century Jesuit deciding to embark on a mission to India or South America to understand what Ignatius is saying about not preferring health to sickness or a long life to a short life. Sickness was an inevitable consequence of choosing to go on mission. A person who wasn't indifferent to sickness or health wouldn't have the ears to hear a call to the missions. Or, to take a more modern example, Father Damian was able to decide to go to Molokai to minister to the lepers because he was indifferent: not preferring sickness to health or a long life to a short life. He did not, however, think leprosy was a good thing. Ignatius is not saying that sickness is an objectively good thing. He is, however, saying that a healthy life is not the Christian's highest priority.

Again, it's important to note that making ourselves indifferent to all created things does not mean becoming indifferent to other people. The exercitant does want to make himself indifferent to all the potential means for achieving his purpose, but, as we have already noted, other people are not means. Sometimes an exercitant will ask if he should become detached from other people. Or, if he is familiar with the concept of inordinate attachments, he may ask if it's possible to be inordinately attached to someone. Strictly speaking, the answer is yes. It is possible to love a person inordinately, that is, to love a person more than God. Jesus himself is aware that people can love "father or mother more than me" or "son or daughter more than me (Mt. 10:37). Often, however, what appears at first glance to be an inordinate love of a person is actually something else. Many of our loves have a strong implemental component to them. For example, I love you because of the pleasure you bring me or the financial security you provide for me. In other words, I can be inordinately attached to the money or pleasure that I get from the relationship.

If someone asks such a question, it's a good idea for the director to pause and ask lots of questions. The exercitant could feel uncomfortable about a relationship and is expressing himself awkwardly. For example, a mother might ask whether she can love her children too much. The director should find out what she means by that. Perhaps she's wondering whether she spends too much money on her children or whether her decision to go to every one of her child's sporting events is a good one. If a young person asks if it's possible to be inordinately attached to his friends, he might mean any number of things. Perhaps he's thinking: If this Principle and Foundation is true, I've got to start hanging out with other people. Perhaps he's realizing in a somewhat inchoate manner that a love for honor has inspired most of his choices up till now. A question about indifference as it relates to other people is a signal that more conversation is needed.

The last part of the Principle and Foundation highlights the fact that choosing what is more for the glory of God isn't a philosophical or ideological choice. In this regard, Puhl's translation of it is somewhat misleading. His translation reads, "Our one desire and choice should be what is more conducive to the end for which we are created." Mullan reads, "desiring and choosing what is most conducive for us to the end for which we are created." The exercitant shouldn't be desiring and choosing what is more for the glory of God in the abstract. He should be choosing what is more for the glory of God in his particular situation and with his particular character.

The early directory dictated "at least in substance" by Ignatius makes a similar point about "the Foundation." It notes how some "persons who took the path of religious life and did not persevere in it" ended up hating God and renouncing the faith. Taking vows of poverty, chastity and obedience didn't help them reach the end for which God created them. Then it notes how "others entered religion after having been unable to live in the world without sinning" and they became really holy. If they had stayed "in the world" and pursued marriage, they might have ended up hating God and renouncing the faith. Likewise, it notes that some who possess riches end up in heaven and some who possess riches end up in hell. It then cautioned the exercitant against "embarking on things unthinkingly and inclining our minds without reflecting whether this is right for the service of God, whether it is my calling, whether this is the best path for me to travel and so reach the end for which God created me."[37]

When the director gives the Principle and Foundation, he has to do more than simply recite it. He needs to explain it. On the other hand, he shouldn't talk too much. He certainly shouldn't say everything we've said here. He has to introduce the Foundation, knowing that he will keep explaining it throughout the retreat. As he's explaining the Foundation, the director should be speaking directly to the exercitant, not reading from his notes or from the manual itself. The director is the authority, not some written text.

What happens after the director introduces the Principle and Foundation? Ignatius doesn't give any fixed time for the exercitant to consider the Principle and Foundation nor does he offer a method for digesting it. The Principle and Foundation isn't really a meditation, but a person should spend considerable time thinking it over, making sure he understands it. Ideally, the exercitant should understand it enough to be able to explain it to someone else. Not only should the exercitant have a preliminary understanding of the Foundation, but he should also begin to make a personal synthesis of it. He should begin to look at his life in light of the Principle and Foundation. How all this happens is up to the director.

After explaining the Foundation, the early Jesuits often sent an exercitant off to think about what use he had made of "the means" in his life. Sometimes they directed a person to consider the things in his life one by one—food, clothing, property, job, etc.—and ask himself how he had made use of these things to achieve his end.[38] Sometimes they recommended a more general strategy: "the exercitant can meditate on how much he has strayed from this goal in his life so far, what was the direction of his endeavors, and how many creatures he has abused which were supposed to help him in attaining his final end."[39] Sometimes they simply sent an exercitant off to think about the Principle and Foundation. We, too, have sometimes simply instructed an exercitant to think about it. Sometimes we've sent him off with one question: What are you living for? On occasion we've asked an exercitant to rephrase the Principle and Foundation in his own words.

We've also given some exercitants an assignment, similar to some of those recommended by the early Jesuits, which helps them evaluate their own lives in light of the Principle and Foundation. We ask the exercitant to make a list of things he values. In order to help him make that list, we give him some questions to consider: How do you spend your time? When you have some extra time, how do you spend it? How do you spend your money? When you have some extra money, how do you spend it? What do you daydream about? What makes you mad or irritates you? We then instruct the exercitant to take his list of values and go through it, item by item, asking himself three questions: What purpose does this serve in my life? How have I used this to achieve my end? Can I or would I live without this thing I value? In short, the exercitant is asking himself whether his purpose is the purpose for which God created him. He's also asking himself whether he relates to the things which he values as means or as ends in themselves.

During the first few days of the Spiritual Exercises, the director not only gets to know the exercitant, orients him to the retreat and presents the Foundation, but he also introduces the notion of inordinate attachments. The director has to decide when he wants to do this. He could decide to talk about inordinate attachments in his first meeting with an exercitant. For example, someone might say that he wanted to make the Exercises because he's sick of doing everything out of a love for money. The director then might very well decide to start talking about inordinate attachments. He could also introduce the topic as he is explaining the Principle and Foundation. As the director talks about indifference, it's natural to begin talking about obstacles to indifference. A director might choose to wait until the exercitant has had some time to digest the Foundation before he introduces inordinate attachments. Often, after considering the Foundation, a person will begin talking about his inordinate attachments without calling them such. It's ideal when the director's description of disordered loves and unruly desires comes just at the moment the exercitant is becoming conscious of them.

If the exercitant doesn't give the director an opportunity to bring up inordinate attachments, the director should bring them up anyway at some point. It's not immediately obvious from the text of the *Spiritual Exercises*, but conversation about inordinate attachments should be a part of the First Week. The exercitant might become increasingly aware of his inordinate attachments during the Second Week, but he and the director should at least begin talking about them in the First Week.

As the director talks with the exercitant about inordinate attachments, it's usually a good time to highlight the purpose of the Exercises. The exercitant is beginning to feel the enormity of the task in front of him—taming his disordered loves and unruly desires. The director can then offer the Exercises as a tool designed for just such a task. They are designed to help a person tame his disordered loves and unruly desires and put his life in order. Ignatius puts it this way. The Spiritual Exercises, he says, "have as their purpose the conquest of self and the regulation of one's life in such a way that no decision is made under the influence of any inordinate attachment" (21).[40] In other words, the Exercises enable the exercitant to make every decision out of love for the Lord and not on account of the influence of his unruly desires and disordered loves.

When Ignatius says the Spiritual Exercises are designed to conquer oneself and regulate one's life, he means that they are designed to help a person take stock and then take charge of his life. He doesn't mean that they are a tool for total self-abnegation or an excuse for self-loathing. When the exercitant conquers himself and regulates his life, that is, rules his life, he's taking charge of himself so that he can accomplish the purpose for which God created him. He brings some order into his life. He takes his place in creation, under God and over created things.

Sometimes a person can misunderstand the director's words about inordinate attachments and mistakenly think the whole retreat is about unearthing and conquering them. Although the success of the retreat depends on the exercitant's willingness to fight his inordinate attachments, they are not the subject of the retreat. In his opening conferences, the director has to guard against unintentionally communicating that detachment is the goal of the retreat. Taming one's disordered loves and unruly desires is a means, not an end in itself. It's a means to making decisions with God in love, acting in the world in Christ, as Christ, and doing God's will in the world.

Considering the Principle and Foundation leads naturally to self-evaluation and an awareness that change is needed in order to live it out. There's a charming story told by an English Jesuit scholar, Joseph Rickaby (1847-1927), that illustrates this moment in the Exercises well:

> A sailor-boy came to make a retreat in a Jesuit house. He was given a paper with this Principle and Foundation printed on it, and with some brief explanation was left to himself. When the Father who had charge of him came to see him, he found him in a violent state of agitation. . . . Asked, "what did you do at meditation?" "Do," he said, "I stamped up and down the room, saying, d_mn it, it's true, d_mn it, it's true." He was told that he had made just the meditation St. Ignatius wanted.[41]

Although not everyone who makes the Exercises reacts as colorfully or as consciously as this, considering the Principle and Foundation brings a person face to face with the fact that not everything in his life is ordered toward the glory of God. The next step in the Exercises capitalizes on this moment.

There are several different ways to handle the next step in the Exercises, but in our retreats we normally have the exercitant take some time and do a review of his whole life, calling to mind how he has sinned in thought, word and deed. Many people hear the word "sin" and think immediately of offending God and hurting His feelings. That's not what Ignatius means by sin. For him, sin has to do with disorder. The person who is sinning is out of order, unruly and disobedient. God is ruling the world and the person who is sinning is working against God's rule. It's God's world. Because of sin, things don't go the way God wants them to go.

Before telling the exercitant how to do such an examination of his conscience, the director should give a short teaching about sin, along the lines of Ignatius's teaching (32-42), although updated. Some of Ignatius's concerns can be left out, such as what does and does not constitute an idle oath, but the director should be very forthright and direct about sin. In fact, he should name some sins, following the inspiration of the Holy Spirit. Although he will talk about sins of thought, the director should also name sins that one could videotape or audiotape, avoiding vague generalities. So, for example, instead of mentioning "being angry," he might mention "yelling abusively."

The director's teaching might go something like the following. "I'm sure you are aware that not everything we do serves and glorifies God. In fact, sometimes we sin. If we're honest with ourselves, we know that we sin. As Scripture says, 'all have sinned and fall short of the glory of God' (Rm. 3:23). Would any of us want our whole life story written up in a newspaper or videotaped? All our thoughts, the things we have said, the things we have done in secret, the things we should have done but didn't—would we want all of that to be read by everyone we know? Each one of us has sinned. I'm not talking about wishing you were a better or a different person. I'm talking about doing things that God has specifically said not to do. As Jesus said, 'Do not kill, Do not steal, Do not bear false witness, Honor your father and mother' (Lk. 18:20). Some sins are so serious—Scripture calls them 'mortal sins'—that they lead to death (1 Jn. 5:16-17). There are other things too, maybe not as serious, but things that we are ashamed of and are still wrongdoing.

"So, when I'm talking about sin, I'm talking about thoughts, words and deeds. Let's begin with our thoughts. After all, evil deeds are always preceded by evil thoughts. You can sin with your thoughts if you consent to an evil thought with the intention of carrying it out. That's sinning. If for a while you take delight in considering serious wrongdoing, you may sin even if in the end you discard the thoughts. On the other hand, by resisting evil thoughts as soon as they come to mind, you show your love and commitment to the Lord.

"We can also sin with our words. Taking the name of the Lord in vain is mentioned in the Ten Commandments. We can sin by damaging another person's reputation by our speech. Slander is speaking falsely about someone in a way that damages his reputation. Detraction is speaking truthfully about someone in a way that damages his reputation. There's also gossip and lying and other sins of the tongue. Remember Ephesians 4:29: 'Let no evil talk come out of your mouths, but only such as is good for edifying, as fits the occasion, that it may impart grace to those who hear.'

"And, of course, we can sin with our deeds, for example, fraud, stealing, drunkenness, fornication—that's sexual relations outside of marriage—masturbation, homosexual acts, abortion and involvement with the occult are all sins." As we have noted, the director could end here, but he should mention other sins, if so inspired.

After this introduction, we use a modified form of the examination of conscience (43). This examination of conscience was designed to be used daily (more on that later), but at this moment we use it as a form for a general review of one's life. Our modified form looks like this:

1. Begin by thanking God "for all the favors received." The exercitant should concentrate on some of the big blessings of his life. This shouldn't take a long time.
2. Ask "for the grace to know my sins and to rid myself of them." At this point, the director hasn't taught him very much about prayer, so he should model the heartfelt nature of this prayer for him in words such as: "Lord, will you show me where I'm messing up? Tell me the truth. Let me know what I say and do and think that I shouldn't. Lord, reveal them to me."
3. Make a review of my life, going over one period of my life after another, looking first at thoughts, then words and then deeds. This will be the bulk of the exercise.
4. Ask the Lord's forgiveness.
5. Resolve to amend my life.
6. Say the Lord's Prayer.

We usually have the exercitant spend about an hour on this exercise. He doesn't need to call to mind every sin he's ever committed. The director should remember that at this point the exercitant isn't asking for sorrow for his sins. He's just asking for the grace to know his sins and rid himself of them. Later on in the First Week, the exercitant will return to this exercise and use it as a starting point for his second meditation.

The exercitant should be honest during this exercise. On the one hand, he shouldn't gloss over things. On the other hand, he shouldn't be inventing evil or making things out to be worse than they are. Also, the director should warn the exercitant not to turn something he doesn't like about himself into something really grievous. For example, "being high strung" or "being shy" aren't sins. Again, if a person asks himself whether this is something he can videotape or audiotape (or whether he's thinking about something he could videotape or audiotape), he'll avoid a lot of confusion and make a better examination of conscience.

Although the exercitant may not make a perfect examination of conscience, the director can count on the fact that all people know they have sinned. At Vatican II, the council fathers eloquently described this reality:

> Deep within his conscience man discovers a law which he has not laid upon himself but which he must obey. Its voice, ever calling him to love and to do what is good and to avoid evil, tells him inwardly at the right moment: do this, shun that. . . . His conscience is man's most secret core, and his sanctuary. There he is alone with God whose voice echoes in his depths.[42]

The exercitant's examination of conscience is a meeting with God. He becomes aware of the voice of God in the depths of his being.

Most people have no problem making an examination of conscience, but occasionally the director will run across someone who feels guilty about things which aren't sins. For example, an exercitant feels guilty about all the many things he thinks he ought to do. "I ought to trim my bushes. They're taking over the yard. And I ought to clean out my garage and I ought to answer all my email," and so on. Another exercitant feels guilty because his parents wanted him to become a priest and he didn't. Or a parent who has given his or her child good instruction about God's commandments, combined with love and a good example, might say, "I feel guilty because my son is living with his girlfriend." Someone might say, "I would like to spend some time visiting nursing homes. My present responsibilities prevent this, but I feel guilty because people are being neglected."

We are touching on a complicated subject here. If the director wants to know more, he can read Ignatius's notes concerning scruples (345-351). There is, however, a simple formula that can help most people think straight about sin. Sin = Wrongdoing + Responsibility. Some exercitants feel guilty where there is no wrongdoing. There is no wrongdoing involved in the failure to trim the bushes, clean out the garage and answer absolutely every email. God never said bushes must be a certain height. In fact, the bushes He takes care of are rather unkempt. Likewise, the man who decided his vocation without consulting his parents is not guilty of wrongdoing. His parents have no right to decide his vocation. In both these cases, there is a perceived difference between the way things are and the way they ought to be, but the "ought" doesn't come from God and His Church. The exercitant may wish things were different, but he hasn't sinned.

It can also happen that some people feel guilty about wrongdoing for which they are not responsible. The parent whose son is living with his girlfriend is not responsible for his son's choice. There is wrongdoing present, but the parent is not responsible. There may be lonely people in nursing homes—and perhaps there is some wrongdoing somewhere on someone's part—but the exercitant is not personally responsible for this.

Sometimes a person can mistakenly think he is responsible for something he has no control over. For example, some perverse thought or vengeful feeling might pop into his mind. He is not responsible for that. If he accepts it, encourages it and gives it a home in his consciousness, he is responsible for that. People often experience guilt feelings in the area of sexuality because they find their thoughts or imaginations or fantasies invaded by sexual images. Often these are so vivid or alluring that they experience sexual feelings. Then there is a feeling of guilt. Sexual relations are attractive. People are drawn to them. These are automatic reactions. However, it takes the intervention of intelligence and will to change these reactions to responses, for example, to take pleasure. The response is under a person's control.

At this point in the Exercises, just after the exercitant has spent time considering the Principle and Foundation, the early Jesuits did something slightly different. Normally, they taught the exercitant how to make a particular examination of conscience (24-31) and how to make a daily examination of conscience (43). They gave the teaching on sin (32-42) along with instructions on how to make the daily examen (43). Then, at the end of the First Week, the exercitant did an exhaustive review of all the sins of his life.

The particular examination of conscience is an aggressive and determined way to focus on and root out one particular sin or fault. To practice this exercise, the exercitant does essentially three things. Upon rising, he resolves to overcome the defect. At lunch he reviews his day so far, hour by hour, noting on a piece of paper the number of times he has failed. He then renews his resolution to avoid the defect. After dinner he does the same thing. He does this exercise with the expectation that, as the days pass, the number of times he fails will be fewer and fewer.

The daily examination of conscience is a review of one's life at the end of each day. The exercitant gives thanks for the favors received, asks for the grace "to know my sins and to rid myself of them," examines his thoughts, words and deeds that day, asks for forgiveness when needed and resolves to do things differently. He then ends with the Lord's Prayer.

We prefer to present the particular examination of conscience and the daily examination of conscience when the exercitant begins to feel a need for them. For example, sometime during the course of the retreat, the exercitant may begin to struggle with one particular thing, such as daydreaming during a meditation. If he talks to the director about the problem, it's a perfect moment to teach him the particular examen. Likewise with the daily examen. Often, after making more of the First Week meditations, the exercitant experiences a new heartfelt desire to avoid sin. When he expresses this desire to his director, the director can then present him with the daily examination of conscience. These two exercises make a bigger impact on a person when they are presented as the answer to a felt need. Becoming aware of the choices he is making and then evaluating those choices is a powerful tool for change.

Again and again in the first few days of the Exercises, the exercitant confronts the fact that he is making choices all the time and the fact that different choices are possible. The Foundation is a bold declaration of possibilities for choice and action. The exercitant hears and considers that it is possible to think straight and act decisively to accomplish his God-given purpose. As he makes the examens, the exercitant again encounters himself as a decision-making creature. Sin isn't something that happens to him. He's not a helpless victim of temptation. He chooses what he thinks, says and does, and he can choose differently. He can actually use the things that will help him achieve his end and avoid the things that don't help him, if he wants to. In other words, the exercitant catches a glimpse of the fact that he is free and that he is responsible for his life and his choices.

CHAPTER 5

MAKING MEDITATIONS

After considering the Principle and Foundation and examining his conscience, the exercitant begins a cycle of five meditations. For approximately four days, four or five times a day, he considers sin and its consequences, both in the world and in himself. These meditations of the First Week—and indeed all Ignatian meditations (or contemplations)—have essentially the same structure.[43] They all have clearly defined starting and ending points. The meditations begin with a prayer, followed by two or three preludes. Then each meditation contains anywhere from three to six points for the exercitant to consider carefully. A meditation closes with a colloquy and the Lord's Prayer.

As the exercitant begins to make the five meditations of the First Week, the director has several things to do. He continues teaching about how to make the retreat, using primarily the Annotations (1-20) and the Additional Directions (73-90). Of course, he gives the meditations, but he also has to teach how to make the meditations. He has to listen closely to what the exercitant tells him about his meditations, watching for the work of the Lord and the work of the Enemy, and he has to begin to teach the exercitant how to discern the movements of his soul. In subsequent chapters, we'll discuss the content of the First Week's meditations and all the various movements of the soul a person is apt to experience as he makes the meditations. For now, however, we'll look at the form of a typical Ignatian meditation and the director's guidance of the exercitant as he learns to use this form.

In order to guide someone well, it's important for the director to understand the structure of a meditation and the purpose of each of its parts. Although, in general, the director doesn't explain the strategy behind the Exercises, he does eventually explain a lot about the strategy behind the meditations' form. So for example, he wouldn't explain how the meditation on Hell sets the stage for the exercises of the Second Week, but he should briefly explain why it's important "to ask God our Lord for what I want and desire" (48).

A meditation always begins with the same prayer: "to ask grace of God our Lord that all my intentions, actions and operations may be directed purely to the service and praise of His Divine Majesty" (46). Ignatius calls this "the preparatory prayer." It's an echo of the first lines of the Principle and Foundation, "Man is created to praise, reverence and serve God our Lord" and is meant to call to mind the whole Principle and Foundation. Normally the exercitant prays this prayer five times a day, calling to mind his purpose in life. No matter what he ends up willing in a particular situation, he should always be willing the praise and service of his Lord. He's asking God, even begging God, that this will always be true of him.

When Ignatius speaks of "intentions" here, he means a purposeful determination to act in a certain way or to do a certain thing. He doesn't mean a mere velleity or some kind of slight wish or inclination. Commentators on the *Spiritual Exercises* aren't certain why he makes a distinction between actions and operations. Some say that actions can be understood as exterior activities and operations as interior activities. Once a person understands what he is praying in this opening prayer, it's fine for him to put it in his own words. For example, someone could pray that all that he is and all that he says and does may make his Lord louder, brighter and firmer in the world—more visible, more manifest, more glorious.

Following his opening petition, the exercitant makes two or three preludes. The exercises of the First Week have two preludes, while most of the subsequent exercises have three.[44] "Prelude" is sometimes translated as "preamble" or "introduction." It has the connotation of "entering." The preludes, along with the preparatory prayer, serve the same function as tuning an instrument before playing. They prepare and dispose the exercitant for what follows. They give him a chance to recollect himself and enter the meditation with more attention and reverence.

In the first prelude the exercitant makes a "mental representation of the place" (47) by seeing it in his mind's eye. This becomes more important in the Spiritual Exercises of the Second, Third and Fourth Weeks when he is contemplating events in the life of Jesus. Ignatius isn't asking the exercitant to ponder truths about the life of Jesus; he's asking him to ponder events in the life of Jesus, things that happened. The Gospels are not stories designed to illustrate ideas that can in principle be stated without recourse to the vehicle of narrative. Quite the contrary. In fact, if someone doesn't make an attempt to see the Gospel scene in his mind's eye, he runs the danger of missing the revelation of the Gospel: the Word made flesh. He's less likely to recognize Christ alive today in the flesh of his brothers and sisters or, indeed, his own flesh. The exercitant's "representation of the place" might not be historically accurate, but without it his prayer is likely to become speculations about God, rather than a personal encounter.

During the First Week, the first prelude happens to be somewhat different. As Ignatius himself says, the subject matter isn't as easy to visualize as events in the life of Jesus. The exercitant is meditating on sin and its consequences, so Ignatius has him picture himself as someone who daily experiences the effects of sin. The place is, so to speak, being a part of sinful humanity. In all the meditations, however, taking time to make a mental representation of the place is a way of becoming present to the subject matter of the meditation. Having a picture in his mind also helps the exercitant when he is distracted. If his mind wanders and he finds himself asking, Where was I?, he can return to his mental image and reenter his meditation.

After making a mental representation of the place, the exercitant asks "God our Lord for what I want and desire" (48).[45] Ignatius directs him to diligently ask for certain graces. Sometimes the exercitant asks God for sorrow with Christ in sorrow, or joy with Christ in joy. At other times he implores God for more love for Jesus or sorrow for his sins. The exercitant is asking for a grace. It turns out that the gift he is asking for is most often some kind of emotion.

It's a remarkable strategy on Ignatius's part. He's working with a person who is well-disposed to the Lord. After all, the exercitant is willing to make a 30-day retreat and has been praying for an open and generous heart. He wants, at least theoretically, to be friends with his Lord and to make all his choices in union with his friend. After helping him think straight about his God-given purpose and examine his life in light of that purpose, what does Ignatius do? He gives the exercitant 30 days of exercises in which he begs God to enkindle his heart with love.

Ignatius knows that God alone gives graces and that a person can't get the graces of the meditations by sheer willpower. The whole retreat relies on the fact that God is always ready to pour out His graces on the exercitant. One of the early Jesuits put it well:

> Not without reason, there are persons who wonder what accounts for the fact that the Exercises are able in so short a time to bring about such extraordinary progress in the spiritual life and such remarkable transformations of life and behavior, and in a sense of the entire person. On closer inspection, however, it is not difficult to grasp the cause of this lavish outpouring of the grace of God—from whom comes every best and every perfect gift. Anyone who thinks of God loftily and reverently, as is meet, ought to hold this of him above all: that the sun is not so ready to shed its light, or any other secondary cause to produce its natural effect, as God himself, the sun of all wisdom and justice, entirely free but also by his very nature (which is goodness) utterly generous, is ready to enlighten and perfect our minds with the rays of his grace. In fact, we ought to hold that within the limits of his creatures' capacity he is on his part more eager to bestow greater gifts than lesser ones, as beseems his divine majesty and magnificence.[46]

Asking for "what I want or desire" disposes the exercitant for the grace he desires. Making the meditations helps create an environment in which he can recognize God's action. Making the meditations does not cause God's action. Anyone who has made the Exercises can testify to this fact. When the exercitant experiences the grace he is asking for, he experiences it as sheer gift.

Even though this part of the exercise is in some sense preparatory, it is a very important part of the meditation. It's like the gas for an engine. The director should encourage the exercitant to pour all his energy into asking for the grace of the meditation. It's also helpful for a person to be mindful of the grace he's asked for throughout the rest of the meditation. As he considers the various points of the meditation, the particular grace of the meditation can serve like a point on the horizon toward which he is heading. The exercitant "should understand the end and fruit to be garnered in each meditation so that he may acquire it, keeping his eye on the target throughout the entire meditation."[47] So, for example, in the first meditation, as he considers three very real sins, the exercitant should occasionally eye his target—shame and confusion.

After the preparatory prayer and the preludes, Ignatius gives the exercitant three to six points to consider. To begin with, the exercitant considers these points, using first his memory, then his understanding, and finally his will. Ignatius calls these the "three powers of the soul." Today people don't usually think in terms of "powers of the soul," but they can easily catch on to what Ignatius has in mind here. Ignatius wants exercitants to consider and respond to Gospel events with their whole selves.

In a meditation, the exercitant uses his memory to recall the facts. If, for example, he's meditating on Adam and Eve's sin, he briefly calls to mind the facts of the Genesis narrative. Ignatius does not envision a person taking time during an exercise to read the scriptural account or accounts of a certain event. *Lectio divina*, the slow, meditative reading of Scripture, is a wonderful practice, but that's not what Ignatius is directing a person to do here. The exercitant should prepare for his meditation by reading the pertinent Scripture passage ahead of time. At the appropriate moment in his exercise, he should simply call to mind what happened. If he uses his Bible, he uses it only as an aid to his memory.

After calling to mind the facts, the exercitant then uses his mind to think over the facts and to gain insight into them. Ignatius calls this making "use of the acts of the intellect in reasoning" (3). Ignatius wants the exercitant to digest the facts, but he isn't recommending an academic study. For example, when considering the sin of Adam and Eve, a person shouldn't be comparing translations, looking up cross-references or doing a word study. When Ignatius talks about using the mind to consider certain points, he's not talking about using the mind to accumulate more facts. A person should also avoid pondering hypotheticals, such as what would have happened if Eve had eaten the fruit and Adam hadn't? Ignatius thinks it's ideal when one "takes the solid foundation of facts, and goes over it and reflects on it for himself" (2). If he does this, the exercitant "may find something that makes them a little clearer or better understood" (2).

Let's say someone is pondering the sin of Adam and Eve. He calls to mind the facts of the narrative. He's thinking about the consequences of their sin. He remembers the words of Adam and Eve after their sin. Adam said, "The woman whom thou gavest to be with me, she gave me fruit of the tree, and I ate" (Gen. 3:12). Eve said, "The serpent beguiled me and I ate" (Gen. 3:13). Then, according to Ignatius, "the understanding is to be used to think over the matter in greater detail" (51). So the exercitant begins to think about what they said. He notices how Adam blames Eve, and Eve blames the serpent. He might think about instances when he has blamed someone else. He thinks about blaming. He might ask himself, What else could they have done? He ponders this for a bit and comes to the conclusion that they could have taken responsibility for their actions. A light goes on for him. He thinks a new thought: Ohhh. A fruit of sin is a failure to take responsibility for one's action.

Although a person may relish the insights that come from his meditation, Ignatius wants him to go one step further. He wants the exercitant to respond to the facts with his heart. Ignatius calls this making use "of the acts of the will in manifesting our love" (3). One's perception of an Ignatian meditation could be skewed if one understands by "will" simply the ability to will and make decisions, apart from any affectivity. For Ignatius the will is the seat of what we commonly refer to as "feelings" or "emotions" or "affections." When Ignatius speaks of "memory, understanding and will," one could just as easily say "memory, understanding and heart." Ignatian meditations are not meant to be cerebral. The goal is an affective response.

So, after getting insight into an event, the exercitant should respond with his heart to what he is contemplating. For example, after realizing that a fruit of sin is a failure to take responsibility for his actions, a person might feel shame and even stir up shame by thinking of all the times he's failed to take responsibility for his own actions. He uses "the will to rouse more deeply the emotions" (50). It's important for him to release his affections into the meditation. To grow in love of the Lord, the exercitant needs to do more than to see and to understand. An exclamation is needed, a cry of the heart. It could be a cry of wonder or pain or joy or shame or compassion or sorrow or admiration—whatever might be triggered by the subject of his meditation.

Sometimes people become enamored of all their new insights into the life of Jesus and the facts of salvation. While it's important for a person to use his understanding to gain insight, the meditations are for more than insight. They are aimed at the heart. The early Jesuits were well aware of this. One early Jesuit, a novice master in Spain for most of his life, commented:

> Regarding meditation, he [the exercitant] should be told to endeavor to avoid in this exercise too much intellectual speculation and to try to handle this matter with the affections of the will rather than reasonings and speculations of the mind. For this, one should be aware that the intellect both helps and can hinder the working of the will, which is love for divine things. For, while it is necessary for the intellect to precede the will, guiding it and giving it knowledge of what it is to love, nevertheless when the speculation is excessive it hinders the affections of the will, for it does not allow it room or time to work.[48]

The exercitant's insights are meant to fuel the fire of his love. They are meant to enkindle the affections. On the other hand, even though the meditations are aimed at stirring up the heart, it's a mistake for someone to run to love too quickly, without stopping to ponder and understand first. Knowledge is the gateway to love. The exercitant's experience will deepen if he first ponders a point, but he shouldn't stop at insight.

One early Jesuit described the process of meditating:

> He should behave like someone who, in the faint light of dawn, deeply yearns to see the content of a picture he holds in his hands, eagerly awaiting the sun's rays, and turning the picture again and again toward where the approaching light will enable him to see it better. Meditating in this fashion, he keeps turning over the points interiorly in different ways, ardently longing for spiritual light to come. He should keep beseeching strongly until aroused to attention and devotion.[49]

However he chooses to turn the picture, the exercitant should make sure he is using his memory, intellect and will/heart when he is meditating, all the while keeping in mind the grace he's asked the Lord for according to the particular meditation.

After considering the points of the meditation, the exercitant makes what Ignatius calls a "colloquy." The word comes from Latin and means "a mutual discourse." At this point in the exercise, among other things, Ignatius wants a person to speak with the Lord "as one friend to another" (54). In the First Week, Ignatius gives the exercitant rather specific instructions for his conversation with the Lord. He directs the exercitant, in general terms, what to talk about. In subsequent weeks, he usually just tells the exercitant to make a colloquy, although occasionally he'll give him some instructions for his colloquy. Whether Ignatius gives instructions for the colloquy or not, he always intends for the exercitant to speak with the Lord from his heart.

The colloquy is meant to be the culmination of the meditation, as one early Jesuit noted: "Since all the activities of meditation culminate in prayer, this prayer comes at the end of our exercises; it is carried out in the form of a conversation. Everything that precedes it—mental reasoning or knowledge of the truth; affections of fear, hope, love, trust, zeal, etc.; holy desires and resolutions—is a kind of preparation for this act of prayer."[50] During a meditation, the exercitant uses his mind to enkindle his affections. He enkindles his affections so that he can then speak to the Lord from his heart.

What's the subject of a colloquy? It varies from day to day and even from meditation to meditation. Although the exercitant can talk to the Lord about anything, he often speaks about what's happened in him as he's made his meditation. He has just experienced something—most often an event from the life of the Lord—with his mind and heart. It's somewhat natural for the exercitant to then turn to the Lord and tell Him about what he's just experienced. He might, for example, describe to the Lord how his consideration of Adam and Eve's sin made him feel. At other times, the exercitant's colloquy may have nothing to do with the meditation per se. He might, for instance, choose to talk to the Lord about his daily life beyond the retreat, "now asking some grace, now blaming oneself for some misdeed, now communicating one's affairs, and asking advice in them" (54, Mullan).

Whatever the topic of the colloquy, it's meant to be a moment of self-revelation in which the exercitant reveals his inward life to the Lord, believing that the Lord wants to hear everything he is revealing. Likewise, since it is a colloquy, not a soliloquy, God is also working to reveal Himself the best He can, given the limits of the exercitant's mind and heart. Usually, during the course of the Exercises, with the director's help, a person grows in his ability to discern the Lord's actions, gestures and words in his prayer. By this mutual intimate self-revelation, love and friendship grow.

Although Ignatius says that the exercitant should speak to God as "one friend to another," he doesn't mean that the exercitant should approach God as an equal. He says, in fact, that the colloquy is made "by speaking exactly as one friend speaks to another, or as a servant speaks to a master" (54). In our egalitarian culture, this might sound puzzling—speaking in one breath of the relationship of friends and of the relationship of servants and masters. It wasn't so odd to Ignatius. The tradition of chivalry gave him a picture of knights serving their lord and king in true friendship. Today we might use the image of an employer and a longtime trusted and valued employee who serves as an alter-ego to his boss, or the image of a much-loved coach and his dedicated player.

As a rule, Ignatius is very aware of a person's place before God as creature and servant. Even while he is pouring out his heart to his Father, the exercitant shouldn't forget who he is and who his Father is. In his introductory observations on the Exercises, Ignatius notes that, when "we address God our Lord or His saints either vocally or mentally, greater reverence is required on our part than when we use the intellect in reasoning" (3). The exercitant should, then, be reverential in his colloquy.

What does Ignatius mean by "reverence"? We can answer this question by looking at how he uses the word in the Exercises and by looking at his own behavior. He uses "reverence" in the Principle and Foundation. Man is created "to praise, reverence, and serve God our Lord" (23). The angels reverence and obey their Creator (50). Before making a meditation, the exercitant is instructed to make an act of reverence or humility (75). Subjects reverence and obey a temporal king (92). While meditating on the Nativity, the exercitant is to imagine himself a servant who serves the needs of the holy family with homage and reverence (114).

Laynez, one of Ignatius's early disciples, left a beautiful picture of his friend's reverence. When in Rome, Ignatius would customarily go to a terrace where he could see the open sky. Then, according to Laynez,

> He would stand there and take off his hat; without stirring he would fix his eyes on the heavens for a short while. Then, sinking to his knees, he would make a lowly gesture of reverence to God. After that he would sit on a bench, for his body's weakness did not permit him to do otherwise. There he was, head uncovered, tears trickling drop by drop, in such sweetness and silence, that no sob, no sight, no noise, no movement of the body was noticed.[51]

This reverence, of a subject for a superior, should be cultivated by the exercitant and encouraged by the director, even though it is countercultural. Sometimes even telling the exercitant to practice good manners in his colloquy helps.

A meditation always ends with the Lord's Prayer. Although the exercitant may not be aware of it, when he is praying this prayer he is praying in Christ, as Christ. He's identifying with Jesus' point of view and making Jesus' desires his own. It's a foretaste of things to come. The exercitant's prayer and Jesus' prayer are one. He's praying the Lord's prayer.

So what does the director do when, during the First Week, it's time for the exercitant to begin meditating and making colloquies using Ignatius's method? The director, of course, needs to teach him how to make an Ignatian meditation. This can't be done in a single meeting, but the director still needs to get the exercitant started.

There are a couple of strategies available to a director. Some directors like to give the exercitant a general overview of an Ignatian meditation, saying one or two sentences about each of the parts. Exercitants are usually all ears, especially if they know that they are going to be using this particular form for the next few weeks. Then the director gives the exercitant the particulars he needs to make the first meditation. Other directors like to get the exercitant started without doing much explaining. They simply tell the exercitant: pray this prayer and then think about this point and then think about this, and so on. After the exercitant has made one or two meditations, the director then begins gradually to explain to him what he is doing. "You'll notice that you began by praying that all your actions, intentions and operations may be directed purely to the praise and service of His Divine Majesty. That's called a preparatory prayer. You'll begin every meditation with this prayer. You might have noticed that it echoes the Principle and Foundation. You're praying that God will give you the grace always to be true to the Principle and Foundation." These directors move from the particular to the general. Their strategy is to explain the form after the exercitant has experienced it.

Introducing someone to this new format for prayer is a big job. At this point in the retreat there is so much information the director needs to convey to the exercitant that he may decide to meet with the exercitant more than once a day. Eventually, though, the exercitant and the director settle into a rhythm of meeting about once a day. Then the real work begins. In a way, the whole retreat is a process of learning how to meditate and make colloquies. When the early Jesuits traveled into Germany, people there "rejoiced that teachers of affectivity had been found."[52] As the director meets with the exercitant, he's taking up the mantle as a teacher of affectivity.

As the director introduces someone to an Ignatian meditation, it's helpful to emphasize two things. The director is beginning to teach him that meditating on the various points is not the most important part of an exercise. The aim is to make the colloquy and to experience the grace. So, early on, the director should highlight for the exercitant the importance of the second prelude, where the exercitant prays for a particular grace. Eager to get on to what they perceive as the meat of the meditation, novices tend to gloss over this prelude. The director should encourage the exercitant to pour himself into this prayer, asking, even begging God for the grace. The exercitant needs to understand that this prelude powers the meditation as gasoline powers an engine. It's also helpful to remind him that as he makes the meditation he should be aiming for the grace he is asking for.

Early on, the director should also highlight the importance of the colloquy. In order to meditate well on all the points, people tend to cut short the colloquy or leave it out altogether. The director needs to make sure the exercitant knows not to cut the colloquy short for the sake of finishing a meditation. It's tempting for the director to explain that meditation is for the purpose of prayer and therefore the meditation is all about the colloquy. Yet he shouldn't do this, because he'll be setting the exercitant up for failure. At first the exercitant won't be very good at making a colloquy. Normally it takes the whole retreat for someone to experience a good colloquy. In the First Week, then, it won't help the exercitant to stress the importance of the colloquy. It's enough for him to know that he should always have a colloquy, even if that means not finishing all the points.

The exercitant might initially find these structured exercises awkward or cumbersome, but the director should encourage him to persevere. One of the best ways to encourage perseverance is to speak with confidence about the long-term benefits. Once the exercitant gets used to them, the meditations prove to be a gateway to love and friendship with God. They aren't just a gateway to good prayer times. They are a gateway to shared life. Conversations are just a part of life.

Some people begin to make meditations and colloquies gladly and eagerly. As time passes, however, they slowly revert to their normal way of praying, or they syncretize making meditations and colloquies with their former way of praying. Take, for example, the person who, prior to the retreat, was accustomed to a stream-of-consciousness conversation with the Lord. After three or four days of making meditations and then having a colloquy, this person gradually reverts to having a running conversation with the Lord as he considers the points of the meditation. The colloquy is no longer a distinct part of his exercise.

What can the director do in such a case? The director may have doubts about the exercitant's normal way of praying, prior to the retreat. He might suspect, for instance, that the exercitant was actually talking at the Lord rather than talking with the Lord. Nevertheless, the director shouldn't comment on the exercitant's prayer prior to the retreat. Instead, the director can reiterate how to make a meditation and remind the exercitant to put his colloquy at the end of his meditation. Often, in such cases, it's helpful to ask the person to put aside, for a time, his habitual style of prayer. If the director decides to do this, he should do it in a straightforward and clear way, without passing judgment on the exercitant's habitual way of praying. Eventually, the exercitant himself will, on the basis of new experiences making the Exercises, make his own good judgment about his habitual way of praying.

As the retreat progresses, some find their minds wandering a lot. When this happens, exercitants often get discouraged. This is especially true for those who are accustomed to using spiritual reading as a cure for distractions. In the past, when they've experienced wandering thoughts, they pick up a book. During the Exercises, however, they have to face five approximately hour-long exercises a day without a book. They can feel defenseless and defeated. The director should communicate hope to these exercitants, telling them that things will get better. Things will, in fact, get better for them, once they learn how to discipline their wandering minds instead of placating them. Such exercitants need to keep struggling in the work of prayer, just as Jacob struggled throughout the night with the angel of the Lord. Eventually the struggle will end and the victory will be won.

An exercitant might complain of being bored. If this happens, the director should ask him about his meditations. Of course, the director and the exercitant are always talking about his meditations, but the director should take boredom as a sign that he should try to get a better picture of what is actually happening during the meditations. So, for example, if someone is meditating on Palm Sunday, the director might ask him about his mental representation of the place. "Tell me, how did you picture the scene?" The director is checking to see how present the exercitant is to the scene. Some exercitants relate to the scene as a spectator, as if they are watching a movie. These exercitants tend to get bored, eventually. It's more effective for the exercitant to actually place himself in the scene so that he is somehow present to it. The exercitant who sees his own jacket on the ground before Jesus and then sees the donkey's hoof stepping on his jacket is less likely to get bored.

If the exercitant isn't very present to the scene he's meditating on, the director should avoid saying things like, "Look, you're not doing this part of the meditation well." He should merely tell him to add something to his next meditation. He might say, "I can help you with the boredom. In your next few meditations spend more time picturing the scene. Try to place yourself in it as a participant in the action." The director might have to give an example of what he means. When the exercitant has a better experience in the following meditations, the director can then lead him in reflecting on what he did and what he experienced. The director isn't holding the exercitant to some standard; he's working with him and his experiences.

Of course, not all exercitants are the same. Some who are bored would benefit from doing some penance. Others are bored because their meditations consist largely of discursive reasoning. They are gaining insight into the subject matter of the meditation, but they aren't responding to it with their hearts. Most people have more experience with knowing about God or even knowing God than with loving God. During the Exercises, their default position will often be a tendency to pursue even more knowledge about God. Eventually, though, without the affective element, this kind of meditation leaves people feeling empty. As Ignatius says, "It is not much knowledge that fills and satisfies the soul" (2).

If someone isn't responding to the meditation with his heart, the director should point him toward the grace of the meditation. For example, the director might ask him if he experienced any sorrow with Christ in sorrow or any joy with

Christ in joy. He could remind the exercitant to keep his eye on the target (sorrow or joy with Christ) as he considers the points. During the Second Week, when the exercitant prays repeatedly for the grace of "an intimate knowledge of the Lord who became man for me so that I might love Him more and follow Him more closely" (104), the director could remind him that he isn't just praying for more knowledge of the Lord; rather, he's praying for an intimate, personal knowledge of the Lord. He's not aiming at insight for insight's sake, no matter how enjoyable that is. He's praying for a knowledge that leads to love. The director should encourage him to literally beg God for the grace of the meditation.

It's also helpful for the director to give the exercitant some questions aimed at helping him respond to the subject matter of his meditation with his heart. When the exercitant gets an insight into the Lord, he can ask himself, how does that move me? Likewise, when he catches a glimpse of the Lord, he can pause to notice whether he is moved to something. In other words, the exercitant can ask himself, How does this insight affect me? This helps bring to his consciousness his affective responses to an insight.

Thinking too much during an exercise is, in fact, a very common problem. After all, new insights are enjoyable and relatively easy to come by, at least in the beginning. "Enter the scene and let your heart be moved" is good advice for many, many exercitants. At a certain point, it's also helpful to tell them that more insight won't deepen their prayer. The director has to be aware, however, that what's good advice for some exercitants isn't good advice for others.

Some need to think more in their meditations. They are quick to praise, reverence and serve their Lord, but they don't truly know Him. Some are living on a past revelation of Him. Some are relying solely on what others have told them about God. Some are still relating to the God of their childhood. The director has to remind such people that they can't love someone with a deeply personal love if they don't know him. "Think more and get deeper insight" is good advice for some people.

The director needs to be alert to what's going on with an exercitant. One exercitant, if he isn't responding to the subject matter with his heart, might talk to his director about his insights because nothing else is going on in his meditation.

Another might be moved by the subject of his meditation, but he doesn't talk to his director about it. He is either unaware of the movements of his heart or he doesn't know how to talk coherently about them. Sometimes, too, an exercitant might fail to mention his affective responses because he values insight more. He might be suspicious of any kind of affective response because he thinks his emotions can lead him astray. Perhaps he has been led astray by disordered loves and unruly desires in the past. This exercitant needs to know that, as he brings order to his life, he can let go of the reins of his heart.

The director shouldn't be giving the same advice to everyone. In his classic work on pastoral care, Gregory the Great commented, "the discourse of a teacher should be adapted to the character of the hearers, so as to be suited to the individual in his respective needs."[53] For example, some need to be reminded that all consolations and all graces are undeserved and given by God at his initiative. Others who are more conscious that they are undeserving might need to be reminded that God is lavishly pouring out His grace and "that he is on his part more eager to bestow greater gifts than lesser ones."[54] Those who pray for the grace of a meditation halfheartedly might need to be reminded that it is possible to "dispose themselves for his gifts listlessly and offhandedly and so to fail to win any grace, or any great grace."[55]

As exercitants settle into a routine of making meditations, the director will have to tell some to relax and others to be more disciplined. When people learn to ride a horse, some hold the reins too tightly and the horse rears up, trying to throw the rider. Others hold the reins too loosely and the horse runs wild. The same is true of making meditations. Some exercitants tire themselves out because they are trying so hard. They are in danger of giving up unless they relax a bit. Others are more lax and they run the danger of wandering aimlessly through a meditation, touching many things but never focusing on anything. The director needs to figure out what kind of person he is talking to and tailor his direction accordingly.

Sometimes the director gives the same person different advice at different moments. In other words, he tailors his advice not only according to the exercitant's character, but also according to what is happening in his meditation. For example, someone might tell his director about a moment when he was particularly moved by a point he was considering. The director realizes that he didn't "remain quietly meditating on the point in which I have found what I desire, without any eagerness to move on till I have been satisfied" (76). Instead, the exercitant moved on to the next point so as to consider all the assigned points of the meditation. The director could then tell the exercitant, "Next time that happens, just pause and stay in the moment. Pause as long as your heart is being moved, even if you don't finish all the points."

So, on one occasion the director might tell someone to pause in his meditation and not to move on to consider the rest of the points. On another occasion he might tell him to move on. For example, someone might tell his director about how he got stuck making a certain point. After making a few inquiries about what was going on in the meditation, the director might say, "Next time that happens, just move on, consider the rest of the points and talk to me about where you got stuck." Sometimes a person can get stuck on a certain point because of ignorance or a certain lack of understanding. It's important that the exercitant doesn't develop the habit of quitting the minute a meditation gets difficult. On the other hand, if he encounters a closed door, sometimes it's best, after knocking a few times, to just go around it and find another way in. Sometimes, too, a person can get stuck on a certain point on account of the work of the Enemy. Again, it's important to fight the Enemy, but he's won a skirmish if the exercitant spends his whole meditation spinning his wheels on a particular point and doesn't move on. Moving on is good advice in some situations.

A person learns how to make meditations and colloquies gradually. He learns by doing, by reflecting on what he is doing and by talking with his director about what he is doing and experiencing. Ideally, the director gives him what he needs to know when he needs to know it. The director has to be careful not to overwhelm the exercitant with too much information or advice about making meditations and colloquies. He certainly doesn't want to shed light in a way that blinds the exercitant.

It's common for a director to be tempted to talk too much. He's made the Exercises himself and each exercise has a particular meaning for him, so he may consciously or unconsciously want the exercitant to reap the same fruit as he did. Nevertheless, as the director gives a particular exercise he shouldn't be elaborating on what the exercitant should think and feel as he makes the exercise. The director "should permit the Creator to deal directly with the creature, and the creature directly with his Creator and Lord" (15). On the other hand, sometimes a person is slow to catch on to making meditations, and the director needs to demonstrate how to do it. It's helpful for such people to see what a meditation looks like. Ignatius himself gives such demonstrations in the first exercise of each week. Sometimes an exercitant might need more examples.

Usually exercitants don't ask too many questions about making a colloquy during the First Week. There are several reasons for this. They are busy learning how to make meditations by using their memory, intellect and heart to consider the points laid out by Ignatius. They are also busy wrestling with the subject matter of their meditations—sin. Making a good colloquy isn't an issue for them yet, especially since Ignatius gives rather specific directions for the colloquies in the First Week.

As we've already noted, as a person begins making meditations and colloquies, it's usually enough for the director to tell him three things about making colloquies. First, he needs to know that he should always have a colloquy, even if it means not finishing all the points. Second, he needs to understand that the instructions he has for a colloquy are like an outline, and it's his job to fill in the outline with his own words, speaking from the heart, as one friend to another. Or, to use a different metaphor, the exercitant's job is to take the black and white photograph provided by Ignatius and turn it into one with color. Finally, the director needs to tell the exercitant to be respectful in his colloquy.

A person's questions about the colloquies usually increase as the retreat progresses. After the First Week, Ignatius occasionally gives specific instructions for a colloquy, but most of the time he simply tells the exercitant to close his meditation with a colloquy. At some point in the Second Week, the exercitant begins to wonder about what he is supposed to be doing in the colloquy. The director, for his part, watches for this moment, and when it arrives he begins to give the exercitant more instructions about his colloquy. In essence, the director gradually unpacks what it means to speak to God as one friend to another.

This is a part of the retreat that requires great skill and artistry on the part of the director. He'll be tempted to explain friendship with God, so that the exercitant will be able to figure out what to do in his colloquy. That is not, however, what is required of him at this moment. His job is to give the exercitant some pithy, brief piece of direction that will enable him to take a step along the road of friendship. Then, after a few more days, the exercitant will probably need another piece of direction, and so on. In other words, the Spiritual Exercises aren't designed to help a person understand friendship; they are designed to help a person become a friend. The director has to understand the difference.

In the meditations, Ignatius is providing the exercitant with an opportunity to become aware of the Lord—His words, actions and gestures. What is happening in a meditation is actually richer and more complex, but harder to describe. In fact, in the meditation, the Lord reveals Himself to the exercitant. He shares with the exercitant His own experiences. Jesus is, after all, God's self-revelation. He is the Father's Word. On the other hand, as the exercitant makes the meditation, he has his own set of experiences. He responds to the subject of his meditation with sorrow, or with a determination to change something in his life, or with a desire to do penance, or sometimes with boredom, or with fear, and so on.

In the colloquy a person reveals, among other things, his own response to the Lord's self-revelation. Ideally the exercitant's heart is enkindled in the meditation and then he moves into the colloquy and speaks to the Lord. Prayer is always best when it arises from the heart. Nevertheless, even if a person is not very moved, he can still reveal to the Lord what he experienced as he made the meditation. He can also use the moment to speak to the Lord not just about his response to the meditation but about anything at all. It is a radically free moment and an intensely personal one. Colloquies will vary greatly from person to person, and they will vary from week to week in the retreat and even from hour to hour. There's no formula or law or program for the colloquy. The director's job would be a lot easier if there was.

Although the director can't give him ten easy steps to a good colloquy, there are a few things he can tell the exercitant that will be very helpful. First and foremost, when someone begins to inquire about the colloquy, the director should make one thing clear. Speaking to the Lord as one friend to another means that the exercitant is telling the Lord what he is experiencing. In other words, to put it colloquially, the exercitant should be telling the Lord what's going on with him. A person might say, O Lord, I can see how much you cared about the Temple. I just can't identify with that. Another person might begin a colloquy, O Lord, I would have gladly put my jacket on the ground before you as you entered Jerusalem. What can I do now? I could spend less time on the Internet and do more stuff around the house. Would that give you glory? And still another might say, O Lord, there's a situation at work I think I need to correct.

Most people need to be encouraged to speak directly to the Lord. In fact, when exercitants begin to inquire about the colloquy, the director shouldn't assume that they are actually speaking to the Lord. Often, a person will be ruminating during his colloquy and even thinking about talking to the Lord, but won't actually be speaking to Him. Sometimes, too, a person will be speaking words of praise or words of thanksgiving or words of petition to the Lord during his colloquy, but he won't be revealing much of himself to the Lord. Such exercitants aren't revealing "their significant or at least interesting experiences, their most intimate loves and hates, joys and sorrows, satisfactions and disappointments, fears and hopes" and their "most secret thoughts about what is most inward and important in their lives."[56]

Some people assume that the Lord knows what's going on with them; therefore they don't need to tell Him. Although the director should avoid theological discussions about what God does or doesn't know, he should do everything he can to help exercitants over this stumbling-block. Whether they already know it or not, the Lord wants to hear the exercitants talk about what they are experiencing. Friendship doesn't grow without mutual, intimate self-revelation.

Some people may be in the habit of trying to talk to the Lord as one friend to another, but they are inexperienced in personal friendship. They speak to the Lord, but they speak almost exclusively about their own personal needs. For the most part, they relate to the Lord as to someone who fulfills their needs. He is the one who forgives them and provides for them. He is the key to their becoming better persons. He is someone whose job is to love them. In other words, exercitants relate to the Lord in an implemental way.

The simple act of meditating on the life of Jesus first and then turning to Him to have a colloquy can go a long way toward helping a person's love expand beyond implemental love. Although the exercitant can talk about anything in the colloquy, he frequently chooses to talk about what he just experienced as he considered an event in the Lord's life with his mind and heart. By doing so, his prayer gradually becomes less self-centered and more mutual. An exercitant often experiences this as revolutionary. The director can help this process along by encouraging him to talk about everything he is experiencing, not just his needs.

Besides encouraging a person to speak directly to the Lord, a director can also help him to listen for and recognize the Lord's response. Some people may need help recognizing the Lord's voice. His voice sounds so much like the exercitant's own that it's easy to miss. "It may be compared to a drop of water penetrating a sponge" (335). It's not very noisy, and so the exercitant thinks the Lord isn't responding to him. Other people fail to distinguish their own voice from the voice of the Lord and mistakenly think nearly every thought is a communication from Him.

Many exercitants expect words to be the fruit of their listening and so they miss the Lord's consolations. Often, the important things you know about people are not necessarily the things they say to you, so it's important for exercitants to pay attention to what they are experiencing during the colloquy, because the Lord communicates in all sorts of ways.

It takes time for a person to learn how to recognize the Lord's responses to his self-revelations. Helping him grow in his discernment of the Lord's actions, gestures and words is probably the most important thing a director does during the Spiritual Exercises. Once the exercitant becomes accustomed to making meditations and colloquies, he and the director spend most of their time talking about what he is experiencing during the colloquies.

Fortunately, Ignatius has left extensive materials to help the exercitant understand what he is experiencing during prayer. The Rules for Discernment (314-336) are like a manual within a manual. They are Ignatius's instructions on prayer. During the First Week of the Exercises, the director begins to teach this material to the exercitant. Before that, however, he gets the exercitant started making the five meditations of the First Week.

CHAPTER 6

FIVE MEDITATIONS

The First Week of the Exercises begins with a ringing declaration of our freedom and a call to use that freedom effectively, but the week focuses on the misuse of freedom. After considering the Principle and Foundation and examining his conscience, the exercitant spends approximately four days meditating on sin and its consequences, both in the world and in himself. He prays repeatedly for three graces: "shame and confusion," "a growing and intense sorrow and tears for my sins," and "an interior sense of the pain that the lost suffer."

Why all this emphasis on sin? Ignatius is a keen psychologist. He's also a friend of God. He knows that a growing and intense sorrow and tears for one's sins are a great grace. This is foundational for a person's life in Christ. More importantly, heartfelt sorrow for sin is a window into God's heart. During the First Week the exercitant moves toward unity of mind and heart with his Creator with regard to sin. Meditating on sin gives him a horror of sin, a determination to avoid it in the future and a desire to save those who are lost in sin. Ignatius certainly isn't trying to inculcate fear or an abiding sense of guilt. He is, however, a realist. The reality of sin is central to the gospel. "The Son of man came to seek and to save the lost" (Lk. 19:10).

Ignatius wants the exercitant to face his sin and assume responsibility for it, but he also wants him to renounce his past sin. The exercitant who has never really renounced his past sin is in a dangerous place, even if he is not currently sinning. People who have said yes to God's saving action and who have been led out of Egypt, but have never really renounced their former life in Egypt, are common. Ignatius knows that, when the going gets tough, when they are without familiar food in the desert, they will long for the cucumbers and onions of Egypt. "Now the rabble that was among them had a strong craving; and the people of Israel also wept again, and said, 'O that we had meat to eat! We remember the fish we ate in Egypt for nothing, the cucumbers, the melons, the leeks, the onions, and the garlic; but now our strength is dried up and there is nothing at all but this manna to look at'" (Num. 11:4-6). Ignatius wants the exercitant to renounce utterly his Egyptian life and all its benefits.

Sometimes exercitants have left behind a sinful life and begun a new life with Christ, but their sense of personal wrongdoing isn't strong. They talk about abandoning their former way of life because it wasn't working for them or because it wasn't making them happy. It's as if they are a snake shedding its skin. There's nothing inherently wrong with the old skin; it was just old and didn't fit right. They speak of their new way of life as a lifestyle change, and they are truly grateful for their new, more fulfilling lifestyle. Ignatius thinks it's not enough for the exercitant to be sorry for his past and leave it behind. He wants him to detest his past sins. In other words, an explicit, voluntary rejection of past sin is crucial. The exercitant who has renounced Egypt and all its benefits isn't likely to return to Egypt. If he detests his past sin, he'll relate to the Lord as his Savior and King. "Look what He's saved me from! I want to do things His way." The exercitant who knows Christ as his Savior is much more likely to want to join Him in His saving work. Because Egypt is an awful place, he wants to lead other people out of Egypt. On the other hand, the person who has left behind an unsatisfying life for a happier, more fulfilling one might very well return to his former life or a different type of sinful life when it suits him. Such a person tends to relate to the Lord as to a personal counselor. His Lord and friend is always there for him to help him feel better, and after death to provide the ultimately fulfilling life. Egypt is merely a former lifestyle. He's not ashamed of it; he's simply moved on from it. Such a person doesn't set out to save other people from sin. He wants to help them feel better and make choices that suit them better.

Ignatius knows his friend; he knows that God is very much a Savior. For example, the Second Week opens with a powerful and memorable meditation on the Incarnation. In that meditation, Ignatius has the exercitant call to mind "how the Three Divine Persons look down upon the whole expanse or circuit of all the earth, filled with human beings. Since They see that all are going down to hell, They decree in Their eternity that the Second Person should become man to save the human race" (102). God isn't sending people to hell. He's saving people from hell.

Ignatius thinks that without Christ mankind is "in great blindness going down to death and descending into hell" (106). One unrepented sin is all it takes to separate us from God, not because God is a mean, vindictive judge but because that's the nature of sin. We can't escape the story of Adam and Eve. It's our story. The human condition is a shipwreck, a tragedy, but we are the ones responsible for it. The *Catechism of the Catholic Church* puts it well. Mortal sin (our choice) "causes exclusion from Christ's kingdom and the eternal death of Hell, for our freedom has the power to make choices forever, with no turning back" (1861). God, on the other hand, is doing everything He can to save us from the consequence of our choices. He doesn't want "any to perish, but all to come to repentance" (2 Pt. 3:9). Even so, human freedom is so great and so real that God Himself will not force us to remain in His house, among His people, under His rule. The choice is ours.

Sometimes a person can turn the subject of our eternal destiny—eternal life or eternal death—into an issue of whether or not we are accepted or rejected by God. This is a false issue. We are totally accepted. The real issue is: Do we accept or reject God? Again, the *Catechism of the Catholic Church* puts it well. It says hell is a "state of definitive self-exclusion from communion with God and the blessed" (1033).

The First Week is in many ways an invitation to have God's mind and heart about sin. It is a commonplace that, whereas God loves the sinner, He hates the sin. He causes His rain to fall on the just and the unjust, but He is not indifferent to the reality of sin. He is constantly laboring and suffering to save us from sin and to deal with its effects. Sin is like a cancer, endangering His beautiful and good creation. It is an ugly abomination. The exercitant can't be friends with his Lord and be nonchalant about his sin.

Typically, at the beginning of the First Week, the exercitant doesn't abhor and detest his sin. He may vaguely regret some of his actions and feel sorry he did certain things, but deep down inside he doesn't think his actions were all that bad. How does a person begin to abhor and detest sin? By making the exercises of the First Week and by God's grace. In fact, by the end of the First Week, many exercitants have reached what Ignatius calls "the second kind of humility," which "supposes that not for all creation, nor to save my life, would I consent to commit a venial sin" (166). If the exercitant hasn't reached the second kind of humility, he has usually reached the first kind. "It consists in this, that as far as possible I so subject and humble myself as to obey the law of God our Lord in all things, so that not even were I made lord of all creation, or to save my life here on earth, would I consent to violate a commandment, whether divine or human, that binds me under pain of mortal sin" (165).

It turns out that becoming conscious of the true magnitude of one's own sin opens the door to a new consciousness of God's mercy. The exercitant encounters God's mercy in new and unexpected ways, even though the exercises of the First Week are about sin. If the director focuses on mercy, these exercises won't work. The exercitant can't have a profound sense of God's mercy without a profound sense of his own sin.

The dawning consciousness of one's sin is a painful moment, but the director shouldn't be too quick with assurances of God's mercy. It's much better to let God Himself reveal His mercy. He knows just the right moment. Similarly, if an exercitant is slow to detest and abhor his sin, the director shouldn't try to impress upon him sin's heinous nature. It's much better to let the exercitant discover this by God's grace. Ignatius's advice to the director in the second annotation is especially pertinent here:

> Let him adhere to the points, and add only a short or summary explanation. The reason for this is that when one in meditating takes the solid foundation of facts, and goes over it and reflects on it for himself, he may find something that makes them a little clearer or better understood. This may arise either from his own reasoning, or from the grace of God enlightening his mind. Now this produces greater spiritual relish and fruit than if one in giving the Exercises had explained

and developed the meaning at great length. For it is not much knowledge that fills and satisfies the soul, but the intimate understanding and relish of the truth (2).

The director must trust the meditations and the grace of God to do their work.

On the other hand, the director needs to be aware that not only is God at work in the exercitant's soul, moving him to contrition, sorrow and tears for his sin, but the Enemy is also at work. The Enemy sows seeds of a worldly grief that leads to death, harasses with anxiety, afflicts with sadness and hopelessness, and raises obstacles backed by fallacious reasonings which disturb the soul. So, while it's true that the director shouldn't be too quick with assurances of God's mercy when he sees the exercitant being graced with contrition, he should encourage the exercitant who is experiencing the Enemy. "If the director of the Exercises observes that the exercitant is in desolation and tempted, let him not deal severely and harshly with him, but gently and kindly. He should encourage and strengthen him for the future by exposing to him the wiles of the enemy of our human nature and by getting him to prepare and dispose himself for the coming consolation" (7). One time, during the First Week, Ignatius performed a Basque dance for an exercitant to encourage him.[57] It is important, then, for the director to be discerning.

One might expect the first meditation to be about one's own sins, but it isn't. Ignatius has the exercitant meditate on three sins of others: that of Lucifer, that of Adam and Eve, and that of one person who is in hell on account of one definitive choice to exclude himself from God and His people. It's a typical strategy of Ignatius—considering something in other people first. In this exercise, the exercitant looks at the worst effects of sin. He sees that, as a consequence of sin, hell exists, death and suffering enter the world, hell has someone in it and Jesus is on the cross. As he makes this meditation, once a day for several days, the exercitant comes to a growing awareness that sin really matters. In fact, it's a catastrophe and it has grave consequences. Very often a person enters the Spiritual Exercises thinking, perhaps somewhat unconsciously, that sin really isn't all that bad, but as he makes this exercise he begins to change his mind.

The exercitant begins the meditation by making the standard preparatory prayer and then by making "a mental representation of the place" (47). In subsequent exercises on the life of Jesus this is easy to do, because the exercitant imagines a physical place: the desert where Jesus was tempted or a boat on the Sea of Galilee and so on. Ignatius says, however, that "in a case where the subject matter is not visible, as here in a meditation on sin, the representation will be to see in imagination my soul as a prisoner in this corruptible body, and to consider my whole composite being as an exile here on earth, cast out to live among brute beasts" (47). Sometimes a person who is not that familiar with 16th-century language can mistakenly think that we are saying that the body is evil and that physical creation has no value, that it's simply a place of exile. Of course, we believe in the resurrection of the body and the redemption of all creation (Phil. 3:21, Rm. 8:19-23). So, to avoid misunderstanding, we like to rephrase Ignatius's statement in a way that we think captures his intention. We tell the exercitant to see himself in chains because he is a person who daily experiences the results of sin: alienation from himself, from others and from God; suffering; death, and a world out of order.

As Christians we believe that the world was changed as a result of Adam and Eve's sin. Sickness, physical suffering and death entered the world. Also, our psyches were changed. We are no longer at home—or you could say, "at peace" —with ourselves, with one another and with God. Other people—one's spouse, one's neighbor or even God Himself—have become at the very least potential threats. Even our bodies are potential threats to our well-being. We become locked within ourselves. That's what we mean by "alienated." Of course, the situation has changed now. In Christ, union with God, one another and all of creation is possible, even when experiencing extreme adversity. We experience that union as unbounded freedom.

After the exercitant sees himself in chains, weighed down by the daily experience of the results of sin, he asks God for the grace not to take sin lightly. He's not merely asking for the grace to understand sin. He's asking for the grace to experience shame and confusion. What triggers this shame and confusion? As the exercitant meditates on the three sins Ignatius suggests, he sees how hell is the consequence of a single act of rebellion. He then realizes that he has sinned many times and has deserved a similar fate.

Although it is unpleasant, experiencing shame on account of one's sins is a grace. For example, the good thief on the cross experienced shame. He knew he was guilty and was only getting his just deserts. Ignatius uses the example of "a knight brought before his king and the whole court, filled with shame and confusion for having grievously offended his lord from whom he had formerly received many gifts and favors" (74). One can imagine such a knight confessing his disloyalty and being filled with shame. Generally speaking, a person who is ashamed of his actions wants to hide or to hang his head. Sometimes, however, people do something wrong but they have no shame. They flaunt their wrongdoing. For example, think of a drunken fan at a football game or a Don Juan boasting of his sexual conquests. The other thief on the cross, who rails at Jesus, seems to have no shame. People who have no shame for their sins are flirting with the possibility of definitive self-exclusion from communion with God and the blessed.

What does it mean to experience the grace of confusion? In this context, to be "confused" means to be bewildered or disoriented because something unexpected happens. For example, a person experiences confusion if he walks into a seemingly empty room and people jump out yelling, "Surprise!" A child with his hand in a forbidden cookie jar experiences confusion when he unexpectedly hears his mother ask, "What are you doing?" The exercitant experiences confusion when he realizes that some of the things he has done are more serious than he imagined, or when he realizes he has sinned but has been spared the consequences. It's as if a light has been suddenly turned on in a dark room. It's disorienting.

There are many ways to talk about heaven and hell in Christian tradition. Ignatius refers to the people in hell as "the damned." We often refer to them as "the lost," so as to emphasize their own personal responsibility for their destiny. Also, as we're giving the Spiritual Exercises, sometimes we speak of "hell" and sometimes we speak of "eternal death." Just as some people experience the beginnings of eternal life now, so too some experience the beginnings of eternal death now. The phrase "eternal death" has some immediacy that "hell" lacks. So, in this first meditation, we ask the exercitants to pray for "the grace not to take sin lightly and the grace to experience shame and confusion because I see how many have begun to experience eternal death on account of a single act of rebellion, one 'no,' and how many times I've deserved the same on account of my many 'no's.'"

After praying for the grace of shame and confusion, the exercitant considers "the first sin" (50). Ignatius wants him to do this "employing the three powers of the soul" (45). As the director gives the points of the meditation, he should present them in a way that emphasizes the three powers of the soul. So for example, when giving the first point, we might say something like the following:

"First, consider the fall of some angels from grace. Lucifer and some other angels rebelled. They said no to God. Angels are messengers and servants of God (Heb. 1:14), but these did not want to use the freedom God gave them to reverence and obey their Creator and Lord. Some Church Fathers say they rebelled when God revealed to them His plans for the Incarnation. So, falling into pride, they were changed from loving God to hating him and were cast out of heaven.

"Think about what happened. Their choice had real consequences. Hell exists as a result of their choice. You could think about how perhaps they hated the prospect of submitting to Jesus. Or you could think about how their love turned gradually into hatred. There's lots to ponder here.

"Then respond with your heart. Go ahead and try to have the feelings you asked for. For example, you might try to arouse shame by comparing the one sin of the angels to your many sins. Or you might think about how you've escaped serious consequences of your sin, so far, by the grace of God."

Although the director shouldn't make the meditation for the exercitant, it's helpful to give him a form to follow. The director will want to do more than say something like, "consider the fall of Satan using your memory, understanding and will." After all, this may be the first time the exercitant is doing this.

Occasionally a person will ask questions which indicate that he isn't familiar with the tradition about angels and the fall of Lucifer. It's helpful for the director to have a few Scripture passages ready, if he thinks they will help the exercitant. Hebrews 1:14 indicates that angels are servants and messengers of God. Revelation 5:11 illustrates their vast number and their worship and praise of God. Psalm 103:20-21 refers to their obedience. The director may very well have to explain the Christian tradition about Lucifer, namely, that he was created a good angel but, by his own doing, he became evil. Jude 6 and 2 Peter 2:4 refer specifically to the fall of the angels. Traditionally, Luke 10:18, Revelation 12:7-9, Isaiah 14:12-15 and Ezekiel 28:12-14 are also taken to refer to the fall of Lucifer. If the director gives the exercitant any of these passages, the exercitant should read them before his meditation, not during his meditation.

Next, the exercitant considers the sin of Adam and Eve. Ignatius calls them "our First Parents." The exercitant meditates on the result of this one act of disobedience. If he wants to, he can read the story in Genesis 3, but he should do so before he begins his meditation. Again, the director should present this part of the meditation in a way that emphasizes the three powers of the soul. The exercitant should call to mind these facts: God created Adam and Eve, He placed them in Eden, they could eat of every tree in the garden except one, they did what God said not to do; He clothed them with garments of skin and cast them out of Paradise; they lost harmony with themselves, each other and all of creation; they experienced many hard labors and eventually death. Then the exercitant should think about the facts and get insight into them: what's wrong with eating the tree's fruit? Nothing except that God said don't do it. Eve seemed to have only good intentions, and the fruit looked so beautiful and good. She wanted to be able to judge on her own what was right and wrong instead of relying on God, and so on. Finally, the exercitant should stir up his heart. Just one "no" had such huge consequences, but look at my many acts of disobedience, and so on.

The director might not be familiar with a couple of things in Ignatius's description of the fall of our first parents. He says they were "created on the Plain of Damascus." Ignatius is relying on Ludolph of Saxony here. There was an ancient tradition that Adam and Eve were created in area called Damascus, near the ancient town of Hebron, about 20 miles south of Jerusalem. Ignatius also says Adam and Eve "by their sin lost original justice." The *Catechism of the Catholic Church* has a useful explanation of this term. After noting that "The first man was not only created good, but was also established in friendship with his Creator and in harmony with himself and with the creation around him," (374) it goes on to explain original justice. "As long as he remained in the divine intimacy, man would not have to suffer or die. The inner harmony of the human person, the harmony between man and woman, and finally the harmony between the first couple and all creation, comprised the state called 'original justice'" (376).

After meditating on the fall of the angels and the sin of Adam and Eve, the exercitant considers someone who went to hell on account of one mortal sin. While it's up to the exercitant to choose the scenario for this meditation, it's a good idea for the director to give him some suggestions. He could consider Cain killing Abel, or Judas's betrayal of Jesus and subsequent suicide. He could also consider a historical figure or a semihistorical figure. For example, he could meditate on someone in Holland during World War II who discovers his former Jewish neighbors in hiding and turns them in to the Nazis out of envy or greed. After the war, upon hearing about the death camps and the Holocaust, this person is still unrepentant. Sometimes exercitants want to choose Hitler, but that choice dilutes the meditation. Ignatius wants the exercitant to consider someone who commits one mortal sin, not many.

Again, the director wants to give the exercitant some guidelines. The director instructs the exercitant to settle on the facts of his scenario. Then he reminds the exercitant to use his reason to delve into the scene. He might tell him to think about the malice of the sin. Or he could think about how many small choices paved the way for one decisive act. Or he could think about how God lets this person choose his own destiny, and so on. The director should also remind the exercitant to stir up his heart. Considering "the countless others who have been lost for fewer sins than I have committed" (52) is one way Ignatius recommends stirring up the heart.

The meditation ends, as usual, with a colloquy. In the First Week, Ignatius gives exercitants relatively specific instructions for the colloquies. In this meditation, Ignatius instructs the exercitant to "imagine Christ our Lord present before you on the cross." The exercitant comes face to face with the ultimate consequence of sin—Jesus on the cross. Then he should "begin to speak with Him" (literally, "have a colloquy"), asking Him in particular how it is that He humbled Himself to become man, leaving His Father in order to join us in our experience of pain and death on account of sin (53). This moment is different than one might expect. Ignatius is not taking the exercitant to the cross and saying, "Look what you've done to Him." He takes the exercitant to the cross and says, "Look what He's done for you and for all mankind." In fact, one author noted that during this colloquy an exercitant can expect to feel like something like this: I am standing at the bedside of a friend who has just been mortally wounded while saving my life.

While the exercitant is present to the Lord on the cross, he should reflect on himself and ask himself three questions: What have I done for Christ? What am I doing for Christ? What ought I do for Christ? He isn't trying to make a decision here. The question does, however, stir up a disposition in the exercitant to lay down his life out of love for God. It turns out that this particular colloquy, so early in the Exercises, foreshadows many of the things that will be happening later. Ignatius is already emphasizing action. While the exercitant is face to face with the great love of the Lord, Ignatius leads him to respond by looking for something to do for the Lord. After all, "love ought to manifest itself in deeds rather than in words" (230). Ignatius is also subtly pointing to the call to mission and to the apostolic action that follows. The exercitant will not be aware of this, but the three questions of the colloquy put him on the side of Christ, who is saving the world from sin. These three questions echo in the exercitant's mind throughout the Spiritual Exercises and, indeed, throughout his life.

Next is a meditation on "Our Sins" (55). Again the exercitant uses the three powers of the soul to make the meditation, but in a slightly different way. In the previous meditation he used the three powers of his soul to meditate on three different, but related topics. Here he uses the three powers of the soul to meditate on one topic, his sins. He uses his memory to make the first point, calling to mind his sins. He uses his understanding to make the second, third and fourth points, a sustained reflection on his sins. He uses his heart to make the fifth point, "a cry of wonder accompanied by surging emotion" (60).

The meditation begins with the usual preparatory prayer. Again the exercitant imagines himself in chains on account of his sins. In his mind's eye he sees himself as a person who daily experiences the results of sin: alienation from himself, from others and from God, along with suffering, death and a world out of order. Then he asks for the grace of "a growing and intense sorrow and tears for my sins" (55).

The sorrow the exercitant prays for is a gift from God. Sometimes people come into the Exercises with a nagging sense of not measuring up to some ideal. Although they may feel sorry that they don't measure up to their ideal, this is not the kind of sorrow that Ignatius instructs them to seek in prayer. If need be, the director might warn exercitants that this meditation is not about being discouraged with themselves because they have failed to live up to some ideal, imposed by themselves or by someone else. The meditation is not about the distance between exercitants and their ideal. The sorrow they're seeking isn't the sorrow that comes from wanting to be a different and better person. It's about certain actions they have chosen to do—their sins. In other words, exercitants are praying for the grace to be sorry—tearfully sorry—for their sins. They weep on account of the evil they've brought into the world or into their own psyches.

The sorrow a person is praying for doesn't stem from or lead to self-hatred, self-condemnation or self-rejection. The exercitant isn't praying for bitter, hopeless, desolate, despairing tears. The tears he is praying for don't arise out of a felt separation from God and they don't create or accentuate distance from God. Sometimes an exercitant will find himself shedding many tears and in the shedding of the tears he feels moved to the Lord, to the love of God. His tears are an experience of union, not disunion. Also, the depth of the exercitant's sorrow is not dependent on the number of his sins. It is, however, correlated with his awareness of God's amazing grace.

After praying for a growing and intense sorrow and tears for his sins, the exercitant uses his memory to call his sins to mind. In the early directories, Ignatius comments several times that this review is not meant to be exhaustive. In our experience, however, the exercitant often takes about

15 to 20 minutes for this part of the meditation, so the other points are shortchanged. For this reason, we often have the exercitant do this review as a general examination of conscience after the Principle and Foundation and before the first meditation. It's not exactly the practice of the first Jesuits, and it is perhaps stretching the meaning of "general examination of conscience," but it works. When the exercitant gets to this point of the meditation, he's already done the work. He can just call to mind his examination of conscience.

Ignatius uses a specifically legal word in this meditation. He calls the first point of this meditation a "record of my sins." The word "record" means literally the "court record of a trial." With just one word, Ignatius calls to mind the image of a man before a judge. He reinforces this image when he later counsels the exercitant, "Similarly, in the Second Exercise, I will consider myself a great sinner, loaded with chains, that is, I will look upon myself as bound with fetters, going to appear before the supreme and eternal Judge, and I will recall the way prisoners, bound and deserving of death, appear before an earthly judge" (74). It's an uncomfortable image, but it makes the last point of the meditation all the more surprising and wonderful.

The next three points are a sustained reflection on one's sins. First, the exercitant considers the gravity of his sins. It isn't merely that he's broken the law; he's done terrible things. Ignatius wants him to "see the loathsomeness and malice which every mortal sin I have committed has in itself, even though it were not forbidden" (57).

Second, the exercitant calls to mind his place in the universe, thereby humbling himself. He thinks about the fact that God is his Creator and he is a mere creature, lower than the angels. He is just one among many human beings. He might say to himself: Who do you think you are, saying no to God? At this point Ignatius has a person ask himself five questions. We conflate and rephrase the last two, so that the instruction is, "Consider how I've hurt others and infected my relationships, my environment and even my body itself with my sin."

Third, the exercitant further considers who God is and who he is by comparing himself to his Creator. "I will consider who God is against whom I have sinned, going through His attributes and comparing them with their contraries in me:

His wisdom with my ignorance, His power with my weakness, His justice with my iniquity, His goodness with my wickedness" (59). It's an effective strategy for stirring up sorrow and tears for one's sins. Ignatius knows, as one of his compatriots said, "anything white looks whiter against something black, just as black looks blacker against the white."[58]

The last point of the exercise is "a cry of wonder accompanied by surging emotion as I pass in review all creatures" (60). Here the exercitant considers how the whole world has served him: the people who made his clothes, his parents, his teachers, farmers, truck drivers and so on. All these people have been serving him. In fact, all of the natural world, "the heavens, sun, moon, stars, and the elements; the fruits, birds, fishes, and other animals—why, they have all been at my service!" (60). The exercitant realizes that while he was steeped in his sin the whole world has been serving him. The exercitant wonders, How is it that the earth did not open to swallow me up and create new hells just for me? (60). He hasn't gotten what he deserves. Quite the contrary, he's been served and sustained in life.

He ends the meditation with a "colloquy of mercy" (61, Mullan) extolling God's mercy and "giving thanks to Him that up to this very moment He has granted me life" (61). The exercitant realizes, sometimes rather dimly, that it is God who has been laboring for him "in all creatures upon the face of the earth," as the Contemplation to Attain Love will later make clear. He catches a glimpse of his eternal Judge laboring on his behalf and sustaining him in life, even while he was sinning. He then pours out his thoughts to his merciful Father and resolves to amend his life for the future.

The next exercise is usually a relief to the exercitant. The first two meditations of the day contain many ideas and can easily be overwhelming. Usually, he is not accustomed to meditating on sin. There's a lot of unfamiliar material to digest and it takes time for his heart to respond to the enormity of his sins. So, Ignatius has the exercitant go back over the previous two meditations. He doesn't make the meditations again; rather he goes back over and pays attention to the points where his heart was moved. If he experienced even a glimmer of shame or sorrow at a particular point, he goes back to that point to dwell upon it more.

Likewise, he returns to moments in the previous two meditations where he experienced any increase of faith, hope or charity. Ignatius wants the exercitant to derive more benefit from the grace and consolations God has already given him. If he experienced any darkness of soul or turmoil of spirit, he should go back to those moments also, so that he can win a victory. Ignatius wants the exercitant to "accustom himself not only to resist the enemy but even overthrow him" (13).

It is very difficult for a person to experience the graces of the First Week unless he does the repetitions Ignatius recommends. One early Jesuit, Gil González Dávila, comments:

> For it often happens that at first the understanding alone is nourished by the novelty and interest of the topics and there is only very slight interior relish in the will. But later, when the understanding's speculation and interest is largely stilled, there is freer room for spiritual and interior affections. Hence, in these repetitions one should avoid pursuing new trains of thought in the intellect. Instead, once the exercitant has gone over and ruminated his earlier meditations he ought to dwell rather on the internal relish which feeds the will. . . . Again, it often happens that, where we had at first experienced dryness on certain points, in these repetitions we find a rich and lavish source of divine consolation. For to him who perseveres and knocks, the Lord opens the door of mercy.[59]

It takes time for the mind to take in and the heart to respond to the first two meditations.

This third exercise ends with some specific instructions for the colloquy. Actually, the exercitant makes three colloquies. First, he asks Mary to intercede for him and obtain for him three things. He ends this colloquy with a Hail Mary.[60] Next, Ignatius instructs: "I will make the same petitions to her Son that He may obtain these graces from the Father for me" (63). The exercitant might not be used to relating to Jesus as an intercessor. If so, the director could remind him what Hebrews says about Jesus: "he is able for all time to save those who draw near to God through him, since he always lives to make intercession for them" (Heb. 7:25). The exercitant ends this second colloquy with an ancient prayer called the Anima Christi. The text of the prayer can be found in most editions of the Spiritual Exercises. Sometimes the prayer is attributed to Ignatius, but actually the author is unknown. Ignatius, however, popularized the prayer. Finally the exercitant makes the same requests of the Father and ends with the Lord's Prayer.

In these three colloquies the exercitant prays repeatedly for three graces. First, he prays "that I may feel an interior knowledge of my sins, and hatred of them" (63, Mullan). Ignatius knows that if a person hates and abhors his sin, he is much less likely to sin. Ideally, the exercitant will become like someone who has gotten sick eating, say, shellfish, and thereafter can't stand the sight or smell of shellfish, let alone the taste. This kind of repulsion doesn't come from having a clear intellectual grasp of one's sins. It comes from knowing one's sins from the inside, so to speak, and not as an objective observer might know them. This felt interior knowledge of one's sins leads to a hatred of them.

Of course, the exercitant might abhor his sins as best he can, but unless he changes his life he'll probably end up sinning again. In particular, he must put all his various wants in order so that his one desire and choice will be for whatever is more for the honor and service of God. After all, in the end, we always do what we want. If a person wants money more than God's glory, he might very well steal or even kill to get money. Or, if a person wants first to please people and second to please God, he might very well lie or commit other small sins to get what he wants: the approval of his friends or his superiors. Again, a person always does what he wants, so if the exercitant wants to change his actions, he's got to change his wants and desires. In other words, to avoid sin the exercitant must live out the Principle and Foundation. So, besides praying for an interior knowledge of his sins and hatred of them, he also prays "that I may feel the disorder in my actions, so that finding it abhorrent, I may amend my life and put order into it" (63, Ivens).

The third grace he prays for is a "knowledge of the world, in order that, hating it, I may put away from me worldly and vain things" (63, Mullan). By "world" Ignatius doesn't mean the physical cosmos or even human society per se. However, Ignatius is aware that the consequences of sin go beyond the individual and extend to society as a whole. Fallen society is a complex set of relationships, ideas, values and structures woven together in enmity with God. The "world" is the source of many of the exercitant's disordered loves and unruly desires. The exercitant is, thus, praying for the grace to recognize fallen society's values and ways of doing things and to put them aside for the values and ways of God and his people.

This third grace might be misunderstood by some exercitants or directors. The exercitant is not praying for the grace to abandon the world. Ignatius doesn't want him to see the world as an unfortunate theater in which people are forced to live out their Christian lives. He does want the exercitant to recognize the world's negative influences, but he also wants the exercitant to work for the salvation of the world. He thinks the gospel is God's answer to the world's problems: its distortions in thinking, relationships, morals, goals, organizations and so on. He wants the exercitant to work for the day when "The kingdom of the world has become the kingdom of our Lord and of his Christ" (Rev. 11:15). The first step, though, is to pray for the grace that "I may put away from me worldly and vain things" (63, Mullan).

The director should encourage the exercitant to beg for these graces with all his heart. Actually begging for these experiences creates a desire for them. A desire for these experiences then disposes the exercitant to recognize them. Of course, abhorring one's sins, the disorder of one's life and all that is worldly and vain is a gift from God, but the exercitant must rely on Jesus' words: "Ask, and it will be given you; seek, and you will find; knock, and it will be opened to you" (Mt. 7:7). Praying this threefold colloquy is often very powerful for the exercitant.

At this point, we want to pause and make a comment about the colloquies. As we've already noted, Ignatius gives rather specific instructions for the colloquies of the First Week. In the Second, Third and Fourth Weeks he doesn't give as many specific instructions. In fact, he usually just tells the exercitant to make a colloquy, speaking as one friend to another or as a servant to a master. Here, in the First Week, he is giving examples of what colloquies should look like.

In each of the three meditations we've discussed so far, the colloquy is a somewhat natural response to the things the exercitant has just experienced with his mind and heart. Three times, the exercitant considers the consequences of one act of rebellion. Three times, he reminds himself that he has been spared the consequences of his many rebellions. It's a natural response to turn to the Lord and say, "O my Lord, you're dying so that I may live with you forever. Oh, what have I ever done for you?" Likewise, the exercitant becomes conscious of his Father sustaining and serving him, even while he was sinning. It's natural to extol God's mercy and to respond to that mercy by changing one's life. So too, it's a natural response to the meditations to beg over and over, in several different ways, for the grace to avoid sin. One can, then, learn a lot about colloquies in general by studying the colloquies of the First Week.

In the fourth meditation, the exercitant again goes back over the previous meditations of the day. Both the third and fourth meditations are called "repetitions," but the exercitant goes back over the previous meditations in different ways. In the third meditation he pays special attention to places where he experienced consolation or desolation. In the fourth meditation, he concentrates not so much on his subjective response to the material but on the material itself. Ignatius recommends that "the understanding, carefully and without digressing, should range over the memory of things contemplated in the previous exercises" (64, Ivens). The exercitant isn't supposed to be developing new insights here. The exercise is, rather, an opportunity for him to synthesize and digest the day's materials. Exercitants usually welcome the opportunity. This exercise ends with the threefold colloquy of the previous exercise.

In the last meditation of the day, the exercitant considers the ultimate fruit of sin: the pain and suffering of hell. In this meditation, he begs God for "a deep sense of the pain the lost suffer" (65). He's not asking for an academic knowledge of what happens to the unrepentant sinner when he dies; he's asking for a deep interior sense of the pain the lost suffer. Ignatius has him do this for two reasons. The first has to do with the Spiritual Exercises as a whole, and the second has to do with the goals of the First Week.

During the course of the Spiritual Exercises "a deep sense of the pain the lost suffer" turns into a wellspring of apostolic consciousness in the exercitant. Normally, the deeper his sense of the pain the lost suffer, the more he desires to snatch people from the jaws of hell. He begins to think that saving people from hell is worth doing and even worth dying for. This meditation is then a set-up for what follows. The call of Christ the King to labor with Him resonates with the exercitant. He's open to the possibility of leaving behind his comfortable life, picking up his cross and entering the fray. He identifies with the Trinity, who see "all nations in great blindness, going down to death and descending into hell" (106). He, too, wants to save the lost. This meditation stirs up compassion for the lost.

Experiencing "a deep sense of the pain the lost suffer" also furthers the goals of the First Week. Meditating on the pains that are the inevitable consequence of sin can serve as a deterrent to sin. Although at the moment the exercitant is determined to avoid sin, Ignatius knows that as time goes on small faults can erode his resolve. The exercitant prays for a sense of the pain the lost suffer so that, if his love cools and his determination flags, at least the fear of pain will keep him from falling into sin.

Some people criticize Ignatius for using fear to intimidate the exercitant. Later in the Spiritual Exercises, in the final paragraph, he offers his rationale:

> Though the zealous service of God our Lord out of pure love should be esteemed above all, we ought also to praise highly the fear of the Divine Majesty. For not only filial fear but also servile fear is pious and very holy. When nothing higher or more useful is attained, it is very helpful for rising from mortal sin, and once this is accomplished, one may easily advance to filial fear, which is wholly pleasing and agreeable to God our Lord since it is inseparably associated with the love of Him (370).

Ignatius isn't trying to intimidate the exercitant. Still, if some fear of suffering and pain will help the exercitant avoid mortal sin, so be it. For Ignatius, mortal sin is far more dangerous than a small dose of servile fear.

Besides the usual preparatory prayer and a prayer for a deep sense of the pain that the lost suffer, the exercitant also spends a few minutes imagining "the length, breadth, and depth of hell" (65). In our experience, an exercitant may find this exercise difficult to do, so we usually give two options. He can either imagine hell or he can imagine an earthly vestibule of hell—a hellish place he has seen or heard about. Whatever he does, it's important for him to see in his mind's eye a foul, inescapable place full of people who hate God and His ways. The exercitant should set a scene that will help him receive the grace he is asking for.

Instead of using his memory, understanding and will to meditate on hell, the exercitant uses his five senses to meditate on the very real pain that the lost suffer. First, he should see the real bodily pain the lost suffer—souls enclosed as it were in bodies of fire. Second, he should hear the wailing and the blasphemies against Christ. Third, he should smell the foulest smells: the filth and the corruption. Then, he should taste the bitterness of their tears, sadness and remorse of conscience. Finally, he should use his sense of touch to feel the bodily pain the lost are suffering. The point here is that the consequences of sin are real pain and real anguish.

As always, the meditation ends with a colloquy. Here again, Ignatius gives the exercitant specific instructions. He is to call to mind all the people who are in hell and then thank God that he has not died while in mortal sin. Then he should thank God "that up to this very moment He has shown Himself so loving and merciful to me" (71). So, like the cry of wonder in the second meditation, the exercitant is calling to mind and then thanking God for the fact that at this very moment he is being saved. He is experiencing the mercy of God.

When Ignatius tells the exercitant to call to mind all the people who are in hell, he goes on to categorize them in two different ways. First, he remarks that some are in hell because "they did not believe in the coming of Christ." Others, he adds, are in hell because, even "though they believed, they did not keep the commandments" (71). Then he goes on to say that people in hell can be divided into three classes: those who were lost before the coming of Christ, those lost during

His lifetime, and those lost after His lifetime here on earth. It is not clear to us exactly why Ignatius thought these classifications were so important to include in the colloquy. They don't seem to play a significant role in the rest of the Exercises, as far as we can tell. Still, they do bring home the point that before, during and after the lifetime of Jesus real people have definitively rejected God in some way or another.

Typically, when someone starts doing the meditations of the First Week, he does the first four on the first day, leaving out the meditation on Hell. On the second day he does the full round of five meditations. The director could decide to have him do the full round of meditations for yet another day or two.

What does a person experience during this time? Of course, no two exercitants are the same, but typically the exercitant experiences what he asks for: sorrow, shame, fierce desire to have nothing to do with sin, and a sense of the pain that the lost suffer. He also experiences something else, a dawning consciousness of the mercy of God. He's not specifically trying to have an experience of God's mercy, but the exercises of the First Week awaken him to the mercy he has already experienced.

The realization of God's mercy can be very powerful and very sweet. It is also very piercing, because it is tied to an experiential and affective knowledge of the gravity of sin. One time we were giving the Exercises to someone who was initially wary of the exercises of the First Week. Still, he applied himself diligently to them. As he made the exercises and repeated them, he began to identify more and more with Adam. It was he—the exercitant—who had gone along with someone else's choice. Adam's cowardice was his. It was he who had blamed another for his own sin. Adam's irresponsibility was his. He looked out of Adam's eyes and saw the dead animal at his feet—slain to clothe him. The fruit of his choice was death. "I am Adam" was ringing in his soul, like a death knell.

Then, at the end of the first meditation—a meditation he had already made quite a few times—as he was contemplating Christ on the cross, he remembered a reading from an ancient homily on Holy Saturday. It describes Christ's descent into hell. "He has gone to search for our first parent, as for a lost sheep," says the author, who also describes the Lord approaching Adam and Eve, "bearing the cross, the weapon that had won him the victory." Then the Lord addresses them, "I order you, O sleeper, to awake.... Rise, let us leave this place, for you are in me and I am in you; together we form only one person and we cannot be separated." In the homily, the Lord points to the things He had suffered, saying things like, "On my back see the marks of the scourging I endured to remove the burden of sin that weighs upon your back." This was an unspeakable consolation to the exercitant, who so identified with Adam. But then the Lord says to Adam:

> Rise, let us leave this place. The enemy led you out of the earthly paradise. I will not restore you to that paradise, but I will enthrone you in heaven. I forbade you the tree that was only a symbol of life, but see, I who am life itself am now one with you. I appointed cherubim to guard you as slaves are guarded, but now I make them worship you as God. The throne formed by cherubim awaits you, its bearers swift and eager. The bridal chamber is adorned, the banquet ready, the eternal dwelling places are prepared, the treasure houses of all good things lie open. The kingdom of heaven has been prepared for you for all eternity.[61]

In Adam, as Adam, the exercitant experienced the mercy of God. He had never, up to that moment, thought of Adam redeemed or enthroned in heaven. The experiential and affective knowledge of Adam, with Christ, and in Christ, and indeed one with Christ, was a life-changing moment of grace for the exercitant (and a wonderful grace for his director, too).

Someone just flipping through the text of the *Spiritual Exercises* might be extremely puzzled by the First Week. Can meditating on sin and its consequences really be profitable? The historical testimony is that these exercises were very powerful. Today, too, exercitants and directors will attest to their power. How can these exercises be so powerful? They bring to consciousness the reality of our redemption: our sin and God's merciful response. Usually exercitants respond, in one way or another, with "What have I done for Christ? What am I doing for Christ? What ought I do for Christ?"

Sometimes this consciousness seems to come suddenly, without much effort on the part of the exercitant. One early Jesuit, Cordeses, commenting on the First Week, said that some exercitants experience a "vivid sense of the gravity and loathsomeness of sin . . . accompanied by great amazement and giving rise to deep compunction of will, with much relish and consolation."[62] It's often difficult for the exercitant to describe what he's experiencing. Tears of sorrow are tears of joy at the same time. The exercitant, wounded by sin, approaches his Father, but suddenly he's aware of Christ, bearing in His body the wounds of sin, rising from the dead, returning to His Father. They are one. The experience shatters categories and defies description. The exercitant becomes conscious of his redemption, which is his incorporation into Christ.

Sometimes, however, the exercitant has to labor to obtain the graces of the First Week. He doesn't experience much "relish and consolation" at all. It is harder in these cases for someone to persevere, but, if he does, the Exercises will bear fruit. The fruit is, however, more difficult to discern, at least at first. The exercitant's soul is like a photographic plate exposed to the night sky. If it's exposed for ten minutes, a picture of the night sky emerges. If it's exposed all night, he'll be astonished at the number of stars he'll see.

So, too, with the exercises of the First Week, for some exercitants. Nothing much seems to be happening on any particular day, but at the end of the week they have experienced what they've asked for and are ready to move on.

While all this is happening, the director has to discern what he himself should do. Should he move an exercitant on or have him do another round of meditations? If someone doesn't seem to be getting what he's asking for, the director should inquire about how he is making the meditations and even the retreat itself. If all seems to be going well, the director might have the exercitant move on, even before he has received what he is asking for.

On the other hand, he might have an exercitant make the meditations of the First Week for several more days, because he thinks that will help him receive what he is asking for. In such a case, he might want to encourage the exercitant to persevere in his labors, but with calm and tranquility. Cordeses makes a comment that is pertinent here. "Although this work proceeds from our own striving and effort, you should not think that the striving should be physical or that the meditation should involve any straining of the head or breast, like squeezing an orange."[63]

Similarly, if exercitants are experiencing deep compunction of the will, the director might have them repeat the meditations in order to get as much fruit as possible. On the other hand, he might have them move on. Sometimes exercitants experience the bitter sweetness of compunction and want to stay in the First Week. Their hearts are so inflamed that they don't want to leave the moment. The director might want them to move on. After all, it's not all about the exercitant. There's a world that needs saving.

Besides discerning what he himself should do, the director also needs to be aware that not everything the exercitant is experiencing is from the Lord. Some of it may be the work of the Enemy. For example, the Enemy might sow the seeds of worldly grief. The exercitant weeps, but his tears are not like the tears of Peter, which led to repentance and life. Rather, his tears are like the bitter tears of Judas, which led to his self-destruction. The director needs to discern spirits and teach the exercitant how to do so. We'll look at this area in the next chapter.

CHAPTER 7

DISCERNMENT OF SPIRITS, FIRST WEEK

The exercises of the First Week are challenging for the exercitant. He begins to order his life, by God's grace, so that all his actions, intentions and operations are directed purely to the praise and service of God's divine majesty. In so doing, he comes face to face with his own sin as well as his inordinate attachments. He's practicing prolonged silence, perhaps for the first time in his life. Often he's doing some penance. He's learning how to make the retreat, and in particular he's becoming accustomed to making meditations and colloquies.

As he confronts all these challenges, a lot is happening in his mind and heart. Some of what is happening is pleasant, some not so pleasant. Someone might, for example, find himself thinking, perhaps for the first time, What can I do for God? As he becomes aware of this new thought, he might feel either a thrill of expectation or a wave of terror. As he makes the exercises of the First Week, the exercitant might find himself weeping, or angry, or grateful, or restless or filled with sorrow. On one day he might find himself thinking that he can't love God, and on the next that he wants to do some penance. As the retreat progresses, the exercitant and his director spend more and more time talking about these interior experiences.

Many of the things a person experiences, especially initially, are completely natural. For example, an exercitant might experience peace enveloping him as he begins the retreat. He's been looking forward to the retreat for a long time. The peace he's experiencing is the natural consequence of finally doing what he's wanted to do for a long time. Another exercitant might be experiencing a lot of frustration.

He's been working really hard at the exercises. In fact, he's hardly ever put so much concentrated effort into one thing, and he has nothing to show for all his days of work. Yet another person might be experiencing confusion because this retreat is very different from other retreats he has made. In the early days of the retreat, some exercitants experience disappointment and/or discouragement because their expectations for the retreat are not being met. Perhaps they'd envisioned a relaxing retreat and are shocked at the effort they have to put into it. Or perhaps they were expecting lots of consolations and they aren't experiencing any. Some exercitants are delighted and happy for themselves because they are learning new things about God and themselves. Learning makes them happy. On the other hand, it often happens that exercitants are agitated and emotional because they are overly tired. They can also be sad because they are hungry and they haven't listened to music or used a computer in days. They are accustomed to a life of distractions, and they are experiencing the retreat as a radical departure from their normal way of being. Then again, an exercitant might experience a quiet joyfulness on account of being free from burdensome daily responsibilities. Many exercitants are also experiencing the pain of beginning to order their unruly desires and loves. All of these experiences are fairly self-explanatory, and they don't need a spiritual explanation.

On the other hand, the exercitant also experiences things that are the work of God in his life.[64] The exercitant sees, for the first time or with increasing clarity, "the world" and its vanities. Similarly, he may see, for the first time or with increasing clarity, the disorder of his actions and the reality of his sin. God is enlightening his mind. Another exercitant finds himself ready and willing to make changes in his life in order to live for the praise of God's glory. God is strengthening his will. These works of God can happen inside or outside of the set time for meditations. For some they are rather imperceptible, because they happen gradually. Sometimes exercitants experience warm sentiments of affection for God. Sometimes these sentiments result in tears. Sometimes they result in courage to try to be more or do more for the Lord. Sometimes they give birth to strong urges to make new resolutions or commitments for God's sake. Sometimes exercitants experience God speaking to them from a sermon they hear or from their spiritual reading or even from a chance word their director speaks. Typically, the exercitant is making every effort to redirect or refocus his life toward God. God is making every effort to help him along his way. Ignatius, rather audaciously perhaps, summarizes the effects of God's action in one phrase: "courage and strength, consolations, tears, inspirations and quiet, easing, and putting away all obstacles that one may go on in well doing" (315, Mullan).

The exercitant is also experiencing things that are the work of the Enemy. Generally speaking, the Enemy "seeks to prevent the soul from advancing" (315). The exercitant experiences all sorts of thoughts about how impossible life in Christ will be. In a letter to Teresa Rejadell, Ignatius puts it this way: "In the first place, then, the enemy as a rule follows this course. He places obstacles and impediments in the way of those who love and begin to serve God our Lord, and this is the first weapon he uses in his efforts to wound them."[65] Ignatius experienced this shortly after his conversion. He recounts, very succinctly, "there occurred to him a rather disturbing thought which troubled him by representing to him the difficulty of the life he was leading, as though he heard a voice within him saying: 'How can you stand a life like this for the seventy years you have yet to live?'"[66] In the letter to Teresa Rejadell, he elaborates on this all-too-common experience. The Enemy asks, "How can you continue a life of such great penance, deprived of all satisfaction from friends, relatives, possessions? How can you lead so lonely a life, with no rest, when you can save your soul in other ways and without such dangers?" Ignatius goes on to explain, "he tries to bring us to understand that we must lead a life that is longer than it will actually be, by reason of the trials he places before us and which no man ever underwent. He fails to remind us of the great comfort and consolation which our Lord is wont to give to such souls."[67]

Exercitants experience other things that are also the work of the Enemy. Some experience temptations to disobey God's commandments or to succumb to apparently pleasurable vices. Some are plagued with obscene or sensual thoughts. Some, who tend to overlook their sin, experience being confirmed in that tendency. Ignatius puts it this way, "If he [the Enemy] finds one whose conscience is easygoing and who falls into sins without a thought of their gravity, he does all he can to make venial sins appear no sins at all, and mortal venial, and a very serious mortal sin a mere trifle."[68] Some exercitants have delicate consciences and are bent on avoiding all sin. Sometimes they experience a great deal of confusion about what is and is not a sin. Ignatius says that in these people the Enemy "tries to darken and confuse that good conscience by suggesting sin where there is none, changing perfection into defect, his only purpose being to harass and make one uneasy and miserable. When, as frequently happens, he cannot induce one to sin, or even hope to do so, he tries at least to vex him."[69]

Sometimes the exercitant experiences biting accusations: Your sins are so great, God doesn't want to have anything to do with you. You aren't loveable. You can't love. You are forever alone. Sometimes the exercitant loses his relish for the retreat. He begins to experience distaste for all spiritual exercises. It's as if filet mignon suddenly turns to sawdust in his mouth. He experiences a pervasive sadness and apathy. Life in Christ feels burdensome and oppressive. Sometimes a person is greatly disturbed by fallacious reasoning. He's plagued with thoughts that are half true or simply false: You've already made such a mess of your life, there's no fixing it. You'll be a bad witness if you get too serious about this religion stuff. People don't respond well to fanatics. Thoughts and experiences such as these are also the work of the Enemy.

Of all the many and varied things the exercitant is experiencing, Ignatius wants the director to watch for and learn to recognize two experiences in particular. Ignatius thinks it is especially important to pay attention to what he calls "consolations" and "desolations." Consolations are marked by warm sentiments of affection for God, and desolations by a loss of relish for spiritual things. Ignatius discusses consolations and desolations in Annotations 6 to 10, 13 and 14 and in his Rules for Discernment of Spirits (313-336). No other topic in his manual gets as much attention. The rules themselves are divided into two sets. The first set (313-327), upon which we are relying in this chapter, are especially suited for exercitants in the First Week, and the second set (328-336) are more suited for exercitants in the Second Week. Generally speaking, the first set of rules for discernment deal more with the desolations and the work of the Enemy.

Although the second set also deals with the deceptions of the Enemy, they focus more on consolations. We'll take up the second set of rules in a later chapter.

Ignatius discovered consolations and desolations at Manresa shortly after his conversion. He described how he "began to experience great changes in his soul. Sometimes his distaste was so great that he found no relish in any of the prayers he recited, or in hearing mass, or in any kind of prayer he made. At other times everything was just the contrary, and so suddenly that he seemed to have got rid of the sadness and desolation pretty much as one removes a cloak from the shoulders of another."[70] The experience of alternating consolations and desolations is not unique to Ignatius, however. It is in fact quite common. For example, in one of Cassian's Conferences there's "an investigation of the origin of a sudden change of feeling from inexpressible joy to extreme dejection of mind."[71] In this account some desert monks begin to wonder "why it was that as we sat in the cells we were sometimes filled with the utmost gladness of heart, together with inexpressible delight and abundance of the holiest feelings" while at other times "for no reason we were suddenly filled with the utmost grief, and weighed down with unreasonable depression, so that we not only felt as if we ourselves were overcome with such feelings, but also our cell grew dreadful, reading palled upon us, aye and our very prayers were offered up unsteadily and vaguely." According to Ignatius, these kinds of experiences demand an explanation. When he experienced them, "he began to marvel at these changes which he had never before experienced, saying to himself: 'What new kind of life is this that we are now beginning?'"[72]

Why was Ignatius so interested in consolations and desolations? For one thing, they are potentially life-changing experiences. They can be deeply moving, and as such they can provide a direction for a person's choices. There's nothing mysterious about this. Deeply moving experiences often provide a direction for a person's life. For example, an encounter with a suffering cancer patient can motivate a person to become a hospice nurse, or the beauty of a snorkeling expedition can move a person to become a marine biologist.

Consolations and desolations are not, however, simply deeply moving experiences. They are experiences caused by

God or Satan. The exercitant needs to become aware of them so that he can effectively cooperate with God's action in his life and overcome the Enemy's attempts to harass, derail or trick him. The structured environment of a retreat is an ideal place to learn to do this. As the exercitant examines the various things he is experiencing, he isn't simply getting in touch with how he feels about God. Rather, he's learning how to get in touch with God so that he can unite himself to Him and join Him in His work of saving and redeeming this world. This concern for the work of the Enemy and the work of the Holy Spirit in consolations and desolations is, in fact, the most important operating principle in the Spiritual Exercises.

In the Annotations and the Rules for Discernment, Ignatius says a lot about the Enemy and how he works, and how the exercitant can avoid being fooled by him. He also gives helpful advice about dealing with consolations, but he actually says very little about consolations themselves. Ignatius is, in fact, quite terse about them, sometimes frustratingly so. We also know, from the fragment of his spiritual diary that we possess, that he was not only terse, but sometimes practically inarticulate when talking about his own consolations. It's not surprising that in his letter to Teresa Rejadell about discernment of spirits he notes that he is dealing with matters that "could better be felt than put into words."[73]

Some consolations an exercitant experiences are encounters with God.[74] God does something to reveal Himself, and the exercitant responds. The consolation, the love the exercitant experiences, is his response, but it's a response called forth in him by God. Often, however, an exercitant isn't very aware of the person he's just encountered. This is especially true of an exercitant who doesn't have much experience of prayer. He's more aware of what he is experiencing as a result of that encounter. He's more aware of his feelings and thoughts and desires—the movements of his soul.

Consolations are, then, essentially felt experiences of loving God that arise out of an encounter with Him. They are difficult to define because love is difficult to define. As an exercitant meditates on God's actions and gestures and words, occasionally he feels love for Him. His heart is enkindled or moved by God. Usually in the First Week and well into the

Second Week, the exercitant's consolations are experiences of what we are calling "semipersonal" love for God. He loves God because of the kind of person He is—merciful and patient and almighty, for example. The exercitant is loving God as a person, not as a means to his well-being or pleasure, but his love is not yet the fullness of personal love. In a way, he's still relating to God as an admiring spectator. During the course of the retreat, the exercitant can also experience loving God with personal love, but we'll discuss this when we take up the second set of rules for discernment.[75]

It would, of course, be a big mistake to conclude that a person who is not experiencing consolations is not loving God. Feelings of love are not essential for love. In other words, one can love deeply and firmly even when it seems that feelings of love are for all practical purposes absent. On the other hand, it's also a mistake to say that feelings of love are insignificant and that they somehow don't matter. Feelings of love are necessary for a full or integral response of human love. Consolations are experiences, not only of love, but of integral love.[76]

Consolations are then marked by affective feelings. The exercitant is moved by God's attributes: His mercy, His self-sacrifice, His patience, etc. He responds with love and feels warmth, tenderness, devotion, sweetness, sadness, regret and so on. The feelings vary with the person and the situation, but the exercitant does feel the kinds of things we normally associate with love. It's not uncommon for the exercitant's eyes to well up with tears. Tears are often the sign of deep feelings. That is perhaps why Ignatius associates them with consolations: "It is likewise consolation when one sheds tears that move to the love of God" (316).

Often, joy and tranquility of heart accompany consolations. The exercitant rejoices over his Lord's splendor. Likewise, it fills him with joy that his Lord is known, loved and served by at least some people. Because he is in some sense experiencing the one he loves, the exercitant's heart is tranquil. He experiences joy, quiet and rest because he possesses, in some small sense, the one he desires. Ignatius puts it this way: "I call consolation . . . all interior joy which calls and attracts to heavenly things and to the salvation of one's soul, quieting it and giving it peace in its Creator and Lord" (316, Mullan). The peace Ignatius is talking about isn't simply the absence of anxiety, worry and conflict. It entails a quiet, joyful abiding in God. There is no need to pursue Him and strive after Him because He is experienced as present.

When someone encounters God and finds his heart enkindled, often he experiences impulses to faith and hope. He finds himself thinking things like, I can trust Him. I want to trust Him. He is faithful and true. In other words, he experiences not the intellectual assent to the dogmas of our faith, as important as those are, but rather a type of faith and trust in God which make a relationship possible. Sometimes, then, the exercitant responds with love for God, and the love manifests itself as sparks of belief in and trust of God's commitment to him.

Often, too, the exercitant finds himself thinking things like, No job is too big. No job is too small. He is full of zeal for the work of the Lord, and no obstacle seems too great. Ignatius puts it this way in his letter to Teresa Rejadell: "When this divine consolation is present all trials are pleasant and all weariness rest. He who goes forward with this fervor, warmth, and interior consolation finds every burden light and sweetness in every penance or trial, however great."[77] The exercitant feels more energetic in striving and stronger in facing the troubles and pains of life. He's full of confident expectation and hope.

So, when a person encounters God and responds with an integral love, he's experiencing a consolation. The love he is experiencing manifests itself in warm affective sentiments. Those warm affective sentiments often show up as sparks of faith and hope. That's the way love works. The exercitant's love also manifests itself in the desire to do something for God. Love, after all, manifests itself in deeds. "I call consolation every increase of faith, hope, and love" (316), says Ignatius.

Often, then, when the exercitant is consoled, he finds himself wanting to share what he possesses with the Lord. He wants to give his money, his time and his talents to the Lord. No sacrifice seems too great. Sometimes exercitants find themselves not only wanting to give their material goods to the Lord, and to give of themselves, but even to give their very selves to the Lord. The exercitant's love is marked by giving. Often, too, his love is marked by a desire to be present to the Lord. The exercitant desires to be with Him and to imitate Him. Consolations make him eager for more personal prayer. Of course, the exercitant also feels a strong aversion to whatever draws him away from God. Besides desiring to give to the Lord and to be present to the Lord, he usually finds himself desiring to do things for the Lord as a way of laboring in His service. He might find himself thinking about doing penance or being a missionary or being single for the Lord or pouring out his life in service of his brothers and sisters.

As we've seen, consolations arise out of encounters with God. Ignatius calls such experiences "spiritual consolation" (316). It's important for the director and eventually the exercitant to realize that it's possible to be deeply moved in situations that don't involve a personal or semipersonal encounter with God. For example, a person can be deeply moved by a movie. The movie evokes sweet, comforting tears. Similar feelings of joy and exultation can be caused by a great piece of music or a project completed. People experience great delight and satisfaction from the contemplation of beauty in nature and art or from philosophical, literary or scientific study. One could call such consoling experiences "natural consolations." The feelings which accompany such experiences resemble the feelings that accompany spiritual consolations, but they are not the same experience. Consolations are not simply deeply moving experiences. They are experiences which arise out of an encounter with God and result in an increase of faith, hope and love.

It is possible for one person to listen to a piece of music or gaze at the stars and experience a natural consolation, while another person does the same things and experiences a spiritual consolation. Consider a person who experiences peace, delight and comfort from star-gazing. Maybe he's moved—even deeply moved—by the beauty of the star-studded sky, or maybe all his troubles seem dwarfed by the vastness of the heavens, but it's a nonspiritual consolation. Ignatius, however, experienced spiritual consolations from his star-gazing. "It was his greatest consolation to gaze upon the heavens and stars, which he often did and for long stretches at a time, because when doing so he felt within himself a powerful urge to be serving our Lord."[78] He encountered the Lord in his star-gazing and was powerfully moved by his love to serve Him more.

One of the most important things the director does during the course of the retreat is to help a person learn to recognize spiritual consolations. To do this, the director has to listen carefully to what the exercitant is telling him. The director should, for example, be aware that people can speak very enthusiastically about graces which are not consolations. During the First Week of the Exercises, many exercitants experience a lot of implemental love for God. They see how He saves them from their sins and they love Him on account of what He has done for them. They experience gratitude; they want to serve and obey Him, and they don't want to offend Him. All this is very good and it is a great grace, but it's not a consolation. Consolations are experiences of semipersonal or personal love for God, not experiences of implemental love.

Directors should also realize that consolations vary greatly among exercitants. They vary in intensity. They can happen at any time or in any place. They are not limited to prayer times. A person can experience sparks of love while living and working side by side with his Lord or while he is talking face to face with Him. Consolations are also experienced by people in different ways, according to their temperaments. One person may experience very intense feelings of love, but his demeanor is serene. He's like a deep but powerful river. Such a person may describe his consolations very succinctly. Another person may experience less intense feelings of love, but his demeanor seems less serene. He might speak very animatedly about his consolations.

When the exercitant experiences a consolation, he can use the consolation to draw closer to the Lord, somewhat as a pole vaulter uses his pole. A track and field athlete can, on his own, leap over a bar that is six to seven feet high. If he runs with a pole and then converts his forward momentum to upward momentum, he can get over a bar that is twice as high and sometimes even as high as 19 feet. Ardent feelings of love for the Lord help the exercitant go farther, faster and higher. When someone is moved with love for the Lord, it's a good time for him to look and see if there is something more he can do for the Lord out of love for Him. The Official Directory advises directors to instruct exercitants "how to reap solid fruit from these consolations." In fact, "if nothing further is done, the sweet affection, which usually does not last long, will die away and leave no fruit."[79]

Although the exercitant shouldn't make any "inconsiderate or hasty promise or vow" (14, Mullan), his inflamed love can lead him to make some commitments to the Lord and their work together. Times of consolation are also good times for a person to examine ways he can better keep the commitments he's already made out of love for the Lord. In other words, the exercitant can and should do more than simply enjoy the consolation. After all, when Moses encountered God in the burning bush or Saul encountered Jesus on the road to Damascus, it wasn't so that they could have a good prayer time. If the exercitant only enjoys the consolation, he's likely to miss the grace of the consolation.

Exercitants need to be reminded that consolations are unmerited gifts. It's easy for a person to fall into the trap of thinking his own efforts cause them. As the exercitant makes the retreat, he finds that it is hard work. In fact, the director has to be careful that the exercitant doesn't tire himself out making meditations and colloquies. The exercitant labors with his understanding, and this fatigues his mind. His goal isn't understanding for understanding's sake, however. He's laboring with his mind in order to awaken his love. When his love is awakened, he can mistakenly think that it's the result of his own efforts. He forgets that it is a gift, the gift of a personal encounter. It requires his participation, but it also requires action on God's part. If a consolation could be had simply by virtue of the exercitant's own hard work, he wouldn't be having an encounter with God.

Sometimes a person can be so dazzled by what he is experiencing—the sweetness, the ardor, the peace—that he forgets God and falls in love with the experience. After the consolation, he can even become puffed up, thinking things like, See how much I love God, and looking down on others whom he judges aren't as ardent and zealous as he is. He might think, They are so weak and so prone to discouragement and doubt. If they could just be like me.... The exercitant can begin to believe that he will never be desolate. He can think he is immune from the attacks of the Enemy and that he is unshakably loyal. He can even become a bit like the Apostle Peter. "Everyone else may fall away, but I will not.... Even if I must die with you, I will never disown you" (Mt. 26:33-35).

It's important for the director to remind the exercitant to be grateful and to respond to God's self-gift by humbling himself. "He who enjoys consolation should take care to humble himself and lower himself as much as possible" (324). Ideally, the goal is that "we may interiorly feel that it is not ours to get or keep great devotion, intense love, tears or any other spiritual consolation, but that all is the gift and grace of God our Lord, and that we may not build a nest in a thing not ours, raising our intellect into some pride or vainglory, attributing to us devotion or the other things of spiritual consolation" (322, Mullan).[80]

In times of consolation, the exercitant should even prepare for the time when his ardor is quenched on account of an encounter with the Enemy. A good way to do this is to keep a record of one's consolations and return to it in times of desolation. Ignatius puts it this way: "When one enjoys consolation, let him consider how he will conduct himself during the time of ensuing desolation, and store up a supply of strength as defense against that day" (323).

Desolations often come in close conjunction with consolations. Sometimes, for seemingly no reason at all, the exercitant's love seems to grow cold. At one moment he's full of enthusiasm for the Lord and for the exercises he is doing. The next day, or even the next hour, he's apathetic and listless. It's as if the wind has gone out of his sails. The desolations the exercitant experiences are encounters with the Enemy. In his letter to Teresa Rejadell, Ignatius describes the work of the Enemy:

> We find ourselves sad without knowing why. We cannot pray with devotion, nor contemplate, nor even speak or hear of things of God with any interior taste or relish. Not only this, but if he sees that we are weak and much humbled by these harmful thoughts, he goes on to suggest that we are entirely forgotten by God our Lord, and leads us to think we are quite separated from Him and that all that we have done and all that we desire to do is entirely worthless. He thus endeavors to bring us to a state of general discouragement.[81]

Once the exercitant is brought low and discouraged by his encounter with the Enemy, he's then easy prey for the Enemy's temptations, accusations, lies and vexations.

Faith, hope and love are powerful engines. They propel a person forward. When the exercitant encounters the Enemy, it is as if the motor dies and the energy of his soul is lost. Suddenly the exercitant perceives things differently. The way forward seems beset with insurmountable obstacles. He's disinclined to pursue his relationship with God or with any brother or sister in Christ. God doesn't seem so trustworthy anymore. The exercitant experiences a yearning for more and more selfish concerns. He may begin to find diversion in created things and even comfort in unlawful things. The exercitant is very much tempted to doubt his love for God. He feels separated from God and begins to wonder whether perhaps he has sinned or has in some way become displeasing to God. He might feel unworthy, beyond the reach of God's love, beyond His forgiveness.

In his Rules for Discernment of Spirits, Ignatius describes desolation as "darkness of soul, disturbance in it, movement to things low and earthly, the unquiet of different agitations and temptations, moving to want of confidence, without hope, without love when one finds oneself all lazy, tepid, sad, and as if separated from his Creator and Lord" (317, Mullan). Of course, the exercitant is not separated from God and he is not without love for God. Sometimes, though, when he encounters the Enemy the affective feelings which accompany his love are doused and he suddenly feels desolate.

When Ignatius talks about a desolation, he is usually not referring to a period of dryness in one's spiritual life that lasts for weeks, months or even years. He's talking about an event in time, not a period of time. Often, though, a desolation can, if it goes unchecked, lead to a period of aridity in one's spiritual life. The thoughts, perceptions and feelings that accompany a desolation can take root in a person's mind and heart and begin to grow like a weed. If the exercitant can learn to recognize a desolation when it happens or shortly thereafter, it's a lot easier to fight. It's also worth noting that both beginners in prayer and those well advanced in the spiritual life can experience an aridity in prayer that has nothing to do with desolations.

It is worth noting that sometimes a person's ardor and zeal cool not on account of the Enemy but on account of his own sloth and negligence. Consolation is a response that arises in a person when he encounters God. If a person neglects his relationship with God, he won't encounter God as often and he'll experience fewer and fewer consolations. Of course, often the Enemy takes advantage of such a situation by tempting the now lukewarm person and lying to him, *See, God doesn't love you.* Although the Enemy is active in the situation, he is not the cause of the situation. In this case, the person's sloth and negligence are the cause.

Just as people can experience nonspiritual consolations, they can also experience nonspiritual desolations. For example, grief at the death of a friend is a kind of desolation that's not from the Enemy. A person can also experience an inner turmoil as a result of a chaotic external environment or the demands of many responsibilities. Generally speaking, one can feel sadness, discouragement, listlessness and turmoil as a response to a lot of things, not just as a response to the Enemy. For example, a person can feel dejected and enervated because he is dissatisfied with something about his life and has yet to find an effective way of getting what he wants. So, for instance, sometimes a person's best response to being trapped in a dead-end job are feelings of gloom and a restless discouragement.

It's important to know the difference between a spiritual and a nonspiritual desolation. If a person is dissatisfied with something about his current life situation, no amount of spiritual warfare is going to solve the problem. He will be much better off correctly identifying the problem and then working to better his situation in some way. Of course, nonspiritual desolations can make one prey to the Enemy's attacks and temptations. They can mutate into a spiritual reality.

Ignatius has several pieces of advice for the desolate exercitant. First of all, an exercitant should not, on account of a desolation, change a decision he's already made. He counsels the exercitant "... in time of desolation never to make a change; but to be firm and constant in the resolutions and determination in which one was the day preceding such desolation, or in the determination in which he was in the preceding consolation" (318, Mullan). It's the most natural thing in the world for a desolate exercitant to want to make a change in order to escape the desolation. When the exercitant is desolate, he is sad, confused and in turmoil. He's inclined to question himself. His previous faith and hope and love seem unreal. The psychic energy to live out decisions and resolutions wanes. In fact, the decisions and choices he's made in a better frame of mind now seem unreal. So there is a tendency to make rash, desolation-determined decisions and to abandon good undertakings already begun. That's why the Enemy gives desolations. "He seeks to prevent the soul from advancing" (315). The exercitant should not change direction on account of a desolation. He should stay with previously made decisions and resolutions, even though at the moment they may seem empty and meaningless.

Sometimes, people can mistakenly believe that God is trying to speak to them in a desolation. It is, in fact, an easy mistake to make. The exercitant's fervor suddenly cools off. He's experienced something that begs for an explanation, so he looks for an explanation. He begins to wonder if has done something wrong. He then starts to think that God is not pleased with him and that God is trying to tell him something. So, for example, he might reason, I didn't feel this way before I began the Exercises, but now I've lost all my zeal. God's trying to tell me something. For some reason he doesn't want me to make these Exercises. The desolation is not, however, from God. For people who are earnestly pursuing the Lord, desolations are never from God. Sometimes good people make bad decisions because they misinterpret desolation, taking discouragement, dryness, restlessness as signs of God's will. The reality is quite the contrary. "For just as in consolation the good spirit guides and counsels us, so in desolation the evil spirit guides and counsels. Following his counsels we can never find the way to a right decision," says Ignatius (318). Changing a decision in a time of desolation is following the Enemy's counsel. The desolation is the Enemy's attempt to guide a person.

The second piece of advice Ignatius has for the desolate exercitant has to do not just with resisting the Enemy but with actually overcoming him. When the exercitant recognizes a desolation, it's not time to give up or quit. When he recognizes the work of the Enemy, he should step aside and then strike back, as a boxer would do in a boxing match. He has to summon up all his courage and energy and then counterpunch. The exercitant counterpunches by opposing the Enemy's works: the sadness, the distrust, the tepidity, etc. So, for example, when someone desires to cut back on his prayer time by 10 minutes because he just doesn't feel like praying that long, he should reinforce his commitment by praying an extra 10 minutes. That's a counterpunch. The exercitant is intensifying his action against the desolation. If he feels joyless, he can sing. If he feels flat and apathetic, he can fast more. "Though in desolation we must never change our former resolutions, it will be very advantageous to intensify our activity against the desolation. We can insist more upon prayer, upon meditation, and on much examination of ourselves. We can make an effort in a suitable way to do some penance" (319).

Often a shorthand way of talking about counterpunching is advising a person to do the exact opposite of what he feels like doing; however, this is only partially true. For example, if someone wants to cut short his prayer time, he should pray an extra 10 minutes but he shouldn't spend his whole day praying. Under the guise of counterpunching, an exercitant could inadvertently change directions as a result of the Enemy's work. The Enemy could think, The exercitant's service is really moving things forward for God, so I'll make him desolate. That way, his counterpunch will probably be to pray all day and then he won't be serving anymore.

Directors can and should teach exercitants how to capture desolations for Christ. A person can learn valuable lessons from desolation. When his delightful affective feelings are snuffed out, the exercitant can learn a lot about himself. He learns that it is "not within our power to acquire and attain great devotion, intense love, tears, or any other spiritual consolation; but that all this is the gift and grace of God our Lord" (322). He begins to see how much of what he thinks he is doing for the Lord is actually for himself. After all, it's often a pleasant experience to love the Lord when our hearts are full of warm affection for Him. Desolation comes, and he learns "how little he is able to do . . . when he is left without such grace or consolation." (324).

The exercitant can also capture a desolation for Christ by using it as an opportunity to express his love. He can show his Lord how he will remain faithful through times when he feels no sweetness, no tenderness, no joy in loving. He can pray and do other spiritual exercises "without such great pay of consolations and great graces" (322, Mullan). The exercitant can show his Lord that not only will he remain faithful, but that he is also going to continue to do the things he knows please his Lord. He can renew his commitments, think about what gifts he might give his Beloved when they do connect again and use his memory to think about his Lord's good qualities and attributes. Doing these things helps the exercitant "prepare and dispose himself for the coming consolation" (7). Desolations are, then, opportunities to learn to love unselfishly. They can both strengthen and reveal the exercitant's love. A person should never think the desolation is sent from God, but he should take advantage of the desolation. He can turn it into an effective means for his love to grow and be expressed.

"If he who is giving the Exercises sees that he who is receiving them is in desolation and tempted, let him not be hard or dissatisfied with him, but gentle and indulgent, giving him courage and strength for the future" (7, Mullan). The director can encourage the desolate exercitant by reminding him that God's grace is always sufficient in every situation, no matter how difficult the situation may be. He should confidently assure the exercitant that consolation is just around the corner and encourage him to be patient. The early Jesuits offered this advice to the director:

> He should urge the exercitant to be patient and persevering and not to let himself be overcome by weariness or be deflected from prayer because of the difficulty and toil he is experiencing. If he courageously perseveres in knocking with hope and confidence at the door of divine mercy, it will surely be opened to him, as it is written: "If he delays wait for him, for he will surely come and will not be late" (Hab. 2:3).[82]

The director's confident assurance of coming consolation is a great help to exercitants.

When an exercitant experiences a desolation, the director not only teaches him to persevere in all his commitments and resolutions, to counterpunch and to capture the desolation for Christ, he also exposes to him "the wiles of the enemy of our human nature" (7). Ignatius thought that "It is necessary for us to be aware of our opponent."[83] He touches on this in his first set of rules for the discernment of spirits and returns to it in the all-important meditation on the Two Standards in the Second Week.

Good soldier that he was, Ignatius knew how important it is to know the strategies of one's enemy. The person who sets out to order his life so as to join in the work of uniting all things in Christ isn't fighting only himself.[84] An exercitant could envision the task ahead of him as something akin to climbing a high mountain. He might erroneously think that his principal opponents are himself and his environment. Ignatius is saying something different. If the exercitant wants to envision himself climbing a mountain, so be it, but he has got to understand that he has an Enemy hiding on that mountain, watching for opportunities to ambush him. The exercitant is in a battle. There is no need for him to be afraid, and Ignatius is not recommending an unhealthy curiosity about Satan, but he does want the exercitant to know a few things about Satan's strategies.

The first thing the exercitant needs to know about the Enemy is that he's like a bully. "Your adversary the devil prowls around like a roaring lion, seeking someone to devour. Resist him, firm in your faith" (1 Pt. 5:8-9). He's got a loud roar, but he's a weakling, especially before a show of strength. Even at his vilest, the exercitant can, by faith, resist him. When the exercitant resists him, the Enemy flees.

It's helpful for the director to elaborate about bullies to make sure the exercitant gets the point. If, in a quarrel with a coward, you show determination and fierceness, the coward will lose courage and go away. On the other hand, if you cower, he becomes a tyrant. If you face him, he just slinks away, but if you show weakness, he'll be all over you, like a raging beast. Ignatius says the Enemy is like the proverbially shrewish woman:

> He is a weakling before a show of strength, and a tyrant if he has his will. It is characteristic of a woman in a quarrel with a man to lose courage and take to flight if the man shows that he is determined and

> fearless. However, if the man loses courage and begins to flee, the anger, vindictiveness, and rage of the woman surge up and know no bounds. In the same way, the Enemy becomes weak, loses courage, and turns to flight with his seductions as soon as one leading a spiritual life faces his temptations boldly, and does exactly the opposite of what he suggests. However, if one begins to be afraid and to lose courage in temptations, no wild animal on earth can be fiercer than the enemy of our human nature. He will carry out his perverse intentions with consummate malice (325).

It's important for the exercitant to know that the Enemy feeds and grows strong on the exercitant's timidity, cowardice and discouragement, but that he flees when a person is strong and courageous.

The second thing the exercitant needs to know about his opponent is that he's like a false lover:

> He seeks to remain hidden and does not want to be discovered. If such a lover speaks with evil intention to the daughter of a good father, or to the wife of a good husband, and seeks to seduce them, he wants his words and solicitations kept secret. He is greatly displeased if his evil suggestions and depraved intentions are revealed by the daughter to her father, or by the wife to her husband. Then he readily sees he will not succeed in what he has begun. In the same way, when the enemy of our human nature tempts a just soul with his wiles and seductions, he earnestly desires that they be received secretly and kept secret (326).

It's very important for the exercitant to know that the Enemy works by laying traps, seducing him and trying to keep all his activity in the dark, undercover. "Every one who does evil hates the light and does not come to the light, lest his deeds should be exposed" (Jn. 3:20).

So how does a person fight this seductive, somewhat attractive, suitor? Reveal his advances. If, through fear or shame, the Enemy can persuade someone to keep his advances in the dark, he's won half the battle. He can keep working on the exercitant. So, it's important for the director to encourage the exercitant to talk about the Enemy's advances. "While the one who is giving the Exercises should not seek to investigate and know the private thoughts and sins of the exercitant, nevertheless, it will be very helpful if he is kept faithfully informed about the various disturbances and thoughts caused by the action of different spirits" (17). It's often the case that the Enemy flees as soon as the exercitant brings his activity into the light.

The director should, then, do what he can to make it easy for the exercitant to talk about any temptations he is experiencing. He might remark that it's normal to experience temptations during the Exercises. Or he could remark that very holy people encounter some of the gravest temptations. He could also remind the exercitant that not only was Jesus tempted but that he also must have talked about His temptations in the wilderness. Otherwise we wouldn't know about them.

Not only is the Enemy like a bully and like a false lover, but he is also like a very smart military commander. A commander and leader of an army will encamp, explore the fortifications and defenses of a stronghold, and attack at the weakest point. The Enemy investigates us. He's very smart and very observant. He can understand from the way we act how we are put together. In other words, he gets accurate insights into what makes each person tick. He then uses this knowledge to attack us at our weak points, the places where we are most vulnerable. His lies, accusations and temptations seem tailor-made for each and every person, and so they are. Although the Enemy's normal strategy is to attack the exercitant at his weak points, we've noticed that sometimes he attacks a person at his strongest point. If he can get away with one big punch, the fight is over.

In light of the Enemy's strategy, the director should encourage the exercitant to be equally as shrewd. He should know the weak spots in his defenses and shore them up. Of course, such advice presumes that the exercitant is aware of his weak spots. Self-knowledge is an essential weapon against the Enemy. And if the exercitant experiences a frontal attack, he should remember that the Enemy is a bully and face the temptation promptly and boldly.

How and when does the director teach all this to the exercitant? This question seems to have been an important one for Ignatius. Relatively speaking, a good portion of his preliminary observations about the Exercises has to do with how and when to instruct the exercitant about consolations and desolations. Ignatius's answer to this question—which is that he should teach the exercitant what he needs to know when he needs to know it—can be frustrating to an inexperienced director. Basically, the best time to teach about desolations is just after the exercitant has had a desolation. So, too, with consolations. The director has to be careful not to inundate a person with material on consolations and desolations. He doesn't have to tell the exercitant everything he knows. The goal is to instruct him in a way that will help him with his unique retreat.

As the director talks to a person about consolations and desolations, there are several basic things that the director can keep in mind. First of all, the director does not have to figure out and explain everything that the exercitant is experiencing. Sometimes a director can fall into the trap of trying to neatly identify and categorize each and every experience an exercitant has: Is it from God? From Satan? From natural causes? The director might wonder whether the exercitant's delight in an insight into a Gospel passage is a consolation or simply the natural joy of learning. Or he might wonder whether a person's discouragement is a desolation or his habitual way of responding to challenging endeavors. The rules for discernment are not designed to account for everything the exercitant experiences in his mind and heart as he makes the Exercises. They are not even designed to account for every spiritual experience a person has. They are simply some comments that shed light on some things that some exercitants may be experiencing. The important thing is that the exercitant begins to recognize at least some of the consolations and desolations he experiences.

The director doesn't have to respond to everything the exercitant says. If the exercitant is talking about some experience he's had and the director doesn't know what to make of it, the director can choose not to respond. He can always come back later after he's had time to think and pray about what the exercitant has said. Generally, a good rule of thumb is: If you don't know what's going on, don't say anything. Of course, it's often a good idea to ask the exercitant open-ended questions that will help him better articulate what he is experiencing. It's also helpful if the director can recognize when a person needs a nap or when it might be helpful to lighten the schedule of exercises.

The director also needs to keep in mind some things about the work of the Enemy. It's helpful to remember that not every temptation or every instance of fallacious reasoning is a desolation. Temptations and fallacious reasoning often accompany desolation, but they are not, strictly speaking, desolations. When the director is talking about the Enemy, he doesn't want to give the impression that every bad thought or undesirable emotion is from the Enemy. Such an approach fails to take adequate account of our own responsibility for our actions and their consequences. On the other hand, he does want to impress upon the exercitant the importance of recognizing and then fighting the work of the Enemy. If, for example, a person is plagued by discouragement during the retreat, he might need to persevere patiently, whether the discouragement is caused by the Enemy or by natural causes. If it is the Enemy who is active in the situation, the exercitant is better off knowing it so he can not only persevere but fight back.

There is one more important thing for the director to keep in mind. Normally the exercitants we deal with are "those who go on earnestly striving to cleanse their souls from sin and who seek to rise in the service of God our Lord to greater perfection" (315). Our exercitants may be far from perfect but the general trajectory of their lives is toward God. Occasionally, though, the director may run across an exercitant whose life has been going from bad to worse. The general trajectory of this person's life has been headed away from God. His Christianity is only a veneer. Beneath the surface there is growing corruption.

It turns out that God and the Enemy work differently "in the case of those who go from one mortal sin to another" (314). What does Satan do in such a person's life? He wants to encourage and console such a person in his way of life. In such persons, "the enemy is commonly used to propose to them apparent pleasures, making them imagine sensual delights and pleasures in order to hold them more and make them grow in their vices and sins" (314, Mullan). God, on the other hand, works very differently, "pricking them and biting their consciences through the process of reason" (314, Mullan). In such a person, God appeals to reason and to the conscience, causing guilt and remorse. His action is unpleasant and even painful. He's trying to shake the person up, so that he will wake up and change the course of his life.

It's important for the director to be aware of how God works in the life of someone who is going from one mortal sin to another. One time, a woman came to one of us for help. She was, at least on the surface, a religious person. She was plagued with feelings of guilt and felt bad about herself. She was sure that her feelings of guilt and depression were from the Enemy. After all, she thought, God loved her and wanted her to feel joy and happiness. On the face of it, it looked like she was experiencing a desolation. After a series of conversations, we said, "Actually, those feelings of guilt and depression are from the Lord." The woman was enraged. She believed that God would never do something so harsh. After all, He loved her and wanted her to feel good about herself.

What did the woman say that led us to make such a claim? She was feeling miserable and blamed everyone else for her misery. Sometimes she blamed God Himself for her unhappiness. She was so miserable that she was drinking in secret. She needed money for the alcohol and she didn't want her husband to know about her drunkenness, so she was planning to pilfer some money, just a little bit, here and there. She was making plans to steal. She was going from bad to worse. The Lord was opposing her and her plans. He was not about to reward her plans for evil with feelings of peace and happiness. He was trying to derail her. Her feelings of guilt were due to the action of God in her life. For people who are headed toward God, "it is the way of the evil spirit to bite, sadden" (315, Mullan), but for people who are headed in the opposite direction, it is the way of the Lord to bite their consciences.

Discerning spirits is an art. Ignatius was typically wise when he said that these matters are better dealt with in person than in a letter. The director should make sure he studies the material in this chapter, but the best thing he can do to learn this art is to apprentice himself to a spiritual person. It is a wisdom that is handed on, from Christian to Christian and from generation to generation. The art of discernment is best learned from Spirit-filled people who are grounded in reality.

III

MEDITATIONS ON THE LIFE OF JESUS

CHAPTER 8

THREE KEY MEDITATIONS

THE KINGDOM OF CHRIST

After finishing the meditations of the First Week, the exercitant is ready to move on. Ignatius sets the next meditation between the First Week and the Second Week. Technically, it is a part of neither the First Week nor the Second Week. The exercitant has become accustomed to doing five meditations a day, but at this point in the Exercises there is a break in the schedule. Ignatius wants the exercitant to make the meditation on the Kingdom of Christ only twice during the day. The exercitant experiences this day as a real respite, but it is still very important for what follows. It is a pivotal point in the Spiritual Exercises.

The meditation on the Kingdom of Christ is a foundation for what follows in the rest of the retreat. It has a preparatory function. Some commentators even refer to it as a second principle and foundation. During the Second, Third and Fourth Weeks the exercitant will be meditating on the life of Jesus. The meditation on the Kingdom of Christ prepares the exercitant by providing him a bird's-eye view of Jesus and His mission. After the usual preparatory prayer, Ignatius instructs the exercitant "to see with the sight of the imagination, the synagogues, villages and towns through which Christ our Lord preached" (91, Mullan). The meditation also provides the exercitant with a picture of how someone inflamed with love responds to Jesus.

During the past week the exercitant has been experiencing sorrow and tears for his sin as he has been meditating on the blessings of creation and redemption. He has come face to face with sin and its awful consequences. One might expect Ignatius to offer a person a program of self-improvement or a way to perfect himself so as to avoid all sin in the future. That's not what he does. He has the exercitant consider the call of Christ, and it turns out that it is a call to join Him in a much larger enterprise:

> See Christ our Lord, the eternal King, with the entire human race before him, as to all and to each one in particular his call goes out; "It is my will to conquer the whole world and every enemy, and so enter into the glory of my Father. Therefore all those who want to come with me will have to labour with me, so that by following me in my suffering they may also follow me into glory" (95, Ivens).

The call of Christ is not a call to perfect oneself; it is a call to join Him in His work of bringing salvation and redemption to the whole world.

It is important for the director to remember that a person's struggle with his inordinate attachments is only a subplot of a much larger story. It is all too easy for us to think and act as if the entire story of Christianity consists of our personal salvation, thereby putting ourselves at the center of the story. We can begin to talk as if life in Christ is all about us becoming better persons. Actually, though, our personal salvation and redemption is a subplot of a much larger story. The larger story is about Jesus and those united with Him conquering the world. A person's sanctification is necessary but not sufficient for building Christianity.

Before contemplating the call of Christ the King, the exercitant prays for the grace "not to be deaf to His call, but prompt and diligent to accomplish His most holy will" (91). Sometimes an overeager exercitant can misunderstand what he is praying for here. He's not praying to know the particulars of his vocation in life. He's praying for the grace to hear *whatever* the Lord says. He's also praying for the grace to be prompt and diligent in answering. He doesn't want to be someone who hears the Lord calling and delays in answering.

What might make a person deaf to the Lord's call, and why would a person delay in responding? In today's therapeutic culture we are likely to think that things such as fear and distrust and anxiety make it difficult to hear and respond. Ignatius, however, knows that in this instance fear and distrust and anxiety are merely symptoms of something else, usually some inordinate attachment. A person with inordinate attachments won't hear and respond to the Lord, so Ignatius has the exercitant ask for the grace to do so.

As a help in considering the call of Christ the King, the exercitant first considers the call of an earthly or, as some translations put it, a temporal king. This can be a difficult meditation for some, because kingship plays such an integral role in it, and the mission of the king calls to mind historical enterprises such as the Crusades or the conquest of the New World—enterprises that the exercitant has perhaps been taught to deplore.

Sometimes, when we've given the Exercises, we've instructed the exercitant at this point to imagine a great leader, for example, Churchill. Imagining a great leader instead of a king is helpful for some people, but something is lost too. Because there is more of a sense of equality between a person and a democratic leader, imagining a great leader doesn't capture the sense of obedience and reverence due a king. We've also tried instructing the exercitant to place an imaginary king in a real historical situation. We like to use the story of the 17th-century Jesuit mission to South America. The Jesuits were bringing Christ to the native peoples and rescuing them from the corruption and injustice of the Spanish settlements and from the Portuguese slave traders. We tell the exercitant to imagine a king who decides to make the terrible ocean crossing and bring order to that land. This works well for those who are familiar with the story of the South American reductions and the conditions the Jesuits faced at that time, but not many people are.

It seems to work best to give the meditation as if emphasizing that this is an imaginary and not a historical king. Here's one way to do this: "Imagine a king. I'm not talking about any particular figure in history. He's an imaginary king. He's a really good man, and he's clearly chosen by God. His kingdom is small but he's got many resources available to him. His knights, and in fact all his subjects, trust him. They know him, they've observed him, and they love him. He hears about a distant land of unbelievers engulfed in pain and suffering. This king addresses his knights and all his people: 'It is my Will to conquer all the land of unbelievers. Therefore, whoever would like to come with me is to be content to eat as I, and also to drink and dress, etc., as I:

likewise he is to labor like me in the day and watch in the night, etc., that so afterward he may have part with me in the victory, as he has had it in the labors'" (93, Mullan).

Actually, we're not suggesting that the director repeat the king's call with this somewhat formal language. He can, of course, put it in his own words if he understands it enough not to miss the gist of it. We are suggesting that the director give the meditation with a few unobtrusive bows to modern political and cultural sensibilities.

Next, Ignatius directs the exercitant to consider the response any knight would make to such a call. The image of a knight, as opposed, say, to a common foot soldier, is helpful for two reasons. We associate personal loyalty with knights. Knights have a keen sense of what honor and loyalty demand of them. The image is also evocative of the genuine friendship that can exist between a subordinate and his commander-in-chief. The whole picture is one of friendship, loyalty and shared suffering and victory.

Next, Ignatius has the exercitant consider Christ our Lord, the eternal King. He has assembled before Him the whole world, and He calls to all and to each one in particular: "It is my will to conquer all the world and all enemies. . . ." (95, Mullan). Like the earthly king, Christ eschews all worldly status, power and comfort. He lays aside His kingly position. It is not kingliness that wins this battle. The image is one of a laboring Jesus, not a victorious Jesus. The call is to befriend Him, live with Him and share His life. In fact, the keynote is "with me," in Spanish "*conmigo.*" This word is repeated five times in the meditation. The person who responds to Christ's call doesn't just labor and suffer for Christ; he labors and suffers with Him. Unlike the earthly king, the sphere of this King is the whole world. There is no place or person who is irredeemable or beyond His reach.

Ignatius also notes that Christ's call to join Him in His mission is a universal call. It's given to all, regardless of class, race, gender, state in life, etc. No one is left out, and no one is exempt. This call is also given to each one in particular. This is an important point for the director to keep in mind. Each person is different. The moment when Christ calls John will be different from the moment when He calls Bob, and that in turn will be different from the moment when He calls Sally. This call of Christ is not a one-size-fits-all call. For each person it is unique and unrepeatable, because each person is unique and unrepeatable. Sometimes we can think that God deals with everyone in exactly the same way, but that's a mistake. His dealings with us are personal and full of personal love. The director who has had his own unique encounter with the Lord can't expect the exercitant to respond as he responded and to be moved by what moved him. Each relationship of love is necessarily different because different people are involved. The inexperienced director has to be especially careful not to impose his personal experiences on the exercitant.

Before moving on to examine the responses a person might make to the call of Christ the King, we need to pause and examine the key verb in the call: "It is my will to conquer all the world and all enemies . . . ." For many, it is easier to think of Jesus saving and redeeming the whole world, but conquering? This can sound warlike and even un-Christian to some, and especially, as we'll see, to those who haven't been through the First Week of the Exercises.

Christ the King isn't simply offering people a better way of life. He wants to institute change, and He has enemies. Some commentators on the Exercises make it sound as if the enemies the Christian deals with are his passions, not someone or something outside of himself. However, Ignatius has in mind real enemies, human enemies, people who lure you to worldly values, ruin your good name, put you in jail and order your execution. Jesus had them. His disciples will have them too, if they accept His call. The word "conquer" purposely evokes fighting, but the imagery of the meditation is not warlike. Christ is presented as laboring, not fighting. There is no mention of weapons. This King knows that "A king is not saved by his great army; a warrior is not delivered by his great strength. The war horse is a vain hope for victory, and by its great might it cannot save" (Ps. 33:16-17). This King wins with poverty, insults, contempt and humility.

When Ignatius uses the verb "conquer" he doesn't mean that Christ is going to come into a country and wipe out the inhabitants as, for example, the Assyrians wiped out the Northern Kingdom of Israel. The sense is something more akin to "liberate," yet there's no denying that Christ's mission involves taking over the lands of the unbelievers. He is King and He wants to rule—not for His own benefit but for the benefit of the whole world. The underlying presupposition here is that life is hellish and hellbound unless Christ is ruling. The exercitant who has gone through the First Week and has looked the consequences of sin in the eye knows this. He knows that sin is disorder, and he doesn't want anything to do with it. He wants Christ to be king of the whole world.

After meditating on the call of Christ the King, the exercitant considers two different responses to that call. Both are positive responses. The first response is that of people with "judgment and reason" (96). The second response is that of people who are moved by great love. Ignatius says these people "want to be more devoted and signalise themselves in all service of their King" (97, Mullan), but we recommend referring to them as people who respond with great love. It's clear from the context that this is what Ignatius means, and it avoids misunderstandings. The exercitant is not being directed to meditate on people who want to rise to the top of the pack and outdo everyone else in their response.

Although Ignatius is contrasting those who respond to the call of Christ with reason to those who respond with love, he doesn't mean to present the former as somehow deficient. He's not thinking of a person who is coldly rational—all mind and no heart. The man who responds with "judgment and reason" offers his whole self. You could say that he is wholeheartedly dutiful. He has a personal commitment to the work of Christ, but it is as a collaborator or an associate. Although totally committed, the relationship isn't one of deep personal friendship.

Those who hear the call of Christ and are inflamed with love have a different response. They want to be with their King, no matter where the King is or what He is doing. "Acting against their own sensuality and against their carnal and worldly love" (97, Mullan), they offer themselves for the mission. Ignatius then has the exercitant consider what these folks might offer.

We need to clarify what Ignatius means by "sensuality" and "carnal and worldly love." "Sensuality" doesn't only imply excesses in food, drink or sex. It has a more general meaning. Here it refers to our natural desires for bodily ease and comfort: soft chairs, good food and wine, cool breezes, beautiful surroundings, etc. By "carnal love," Ignatius means not only sexual desires but also natural affection for home and family, and by "worldly love" he means love for what the world loves as opposed to what Christ loves. Those who act against their sensuality and carnal and worldly loves aren't simply on the defensive, resisting temptations. They go on the offensive and war upon anything—however lawful and good in and of itself—that might prevent them from joining their King who is laboring in the field with rough clothes, poor food and sleepless nights. It is the strategy of *agere contra* that we described in Chapter Two.

Those who are moved with love make the following offering of themselves. It is made with great solemnity, in the presence of the heavenly court:

> Eternal Lord of all things, in the presence of Thy infinite goodness, and of Thy glorious mother, and of all the saints of Thy heavenly court, this is the offering of myself which I make with Thy favor and help. I protest that it is my earnest desire and my deliberate choice, provided only it is for Thy greater service and praise, to imitate Thee in bearing all wrongs and all abuse and all poverty, both actual and spiritual, should Thy most holy majesty deign to choose and admit me to such a state and way of life (98).

Although normally the director shouldn't explain a meditation, when giving this meditation he should explain and elaborate a bit on this prayer. He is giving the meditation orally, and the exercitant is taking notes. This prayer isn't intuitively obvious, and the exercitant can easily miss the point.

So what is the imaginary person in this meditation actually asking for? He wants to imitate his King "in bearing all wrongs and all abuse and all poverty, both actual and spiritual." First, it's important to get clear on the vocabulary. "Actual poverty" is the lack of material goods. "Spiritual poverty" is detachment from material goods, whether one has them or not.

What about the word "imitate"? What does it mean to imitate this King? In common parlance, the word "imitate" conjures up some images which aren't helpful in understanding what Ignatius is getting at in the meditation. Think, for example, of the standup comedian imitating a current president, or an end-of-the-year skit where students imitate faculty members. "To imitate" can mean "to mimic." It can have connotations of artificiality. Or think of a young high-school girl imitating—to her own detriment—the clothing, speech, and mannerisms of older, more popular girls. The word can also have connotations of self-abnegation, if a person rejects elements of his own personality in favor of acting like someone else. Or think of the aspiring philosopher who imitates Socrates or the aspiring musician who imitates his favorite musician. There is a distance in time and space implied by this kind of imitation. Is this the kind of imitation Ignatius had in mind? Is the person who is making the offering in this meditation saying, in effect, "My King, You bore all poverty, wrongs, and abuse, so I will too. You set the pattern, and now it's my job to copy it"?

That's not what the person inflamed with love wants. He's not asking to endure poverty and hardship *for* his King. He's asking to endure all poverty, abuse and wrongs *with* his King. The operative phrase in this meditation is, after all, "with me." Of course, none of this makes any sense if the King isn't alive now.

The man who responds to the call of Christ the King with love wants to join Him. Because of some of the connotations of "imitate," we highly recommend that the director substitute the word "join" when he's giving this meditation. In fact, anywhere in the text where Ignatius uses the word "imitate" the director can efficaciously use the word "join."

The one making the offering wants to join Jesus and share His life—not just the final triumph, but all the labors and hardships. He's apprenticing himself to his King. He wants to live His King's life, the way his King lives it. He's looked around, and he's chosen this man to follow. He aspires to be a true disciple of Jesus. He doesn't desire a classroom situation where he listens to a few lectures and then goes on his way. He wants to know everything about this man: how He dresses, what He eats, how He spends His spare time, how He handles troubles and disappointments . . . everything. The moment portrayed in this offering is akin to what happens sometimes between fathers and sons. Think of the boy who sees his father with a hammer and wants one too. He wants to join his father. He wants to share his father's life. He's saying, I want to do what you are doing.

There's one last detail about this offering that needs some treatment. The one who hears the call of the King and is moved with love offers his entire self to the King in great solemnity, but twice he offers caveats: "Provided only it is for Thy greater service and praise" (98) and "should Thy most Holy Majesty deign to choose and admit me to such a state and way of life" (98). What's going on? The one who makes this offering protests that it is "my earnest desire and my deliberate choice . . . to imitate Thee in bearing all wrongs and all abuse and all poverty, both actual and spiritual" (98), but he's not about to make a decision unilaterally. Neither subordinates, nor friends, nor friends who are also subordinates make decisions unilaterally, much less a servant of the King. They don't make their decisions on their own.

So the person who makes the offering is saying, in effect, that he won't make any decisions unilaterally and that he isn't ruling anything out. "Lord, I want to join your campaign and your work of conquering the world. I'm totally available. Not only that, but you can count on me to do the heavy lifting. I'm volunteering for the hardest duty and the dirtiest work. I really desire this, but you decide where you want to put me. After all, you are King." He's not choosing trench duty on his own. When he says, "if you deign to choose me," he's saying, "It's your call. I'm placing myself in your hands." He's willing to be a medic or to peel potatoes, if his King will be better served in these ways.

The careful reader will probably have noticed that this meditation doesn't end with a colloquy. In this regard it's like the Principle and Foundation. The exercitant is to reflect on and consider the Principle and Foundation, but it doesn't end with a colloquy. Even though the salvation of the whole world depends on people volunteering and offering themselves for the labor, Ignatius doesn't ask the exercitant to make the offering. He simply presents the possibility and asks the exercitant to observe and reflect upon the offering.

THE TWO STANDARDS

After considering Christ the King, the exercitant begins to meditate on the life of Christ in earnest. By the time the retreat is over, he will have considered events in the life of Jesus beginning with the Incarnation and ending with the Ascension. The exercitant spends three weeks contemplating his King with only one break in the routine. Three or so days after the exercitant begins, the director changes the routine for a day. The director tells him that as he contemplates the life of Jesus he should begin to think about his own life and any changes he wants to make in his way of life. The director is opening the door for him to ask himself, In light of this newfound love of the Lord, how shall I live? The director then says that there are some things a person needs to know about the strategies of the Lord and of the Enemy and some things he needs to know about himself before considering any changes in his way of life.

The Two Standards meditation helps a person recognize both the snares and traps of "the rebel chief" (139) and the surprising strategies of "the Supreme and True Captain" (139, Mullan). This is an important meditation. The exercitant makes it twice in one day and repeats it twice. The day then closes with the meditation on Three Classes of Men. This meditation is designed to help a person discover and deal with his inordinate attachment to money. Even if he doesn't have a decision looming on the horizon, the exercitant should make both these meditations. They are important to the whole retreat.

Although it might seem like the exercitant is changing gears when he stops meditating on events from the Gospels and begins making these two meditations, he is not. During this Second Week of the Exercises he is beginning each of his meditations on the life of Jesus by asking for "an intimate knowledge of our Lord, who has become man for me, that I may love Him more and follow Him more closely" (104). Following Jesus means making choices: big choices and small ones. In order to follow Jesus, the exercitant has to learn how to make choices for Him and for their relationship.

We'll return to decision-making again, but for now let's turn to the Two Standards meditation. Ignatius proposes for consideration two standards, "one of Christ, our supreme leader and lord, the other of Lucifer, the deadly enemy of our human nature" (136). Right away the imagery evokes warfare and two opposing camps, each centered around its own standard, or flag. The exercise is one of contrasts: between the two camps, their leaders and their strategies for victory.

One camp is on a great plain around Jerusalem, and the other is on a plain around the region of Babylon. The cities are themselves evocative of salvation history.

Babylon is the traditional enemy of the people of God. Out of Babylon came the Assyrians, who conquered the Northern Kingdom of Israel, and out of Babylon came Nebuchadnezzar, whose armies burned Jerusalem and the Temple to the ground. (The director might have to say a word or two about Babylon to an exercitant who is unfamiliar with these events from Scripture.) Babylon is "a horror among the nations" (Jer. 50:23). Symbolically, in the book of Revelation, she is "the great harlot" (Rev. 19:2) and "the mother of harlots" (Rev. 17:5), a monstrous parody of feminine beauty.

Jerusalem, the home of the people of God, is "the city of the great King" (Ps. 48:2) and "the joy of all the earth" (Ps. 48:2). Once unfaithful, but now redeemed, she is, in the book of Revelation, "the new Jerusalem . . . prepared as a bride adorned for her husband" (Rev. 21:2) with a "radiance like a most rare jewel" (Rev. 21:11).

The exercitant also considers the two leaders, Lucifer encamped near Babylon and Christ encamped on the plain outside Jerusalem. Ignatius calls Christ "the sovereign Commander-in-Chief of all the good" (138) and describes His appearance as "beautiful and attractive" (144). He calls Lucifer a "rebel chief" (139) and says his appearance inspires "horror and terror" (140). The exercitant is not supposed to choose between the two camps; he's already done that. Rather, he is to understand the character and purpose of the two leaders by studying their tactics and the means they use to draw people to their standards. The exercitant thus prays "for knowledge of the deceits of the bad chief and help to guard myself against them, and for knowledge of the true life which the supreme and true Captain shows and grace to imitate Him" (139, Mullan).

Lucifer sends "innumerable demons" (141) throughout the whole world, making sure that no man is overlooked. He goads the demons to lay snares and traps for men by tempting them first to covet riches "that they may the more easily attain the empty honors of this world, and then come to overweening pride" (142). Ignatius summarizes: "The first step, then, will be riches, the second honor, and the third pride. From these three steps the evil one leads to all other vices" (142). That's Lucifer's strategy. It's important to notice that there is nothing morally evil about riches and honors in themselves. Rather, Satan uses the attraction to them to deceive people.

Christ also sends "His servants and friends" throughout the whole world, making sure that no man is overlooked. He recommends to them that they "seek to help all, first by attracting them to the highest spiritual poverty, and should it please the Divine Majesty, and should He deign to choose them for it, even to actual poverty. Secondly, they should lead them to a desire for insults and contempt, for from these springs humility" (146). Once again Ignatius summarizes: "Hence, there will be three steps: the first, poverty as opposed to riches; the second, insults or contempt as opposed to the honor of the world; the third, humility as opposed to pride. From these three steps, let them lead men to all other virtues" (146).

It's an astounding strategy, to use the poverty, insults and contempt received by those in the Lord's camp to attract people to it. The exercitant might well ask, What kind of marketing strategy is this? We'll zoom in on this strategy later, but for now let a simple answer suffice: It's a strategy for victory. After all, Jesus won by using this strategy. We certainly don't want to demean Jesus' life by implying in any way that He was a fool or a victim of circumstances, and that the poverty, insults and contempt that marked His life weren't a conscious decision. Ignatius is offering the exercitant an opportunity not just to admire and love the person of Jesus, but also to admire and love the way He chose to do things.

Thus, in the colloquy the exercitant asks to be received under the Lord's standard. He's very earnest. He prays three times, asking Mary, then Jesus and then the Father for this experience. The threefold colloquy emphasizes and stirs up the exercitant's earnest desire. He asks to be received under the Lord's standard "first in the highest spiritual poverty, and should the Divine Majesty be pleased thereby, and deign to choose and accept me, even in actual poverty; secondly in bearing insults and wrongs, thereby to imitate Him better, provided only I can suffer these without sin on the part of another, and without offense of the Divine Majesty" (147). Ignatius is offering the exercitant the chance to respond like the man moved by love at the call of Christ the King.

The exercitant doesn't have to turn Ignatius's words into a rote prayer. He can use it as a model for how he can pray to be received under the Lord's standard of poverty, insults and contempt. At the same time, he should be honest. For example, he might pray, "Father, I'm terrified at the thought of people ruining my reputation, but I want to be with your Son in his camp" or other such things. The colloquy calls to mind an experience Ignatius had at the roadside chapel of La Storta. Prior to this incident, he had been praying for some time, begging Mary "to place him with her Son." On this particular day Ignatius saw clearly that "God the Father was placing him with His Son." He saw "Christ with His Cross on His shoulder, and the Father nearby." The Father said to Christ, "I desire You to take this man as Your servant." Jesus said to Ignatius, "I will that you serve Us." After this vision, Ignatius never wavered from his determination to call his band of brothers the "Company of Jesus."[85] He wanted them all to be intimately united with Christ under His banner of the cross.

There is a wonderful passage in the Jesuit Constitutions which captures the spirit of this colloquy. It's rather lengthy, but very helpful. Ignatius says it's important to call to mind

> to how great a degree it helps and profits one in the spiritual life to abhor in its totality and not in part whatever the world loves and embraces, and to accept and desire with all possible energy whatever Christ our Lord has loved and embraced. Just as the men of the world who follow the world love and seek with such great diligence honors, fame, and esteem for a great name on earth, as the world teaches them, so those who are progressing in the spiritual life and truly following Christ our Lord love and intensely desire everything opposite. That is to say, they desire to clothe themselves with the same clothing and uniform of their Lord because of the love and reverence which He deserves, to such an extent that

where there would be no offense to His Divine Majesty and no imputation of sin to the neighbor, they would wish to suffer injuries, false accusations, and affronts, and to be held and esteemed as fools (but without their giving any occasion for this), because of their desire to resemble and imitate in some manner our Creator and Lord Jesus Christ, by putting on His clothing and uniform, since it was for our spiritual profit that He clothed Himself as He did.[86]

Many people get stuck at this point in the Exercises, when they are asked to pray for poverty, insults and contempt. Directors can be tempted to water down this colloquy because it is extremely countercultural. It is so different from what people believe. Yet it is crucial to the Exercises that one aspire to have the disposition exemplified in this colloquy. In fact, it is so central to the Spiritual Exercises that, if someone persists in refusing to make some version of this prayer, the director should consider ending the retreat as soon as feasible. At the very least, such an exercitant should not do any decision-making on the retreat. We'll touch more on these points later.

There are several caveats in the colloquy. The first is somewhat familiar by now. The exercitant prays to be received under the Lord's standard, in the highest spiritual poverty. Spiritual poverty is, as we've already mentioned, a detachment from all material goods, whether one possesses them or not. Then he prays to be received under the Lord's banner even in actual poverty, "should the Divine Majesty be pleased thereby, and deign to choose and accept me" (147). The exercitant should not choose poverty unilaterally. He has a Commander-in-Chief, after all. The person who thinks that proclaiming Christ's banner means he should be poor has misunderstood the Principle and Foundation. The director may need to remind him that his "one desire and choice" (23) should not be poverty; rather, it should be whatever is for the praise and greater glory of God and the eternal well-being of his soul.

The exercitant then prays to be received under the Lord's standard in bearing insults and wrongs, "provided only I can suffer these without sin on the part of another" (147). It's rather difficult to imagine receiving insults without also imagining another person doing the insulting. So the exercitant must be warned. Under no circumstances is he to pray, even unconsciously, that other people might sin so that he might benefit. Thus he prays to be received under the Lord's standard in bearing insults and wrongs, provided it is "without offense of the Divine Majesty" (147).

Ignatius knows that bearing insults and wrongs doesn't always further God's kingdom or glorify Him. For example, on one occasion he did seek to clear his good name and the name of his followers. "[W]e were grieved that our teaching itself was declared unsound, and also that the way in which we were walking was thought bad, because neither the one nor the other was our own but Christ's and His Church's."[87] Although Ignatius had been received under Christ's standard, he did not automatically accept all humiliations. He didn't want humiliations at the expense of God's glory.

The director needs to be intimately familiar with the grace being sought in this meditation, namely, understanding the strategies of the two leaders. He doesn't explain them in detail to the exercitant but, when needed, he should be able to elaborate briefly on them or some aspect of them. He may, for example, need to straighten out a misunderstanding or answer a question. He should, however, keep his comments to a minimum. He may also on occasion want to point to something in the exercise and say to the exercitant, "Look at that again; there's more there for you."

Now we'll look more closely at the strategies of the two leaders. Both our Lord and our Enemy have strategies that involve the way we relate to things (poverty/riches), other people (insults/honors), and God (humility/pride). We'll look first at Satan's strategy and then at the Lord's.

Satan's strategy begins with tempting people to covet riches. By "riches" Ignatius means primarily money and the things that wealth buys. This category could also include other things that lead to honor, such as intelligence, beauty, talents or athletic prowess. What's the strategy here? It's not that money is evil per se. There are lots of good reasons to pursue money: to take care of one's family, educate one's children, provide for one's old age, contribute to the Lord's work, etc. Satan isn't yet tempting someone to disobey God. He's laying a trap, though.

Money gives a person control and power. With money he can take care of himself and his family. He can secure his future. He can do what he wants. Money means security and protection. With money he can live in a good neighborhood near a good school. He can protect himself and his family from the vicissitudes of life. He has the means to cope with and even avoid natural disasters, medical emergencies, unscrupulous people, etc. Money gives him the illusion of self-sufficiency and independence. He can always build another barn. He does not need God for material provision. Gradually, ever so gradually, a person finds himself relying on money and not on his heavenly Father or his brothers and sisters. As the exercitant meditates on the Devil's standard, the issue comes to the fore: Is he going to save himself or trust in God?

Riches lead to honors. There is nothing mysterious about this. It's just the way the world works. If you have money (and therefore power), people court you. They want your money, your power, your protection, so they bribe you with praise and honor. It's their attempt to control you and to get what you have or at least a share in what you have. But, as Scripture says, "a flattering mouth works ruin" (Prov. 26:28). Rich people fall prey to those who praise them because they are flattered by the honors. They begin to like the esteem of others, the praise of others, the reverence of others. They wind up doing things to receive the empty honors of the world, to please people, instead of doing them to serve the Lord.

Just as the rich man's outer security comes from money, so too his inner security comes from honors. He uses them to establish his dignity without God. For example, he ostentatiously gives money to popular social causes so that people will admire him. He becomes defined by what other people think of him and he learns to rely on the good opinion of others for his sense of self. He often finds himself thinking, I can't do that, because people will think . . .

Honors, of course, put a person on a pedestal. One who is honored is singled out and raised up. Gradually, the rich, honored man begins to relate to others as their superior. He begins to believe that he is above others, that they exist to establish him in the universe more firmly. He relates to people as if they belong to him. He uses his superior position to control them. Of course, they are also controlling him by the honor they give to him. They are all caught in a web of control. Yet, the whole thing is ephemeral. Riches result in the *empty* honors of the world. Saying they're empty is really true: they're just like a beautiful gift, which turns out to be nothing more than an empty box once you've taken off the wrapping. That's part of what Ignatius was trying to get at when he put Satan on a throne of fire and smoke. It's a high place without substance.

How do coveting riches and attaining the empty honors of this world lead to pride? With riches comes a sense of control, power and security. The rich man easily thinks he doesn't need God for his material provision. He comes to rely on money, not on his heavenly Father. On account of his riches, he receives honors. He enjoys the esteem of others, the praises of others, the reverence of others. He takes the glory that belongs to God and develops a taste for it. He accepts a superior position to others, and then he begins to forget who he is, a creature. He doesn't recognize God as his Creator; he opts for a godless existence. In fact, he makes enough money and has enough respect to do what he pleases. He is a powerful person. He can run his own ship. He doesn't need God. Thus, he is gradually ensnared. He moves from wanting to possess things to being the center and to being almighty. Sooner or later, he ends up saying no to God. In the end, it's an issue of who's in charge.

Satan's strategy not only ensnares the individual, but it also captures assets that could have been used for building the kingdom of God. Those shackled by desires for riches, honor and power squander their wealth and waste their lives. What a loss for God's kingdom!

Everyone experiences temptations to covet riches, honor and the power that comes from them, in one form or another. Recently, we took a very informal survey of some random college coeds. We asked a handful of women, "What do you want?" Here are some typical answers:

- "Financial security."
  - "A successful career. People don't come to college unless they want to be successful. People come here because they know it will take them places in terms of a career."

- "I want to get to a point where I can be completely independent and unaffected by the rest of the world. I want to get to a point of total financial security so that I don't have to depend on other people for anything. I want to be able to live my life without having to be involved with the rest of the world."
- "I want total independence and freedom. I want to make a name for myself."

These folks seem to be rallying around the banner of riches, honor and pride. They are being seduced by the Enemy of their souls.

It's important to note that this progression from riches to honor to pride isn't just a mind game, although we've been describing what coveting riches and attaining empty honors does to a person psychologically. Pride is a psychological state, but it is very much tied to reality, to wealth and to position in society. It's also important to note that this progression from riches to honor to pride is not inevitable. People can have wealth and receive honor without falling into the trap of overweening pride and then saying no to God.

What about Christ's strategy? It's not as intuitively obvious as Lucifer's. Riches and honors are attractive, but those in Christ's camp don't win with money and they don't win with honor and fame. The disciple in the Lord's camp may be tempted to score a victory for the Lord using Satan's strategies. For example, when the Christian sees how money accomplishes things in the world, he can end up pursuing riches to score a victory for the Lord. "First I'll earn a lot of money, and then I'll use that money to further the kingdom," someone might say. Or a person can see how honors and fame can catch the world's attention and decide to pursue them in order to further the kingdom. Such people are drifting over to the banner of Satan by trying to use the techniques of Satan's camp to benefit the Lord's camp. Riches and honors do not, however, save. In Christ's camp, victories are won with poverty, insults and contempt, the way Jesus won.

Poverty, insults and contempt are not in and of themselves attractive. It's Jesus who is attractive, and the exercitant embraces poverty, insults and contempt on account of Him, because He chose them. Still the question remains, What's His strategy? How are these tools for victory? Clearly something new and different is going on. There's a battle going on between Christ and Lucifer. At first glance it looks like Jesus eschews all weapons, but that's not quite accurate. He has weapons: poverty, insults, contempt and humility. Most Christians think poverty, insults and contempt are things to be endured. They don't think they can win any victories with them, but Jesus uses them to win victory after victory over Satan. He has a very unprecedented and aggressive strategy.

How is poverty useful to Jesus? He wants to help people by attracting them to poverty. Why? Jesus is trying to help people by attracting them to utter reliance on God. People in His camp don't rely on money as a weapon against the vicissitudes of life. Their shield is faith, their sword is the word of God, their helmet is salvation, their breastplate righteousness, and their belt is truth (Eph. 6:14-17). There is an apparent powerlessness that comes with poverty, but history has shown that trusting in chariots and horses is not the way to victory for the people of God. Being poor provides God the opportunity to shine into the world as Father.

Jesus is inviting everyone to a way of life that in its most fundamental form depends on God for everything. He is inviting people to be poor as He Himself was poor. He is not inviting people to a grinding, dirty, stinking, degrading poverty. Everything about His camp is beautiful and attractive. In fact, there are some types of poverty He's trying to save people from. Nor is Jesus inviting people to have a macho, "I don't need anything" attitude, or a stoic, "Having things doesn't matter anyway" attitude. When Jesus talks about the birds of the air and the lilies of the field in the Sermon on the Mount, He is talking about His experience of poverty. "Look at the birds of the air: they neither sow nor reap nor gather into barns, and yet your heavenly Father feeds them. . . . Consider the lilies of the field, how they grow; they neither toil nor spin; yet I tell you, even Solomon in all his glory was not arrayed like one of these" (Mt. 6:26, 28-29). His experience is one of God providing for Him materially. Jesus is, in fact, inviting people to seek first His kingdom and rely totally on their heavenly Father as He did. He's inviting some people to actual poverty, and everyone to spiritual poverty, which is a consciousness that God is providing for them materially and an attitude of dependence on God as Father.

How are insults and contempt a strategy for victory? First, a word about translations and definitions. Several manuscript versions of the *Spiritual Exercises* exist. Both Puhl and Mullan are translating what is traditionally called the autograph version, which is believed to be a copy of an original text in Spanish.[88] Puhl's translation is "insults and contempt." (146). Mullan's is "contumely and contempt." Other versions exist, one of which is a text in classical Latin, commissioned by Ignatius. This text sometimes uses the word "humiliations." Very often in the literature, when referring to Christ's standard, authors will speak of poverty, humiliations and humility, perhaps in part because of the parallelism it affords—three words for Christ's standard and three for Satan's.

The word "humiliations" is, however, open to misunderstanding. Dictionaries tell us that "humiliate" means "reduce to a lower position in one's own eyes or others' eyes" and that "humiliating" means "extremely destructive to one's self-respect or dignity." There are all sorts of translation issues lurking in the background here, but this second rallying cry of the Lord doesn't have to do with self-esteem or with how the Christian thinks of himself. The Lord isn't trying to help people by offering them the chance to think less of themselves. The humiliations of the Lord's camp aren't psychological. They aren't about how one feels when one gets a traffic ticket or makes a mistake. They have to do with a lower position in others' eyes, not in one's own. The insults and contempt of the Lord's camp refer to things such as spit on the face, the loss of one's reputation among friends, the ignominy of being treated as a criminal, etc.

It's not too hard to see how insults and contempt follow upon poverty. Without the security and protection that wealth affords, the poor man will be insulted and experience contempt. Even the man who has riches, but relates to things as belonging to God, opens himself up to insults and contempt. Given the condition of the world and the activity of Satan, he will be insulted. "If you were of the world, the world would love its own; but because you are not of the world, but I chose you out of the world, therefore the world hates you" (Jn. 15:19).

Where is the advantage in this? The Christian who embraces insults and contempt doesn't rely on the opinions of others as a compass. Their praise, their lack of praise, their criticism or their contempt doesn't guide his actions. He's not controlled by other people and what they think of him. He's guided by his Father's opinions and preferences. Furthermore, he's radically free to do good. Normally, when a person does some good, he expects to be honored for it. The person who embraces insults and contempt does good and doesn't ask for honor in return. In fact, he gives to anyone who asks, demanding nothing in return. He becomes an overflowing fountain of beneficence, like his heavenly Father, and streams of living water flow from him, just as they do from his Commander-in-Chief. Everything that he does and everything that he gives is free. He doesn't demand a payback from others. He gets his payback from his Father, in secret. His reward is in God.

It turns out that experiencing poverty (actual and spiritual), insults and contempt creates an environment in which faith can flourish and grow. Who provides for the poor man? God. Who glorifies the humiliated man? God. The person who embraces poverty, insults and contempt will find himself in circumstances where he needs faith to create a way forward. Jesus didn't have money of His own. He was insulted and held in contempt and He relied utterly on His Father. His faith conquered every strategy Lucifer had. It is faith, not riches or honors, that saves the world. Faith is power in the new creation.

Having little, be it money or social status, is the doorway to astounding creativity. Look, for instance, at what Jesus accomplished with nothing at the wedding feast at Cana. Or look at Peter: "I have no silver and gold, but I give you what I have; in the name of Jesus Christ of Nazareth, walk" (Acts 3:6). The Lord's disciples accomplish marvelous things without any wherewithal. It's almost like creating from nothing. Take Mother Teresa, for instance, or the Coptic monk Father Matta. Father Matta was rebuilding a monastery in the Egyptian desert with no material resources to his name, but often, when the monks went outside, they found a deposit of construction materials at their gates. Even in our own small way, we ordinary Christians frequently experience this.

What about humility? How do insults and contempt lead to humility? Does a person begin to believe the insults? Is that what Ignatius has in mind? Not at all. He's not referring to undue self-deprecation. Although sometimes in the Christian tradition the word "humility" describes the state of a person who thinks lowly and unassuming thoughts about himself, it doesn't always refer to how one thinks about oneself. Ignatius is, in fact, tapping into a different sense of the term, one used by Benedict and Bernard of Clairvaux.[89] For Ignatius humility means being submitted to God.[90] This is also the sense of the word in the famous passages from Philippians about Jesus' humility:

> Have this mind among yourselves, which is yours in Christ Jesus, who, though he was in the form of God, did not count equality with God a thing to be grasped, but emptied himself, taking the form of a servant, being born in the likeness of men. And being found in human form *he humbled himself and became obedient unto death, even death on a cross. Therefore God has highly exalted him* . . . (Phil. 2:5-9, emphasis added).

Humility is, for Ignatius, practically synonymous with obedience.

Humility is the rallying cry of the Lord's camp. The way to victory in this world is obedience to God—having the humility to take one's place as subject to one's King and Creator. "Thy will be done on earth as it is in heaven" is key to the Lord's strategy. Again, it's an issue of who has the power. Jesus wants His Father to rule. He wants to bring the whole world under the rule of God.

There's even more, though. Insults, contempt and poverty open the way to humility because they create an environment for faith. The person who has absolute faith and utter confidence in his Commander-in-Chief can put aside his own preferences, will and judgment and choose his Lord's way. The humility of the Lord's camp is loving submission. When it's working right, however, it hardly looks like submission. It looks like love. "Thy will be done." Why? Because I love you.

The meditation on the Two Standards introduces the exercitant to the strategies of Lucifer and Christ. Lucifer's strategy for victory is to offer men a thriving life without God, a life of wealth, honor and self-determination, in the hope that they will eventually say no to God. None of these things, however, is a source of power in the new creation. They can't save a single person. Jesus has a whole new way of doing things. The Lord is conquering the world, but He's not using wealth and social status to do so. He gained His victory by relying on His Father for material provision, by enduring insults and contempt, by trusting in His Father to vindicate Him, and by being utterly obedient to His Father. His strategy is to invite others to join Him, to share His life and become one with Him. All He has to offer is Himself, His Father, the Holy Spirit and all those in union with them.

The exercitant doesn't, of course, see all this immediately. He has just done a few meditations on the infancy and childhood of Jesus, and then he is introduced to the Lord's standard of poverty, insults and contempt, and humility. He will spend many more hours meditating on the life of Jesus, and during this time the Lord will be revealing Himself. As the exercitant works and as the Lord works, the exercitant will come to know and love the Lord more intimately. The director needs to present the meditations remembering Ignatius's admonition:

> The one who explains to another the method and order of meditating or contemplating should narrate accurately the facts of the contemplation or meditation. Let him adhere to the points, and add only a short or summary development. The reason for this is that when one in meditating takes the solid foundation of facts, and goes over it and reflects on it for himself, he may find something that makes the events a little clearer or better understood. . . . Now this produces greater spiritual relish and fruit than if one in giving the Exercises had explained and developed the meaning at great length. For it is not much knowledge that fills and satisfies the soul, but the intimate understanding and relish of the truth (2).

The director needs to be familiar with the Two Standards exercise, which is the purpose of this exposition, but as we said earlier he shouldn't be explaining the exercise to the exercitant. He should be letting the exercitant experience the exercise for himself. The exercitant will have lots of opportunities as he meditates on the events of the Gospels to see for himself how Jesus won with poverty, insults and contempt, and obedience. To this end, throughout the rest of the Second Week he can use the threefold colloquy of this meditation after each of his Gospel meditations.

THREE CLASSES OF MEN

After an exercitant makes the Two Standards meditation twice and repeats it twice, he ends the day by making a new meditation entitled Three Classes of Men. As we've already noted, these meditations typically take place on the fourth day of the Second Week. The week begins with the exercitant begging for the grace "not to be deaf to His call, but prompt and diligent to accomplish His most holy will" (91) and contemplating the prayer of someone who wants to join Christ the King "in bearing all wrongs and all abuse and all poverty, both actual and spiritual, should Thy most holy majesty deign to choose and admit me to such a state and way of life." (98). The week continues with meditations on the life of Jesus, with the exercitant begging for the grace "to follow Him more closely" (104). Then, after considering the strategies of Lucifer and Jesus, the exercitant has the opportunity to pray to be received under the Lord's standard "first in the highest spiritual poverty, and should the Divine Majesty be pleased thereby, and deign to choose and accept me, even in actual poverty; secondly in bearing insults and wrongs " (147).

Ignatius wants the exercitant to be able to consider a life of actual poverty as a real possibility. He wants a person to be able to answer God's call to poverty promptly and diligently, should that call come. Of course, he wants the exercitant to be free to answer any call from God, whatever it might entail, but at this point in the Exercises he is especially intent on preparing a person to hear and respond to a call from God that has to do with how he uses or does not use money.

Ignatius knows that praying to be received under the Lord's standard in all poverty (actual and spiritual) can easily become a mere velleity—a wish or inclination not strong enough to lead to action. He knows that the desire to be poor with Christ is easily squelched by the attraction of the world's riches. This meditation on Three Classes of Men is designed to help the exercitant deal with his inordinate attachment to riches, so that he can be truly free to "choose what is more for the glory of His Divine Majesty and the salvation of my soul" (152). As we've already seen, inordinate attachments make a person deaf to the Lord's call.

When Ignatius introduces this meditation, he notes that it is "in order to embrace what is best" (149, Mullan). What does he mean by "best"? For Ignatius, the best is, objectively speaking, doing what Jesus did, the way he did it—in all poverty, actual and spiritual, bearing all insults and wrongs, and totally submitted to his Father, in all humility. There is no denying the fact that, in one sense, being actually poor is better than possessing riches. Does that mean that a person should choose actual poverty? No. It would be a mistake for a person to assume that what is "better" is "better for me." Ignatius wants a person to hear and respond to a call from God. The "best" is doing what God wants a particular person to do. Whatever way of life God calls a person to is best for him, even if it is not, objectively speaking, the best. An inordinate attachment to riches prevents a person from embracing the best, in both senses of the term.

Before looking more closely at the meditation, the title needs some explanation. The most literal translation of the Spanish is "three pairs of men" (149, Mullan). Why did Ignatius refer to three pairs of men and not simply three men? And why does the Latin version of the *Spiritual Exercises* translate this title as "Three Classes of Men"? Actually, there are quite a few linguistic issues in the background here, but the most likely explanation is as follows:

> Here we should take into account Ignatius's environmental background at the University of Paris. In the fifteenth and sixteenth centuries the moralists, in solving their cases of conscience, used fictitious typical persons and called them a "pair".... Titius and Bertha in a marriage case, or Titius and Caius in one about justice.... The Spanish *binario* ... might mean one typical person (e.g., Titius) or a pair of them (e.g., Titius and Bertha). In either case Ignatius was writing here about persons each of whom is typical of a class or category.[91]

So the Latin versions read "three classes of men." The only thing the director really needs to know is that Ignatius is offering three men to consider, each of whom is typical of a class or category of people.

To begin with (first prelude), the exercitant is to consider three men. "[Each] one of them has acquired ten thousand ducats, not solely or as they ought for God's love, and all want to save themselves and find peace in God our Lord, ridding themselves of the weight and hindrance to it which they have in the attachment for the thing acquired" (150, Mullan). The language here is awkward and difficult to translate. The director must put it into his own words.

What's the scenario that Ignatius is trying to paint? Ignatius estimated that a student could live on 50 ducats a year in Paris, which means that 10,000 ducats was a fortune. So the exercitant is being asked to consider three men, each of whom has come into a fortune. The money is theirs legitimately. They haven't done anything wrong. It's not as if they've stolen the money or been running an illegal business. Nevertheless, they've come into the fortune without any thought of God or His will. They can't say, for instance, that they know it's for God's greater glory that they possess this money. All three men are burdened by the money because they know they are attached to it. They are aware that on account of this attachment they could stop living for God and the salvation of their souls and start living for the money and organizing their lives around the money and the things that it can buy. They sense that they are in danger, spiritually speaking.

In the second prelude Ignatius has the exercitant imagine himself "standing in the presence of God our Lord and of all His saints, that I may know and desire what is more pleasing to His Divine Goodness" (151). It is not enough to know what is more for the glory of God; a person must also desire it. Then he begs for the grace "to choose what is more for the glory of his Divine Majesty and the salvation of my soul" (152). The exercitant is not making a choice in this meditation, but he is preparing himself, by God's grace, to make a good choice.

For the bulk of the meditation the exercitant considers three men, one by one. The first man knows he is attached to the money but does nothing about it. Many people are like this. They decide what to do about the money by not deciding. They want to rid themselves of the attachment "but the hour of death comes, and they have not made use of any means" (153). They know the attachment isn't good for them, but they won't take the necessary steps to free themselves from it. They are caught between conflicting desires—to keep the money or to be free of the attachment—and are seemingly paralyzed. Time passes, and eventually they reach the hour of their death, but they've done nothing more than wish things were different. Most exercitants find it helpful, as they are considering this man, to imagine what kind of excuses such a man might make to justify his inaction.

We would hope that, as the exercitant considers this man, he is repelled by him. He should become aware of the fact that good desires and good intentions aren't worth much if one is unwilling to take the necessary steps to put them into practice. He'll probably be thinking things like this: People like that are not accomplishing the purpose for which God created them. They're hardly in control of their lives at all. They certainly aren't being driven by their desire to praise, reverence and serve God our Lord! These people end up frittering their lives away, endlessly conflicted. What a waste. I don't want to be like that!

If he sees himself like this first man, the exercitant will be motivated to do something about it. It is to be hoped that he will notice that this first man doesn't make use of "any means" available to him to overcome his inordinate attachment, and he will then resolve to make use of the means available to him. In the context of the Exercises this would mean applying himself to the Exercises and making them well. When the director meets with the exercitant after this exercise, he should be prepared to reiterate some or all of the Additional Directions (73-90), as needed (see Chapter Three).

The second man the exercitant considers wants to rid himself of the attachment to the money, but such people "wish to do so in such a way that they retain what they have acquired, so that God is to come to what they desire" (154). Such a person doesn't ask how he can please God; rather, he wants God to approve of him and everything he desires. Instead of joining God, he wants God to join him. Instead of dealing with his inordinate attachment, he wants God to bless his inordinate attachment.

People like this second man perceive themselves as people of faith. They tell themselves and others that they "want to do God's will," but they have other desires which are in fact stronger than their desire "to praise, reverence, and serve God" (23). This type of person wants first of all to keep the money, so he tries to compromise with God. He might think, I'll keep the money and use it to serve you, Lord. Other examples of this way of thinking are: I'll serve you in whatever way you want when I'm married. I'll be a musician and then I'll serve you, Lord and so on. Such people try to use God to baptize and sanctify their own desires. They simply want God to bless what they desire.

Such a person cannot lay aside the issue of money and go to God unencumbered. He does not consider a life of actual poverty a real possibility for himself. There is no determination to embrace poverty, if God should deign to choose him. He certainly isn't saying, "I'll do it, if you call." Actually, he won't do it.

The exercitant will get a lot out of meditating on this second man, who doesn't possess the freedom and love that will enable him to desire and choose what is more for the glory of God. The exercitant will almost certainly recoil from the image of God coming around to such a man's desires. To use one of Ignatius's metaphors, that's not how a noble knight serves his lord and friend. What a loss for the King's mission when men get ensnared by an attachment to riches! The exercitant will probably resolve to make every attempt "to go to God" and he will certainly beg more earnestly for the grace of "an intimate knowledge of our Lord, who has become man for me, that I may love Him more and follow Him more closely" (104). He will want to do everything he can to have a single-hearted love for his Lord.

The third person the exercitant considers is also attached to the money, presumably just as attached as the previous two people. This man, however, not only wants to rid himself of the attachment to the money but he is also willing to take the necessary steps to make sure this happens. It's important to note that giving the money away is not the necessary step Ignatius has in mind. Men of this third type "want to rid themselves of the attachment, but they wish to do so in such a way that they desire neither to retain nor to relinquish the sum acquired. They seek only to will and not will as God our Lord inspires them, and as seems better for the service and praise of the Divine Majesty" (155). Men of this third type want to get to a place where they are truly free and where all things are possible: either keeping the money or giving it away.

This third class of men strive to be indifferent in the Ignatian sense. Once again, it's important to remember that the indifferent person is actually full of desire. In fact, the Spanish word that means "want" or "desire," *querer*, occurs seven times in Ignatius's description of this class of men. What do they desire? Do they desire to keep the money? No. Do they desire to get rid of the money? No. Their only desire is "to be better able to serve God our Lord" (155). In other words, they are not moved by the thought of keeping the money and they are not moved by the thought of relinquishing the money. They are moved by the thought of serving God. Having the money or not having the money doesn't inspire their choice. Serving God inspires them. God inspires them. They are not moved by God the way a chess piece is moved by a chess master. They are moved by God the way one is moved by someone one loves. He calls forth a response in them. They are indifferent both to having the money and not having the money, because they are so focused on the praise, honor and service of God our Lord.

If this third type of person perceives that his attachments are in danger of crowding out this one all-important love, he takes action immediately and aggressively. In fact, those in this third class of men make every effort to conduct themselves as if they are not attached, "forcing themselves not to want that or any other thing unless the service of God our Lord move them: so that the desire of being better able to serve God our Lord moves them to take the thing or leave it" (155, Mullan).

Some exercitants will thrill at the description of this third kind of person and cry, "Me, too"; some will respond soberly, knowing that they have some work in front of them; some will quake at the thought of letting go of their conflicting love. Almost all will be well disposed to what comes next in the colloquy.

It's worth noting that implicit in this meditation are several strategies for overcoming an inordinate attachment to riches: 1) use all means available to overcome the inordinate attachment; 2) make every effort to go to God; and 3) if you are inordinately attached to riches, make every effort to behave as if the attachment were broken. But at this moment in the meditation, as the exercitant enters into the colloquy, Ignatius has yet another strategy ready at hand, the strategy of *agere contra*. In the colloquy Ignatius has the exercitant pray the threefold colloquy of the Two Standards, noting that:

> [W]hen we feel a tendency or repugnance against actual poverty, when we are not indifferent to poverty or riches, it is very helpful, in order to crush such disordered tendency [inordinate attachment], to ask in the Colloquies (although it be against the flesh) that the Lord should choose one to actual poverty, and that one wants, asks and begs it, if only it be for the service and praise of His Divine Goodness (157, Mullan).

The word "crush" is notable here. The director should encourage the exercitant to aggressively pursue overcoming any disordered love of money, by wanting, asking for and begging for its contrary, namely, actual poverty.

Of course, all the advice implicit in the meditation, along with the recommended use of the *agere contra* strategy in the colloquy, holds true for any inordinate attachment, but the director should be careful not to gloss over the issue of money too quickly. The note about crushing a tendency or repugnance against actual poverty, which follows the meditation on Three Classes of Men, is not an afterthought. At the beginning of the Second Week the exercitant is introduced to a prayer in which someone moved by love asks to serve the Lord in actual poverty, if the Divine Majesty deigns to choose him. The exercitant prays the threefold colloquy of the Two Standards four times in one day, asking, in effect, twelve times to be received under the Lord's standard "in the highest spiritual poverty, and should the Divine Majesty be pleased thereby, and deign to choose and accept me, even in actual poverty" (147). Then after meditating on the three classes of men, the exercitant again prays this threefold colloquy, this time begging for a call to actual poverty. In the note which follows the meditation on Three Classes of Men, Ignatius explains the reason for these disturbing prayers. It is a very deliberate strategy of *agere contra*. He knows the desire for riches is a snare for exercitants. He is offering a way for the exercitant to break free into a place where his "one desire and choice" is that which will serve and glorify his King.

CHAPTER 9

THE GRACES OF THE SECOND, THIRD AND FOURTH WEEKS

We've spent a lot of time commenting on and explaining three Ignatian exercises: the Kingdom of Christ, the Two Standards and the Three Classes of Men. They are important exercises which are easily misunderstood, so they merit a lot of ink, so to speak. To people who have gone through the Exercises, they seem to encapsulate the entire experience, but they are not the entire experience. The entire experience is a 30-day experience, and these three meditations take up a total of two days. They color the subsequent days and are integral to the Spiritual Exercises, but one must not forget that spending approximately three weeks meditating on events from the life of Jesus is more integral to the Exercises.

In this chapter we are going to look at the Ignatian meditations on the life of Jesus. We are also going to spend quite a bit of time on what is happening or can happen affectively in the exercitant as he makes these meditations. By now it should be increasingly clear that the Exercises are all about matters of the heart. We've already looked at what a person experiences on account of an encounter with God or with the Enemy, and we've seen that Ignatius calls these experiences "consolations" and "desolations." When the exercitant is moved interiorly, it's very important to discern what is going on in that particular instance at that particular moment in time. Does what the person has just experienced come from God or from the Enemy? We'll return to the subject of consolations and desolations in the next chapter, but the topic here is different. We want to prescind from the particular and describe what usually happens in the exercitant as he meditates on the life of Jesus.

Meditating on the life of Jesus and speaking to Him "as one friend speaks to another" creates a setting in which love can grow. It is, however, difficult to talk in general terms about the three weeks spent meditating on the life of Jesus because love is as unique as the persons loving. No two retreats are alike, because no two people are alike. The retreat is very personal. It is an interaction between two persons—the exercitant and his Lord—at a particular moment in history.

As the exercitant goes through the retreat and meditates on the life of Jesus, he notices certain things, focuses on certain things, as the Holy Spirit reveals them in him. God is revealing Himself, and what He reveals is personal. His self-revelations are, so to speak, governed by the person before Him. They are not one-size-fits-all inspirations. One person is deeply moved by Jesus' care for His mother as He was dying on the cross. Another is profoundly moved by the magi and their generous gifts. Another sees the 12-year-old Jesus returning to Nazareth in a whole new light. Although the revelations are a free initiative on God's part, one could say they are drawn out of Him by the unique person He is relating to. He relates to one person one way and to another a different way. He is responding to the exercitant, to his unique personal being with his unique personal history. He is also responding at a particular moment in time which is different from every other moment because every person's situation is constantly changing.

The exercitant is in turn responding to the Lord as only he can. He is responding with the words he speaks in the colloquies. He's responding with gestures: the reverence he shows, the penances he undertakes and the decisions he makes, for example. His responses are located in time. They vary from day to day and even from moment to moment, and they arise out of his personal history. He's not following a law or a formula. There are no laws or formulas in a loving interaction between two people. Each responds to the other as the other reveals himself or herself. No two relationships look alike, as an experienced director will testify.

One could say that love is the ultimate spontaneous activity. It is highly unpredictable. In 1980, we ran across an excellent analogy by the physicist John Wheeler. He told a very illuminating story about a game of Twenty Questions. At a dinner party, Wheeler was sent out of the room so that his host and the 15 other guests could consult in secret and agree on a difficult word ... or so he thought. Wheeler was kept out of the room for a very long time. When he was readmitted to the room, there was a smile on everyone's face. Wheeler knew that something was afoot, but he played along. He began trying to discover the word.

"Is it an animal?"

"No."

"Is it a mineral?"

"Yes."

"Is it green?"

"No."

"Is it white?"

"Yes."

At first the answers came quickly, but gradually the participants took longer and longer to answer each question. It was strange. All Wheeler wanted was a simple yes or no, yet the person queried would spend a lot of time thinking before answering. Finally he thought he had it figured out and guessed "cloud." He was right, and everyone burst out laughing. They explained to him that they hadn't actually chosen any word. They had agreed not to agree on a given word. Each person, when asked, could answer as he pleased, with the one requirement that he or she should have a word in mind that was compatible with every other previous response.

This game provides a nice analogy for how God interacts with the exercitant, and how that interaction is marked on both sides by freedom. In the interaction, something is created. In the case of the game, it was the word "cloud." Alone, neither the questioner nor the people being questioned had the power to bring that word into being. The word that they eventually arrived at depended on the questions asked, the order of the questions and the replies. What happens in the Exercises is like that game. It is not capricious, but it is unpredictable because one never knows what will be the result of the interaction between the Lord and the exercitant. It depends on what each says, what each reveals, how they respond to each other and the order in which these things happen. Together they bring something new into being.

Although the director simply does not know what will happen with any particular exercitant, it is possible to make some general statements about what typically happens as someone meditates on the life of Jesus. Broadly speaking, the exercitant begins with an implemental love of the Lord, and during the course of the Exercises he takes steps toward a fully personal love of his Lord. During the Second Week the exercitant asks "for an intimate knowledge of our Lord, who has become man for me, that I may love Him more and follow Him more closely" (104). Typically during the Second Week, as he meditates on Jesus' life, the exercitant is growing in knowledge and love of his Lord and making decisions to follow Him more closely. As the exercitant's love of his Lord matures, he identifies with Him more and more. This means that when he meditates on the passion he experiences "sorrow, tears, and anguish with Christ in anguish" (48) and when he meditates on the resurrection he experiences "joy with Christ in joy" (48). There's much to unpack here. As we'll discover, not all knowledge is the kind of knowledge Ignatius is talking about, and not all sorrow is the kind of sorrow Ignatius is talking about.

Most exercitants come to the Exercises with very little personal knowledge of the Lord. Sometimes they come knowing about Him but haven't really experienced Him. The knowledge they have comes via the testimony of others. This is a good starting point if the exercitant is relying on credible witnesses, but it's also likely that the exercitant has some misinformation. In either case, his knowledge isn't personal knowledge. Imagine someone meeting the friend of a friend and saying, "I know you. I've heard all about you." The new acquaintance might rightly think, You might think you know me, but you don't know ME. You've never met me. Knowing about someone is not the same as knowing someone.

Sometimes exercitants come to the Exercises knowing and loving the Lord to some degree. Their love for the Lord is what we've been calling semipersonal love. They've encountered Him. They love His good qualities: His courage, His mercy, etc. Nevertheless, they love Him from a distance, as a spectator would. Their love is on the way to fully personal love, but it's not there yet.

Sometimes exercitants come to the Exercises with a real love for the Lord, but their love is less truthful than it could be because the exercitant is mistaken about who the Lord is. Occasionally an exercitant is seriously mistaken about the Lord. He doesn't actually know Him at all. Think, for example, of a person infatuated with another person. He doesn't really know her. His love is wildly inaccurate, based on psychological projections and flights of imagination. It's still love, but it's a false love. More often, an exercitant is mildly mistaken about the Lord. Think of a mother, for example, who loves her 18-year-old son as if he were still 14. Her love isn't false, but it's not totally truthful either. In a sense, the person she is loving no longer exists. In similar ways, some exercitants approach the Exercises with a love for the Lord which is false to some degree. To the degree that their love is not truthful, they are not loving the Lord. They are not loving the person; they are loving an idea that they have in their heads.

Another exercitant might come to the Exercises with a very implemental view of the Lord. He thinks, for example, that He exists to make his life go well, to bless him, to serve him, to make him happy, to teach him, to set boundaries for him, to make sure he doesn't make any bad decisions, etc. He's simply a tool—a candy machine or an answering machine or a key to a great future, perhaps. It has never even dawned on him that there is a person there to be known and loved.

So, many exercitants come to the Exercises with very little personal knowledge of Jesus, their Lord. They might have an idea of Him or know about Him, but they don't know Him. Effectively meditating on the life of Jesus remedies this situation. The exercitants grow in their knowledge of the Lord, which in turn fuels their love for Him. Before looking more closely at this process, however, we should pause and look at the meditations themselves.

The meditations on the life of Jesus are located in one section near the end of the *Spiritual Exercises* (261-312), just before the Rules for Discernment of Spirits. Ignatius calls them "Mysteries of the Life of our Lord." By "mystery" he means an episode or event in the life of Jesus. Each episode has a title, followed by one, two, three or four scriptural references, although a couple of the episodes have no scriptural reference (299 and 310). Normally the event is summarized in three points, which follow the title and scriptural references. Some episodes have only two points and a few have only one point. The exercitant organizes his meditation around these points.

There is a total of 51 mysteries. Why does Ignatius use these events from the life of Jesus and not others? When Ignatius was recuperating from the cannonball wound in his leg, he read a very popular devotional work called *Vita Christi* (The Life of Christ), by a 14th-century Carthusian monk named Ludolph of Saxony. This book, which emphasizes the words and deeds of Jesus, is a sort of compilation of the Gospels and Gospel commentaries by the Church Fathers. It was pivotal in Ignatius's conversion, and there is evidence that he studied it closely. It looks like Ignatius was following Ludolph of Saxony's list of Gospel episodes. Almost all of Ignatius's mysteries can be found in Ludolph, and in the same sequence.

Ignatius lists more mysteries than can be used during the three weeks of meditations. For example, after the Incarnation (Annunciation) and Nativity meditations, Ignatius suggests meditating on 14 more mysteries during the Second Week: the Presentation in the Temple, the Flight into Egypt, the Obedience of the Child Jesus to His Parents, the Finding of the Child Jesus in the Temple, the Baptism of Christ, the Temptation of Christ, the Vocation of the Apostles, the Sermon on the Mount, Christ Walks upon the Waters, Jesus Preaches in the Temple, the Raising of Lazarus and Palm Sunday. However, the director has a lot of flexibility. He may shorten the week by leaving out some mysteries or he may lengthen the week by adding some mysteries from Ignatius's list of 27 mysteries for Week Two. The director can tailor the retreat more to the individual needs of the exercitant. For example, when we're giving the Exercises to a woman, we often include an episode in the Second Week in which a woman has a prominent role, usually either the Conversion of Mary Magdalene or the Supper at Bethany. During the Third Week, when the exercitant is meditating on the passion, Ignatius recommends not leaving out any of the mysteries. Instead, if the director wants to lengthen the time spent on the passion, he should divide one mystery into two. If he wishes to shorten the time, he should combine mysteries.

The titles of the passion episodes are somewhat surprising. One might expect Ignatius to choose certain events from the passion and use those events to title the meditations.

For example, one might expect a meditation on Peter's Denial or Jesus Carries His Cross or Jesus Before Pilate. Instead, the meditations are entitled, From the Last Supper to the Agony Inclusive (290), From the Garden to the House of Annas Inclusive (291) and From the House of Annas to the House of Caiaphas Inclusive (292), etc. Ignatius seems to have taken all four Gospel narratives and organized them geographically.

For Ignatius, Jesus is on the road to Calvary. One wonders whether Ignatius's own pilgrimage to Jerusalem greatly influenced his reading of the passion narratives. We do know that Ignatius retraced the steps of Jesus through Jerusalem on his own pilgrimage. In any case, the image of a road comes up rather frequently, not only in the passion meditations but in all the meditations. For example, when he meditates on the Nativity, Ignatius directs the exercitant to see "in imagination the way from Nazareth to Bethlehem. Consider its length, its breadth; whether level or through valleys and over hills" (112), and when he meditates on the Last Supper he is to "consider the way from Bethany to Jerusalem, whether narrow or broad, whether level, etc." (192). It's not too surprising that Ignatius refers to himself as "the pilgrim" in his autobiography.

From the examples Ignatius provides, the exercitant learns how to take the three brief points and turn them into an hour-long meditation. At the beginning of weeks two, three and four Ignatius provides one or two sample meditations to serve as guides for the week's meditations. Thereafter, the exercitant takes the three points and constructs his own meditation around them, using the form Ignatius provides. He always begins with the preparatory prayer, which calls to mind the Principle and Foundation. He makes three preludes, two of which are like the preludes of the First Week. He makes "a mental representation of the place" (47) and asks "God our Lord for what I want and desire" (48). First, however, he makes a prelude which Ignatius calls "the narrative of the thing which I have to contemplate" (102, Mullan). This prelude is found only in the Second, Third and Fourth Weeks.

This first prelude consists of briefly calling to mind the sequence of events in the mystery the exercitant is considering. For example, if someone is considering the baptism of Jesus, he might fix in his mind the details of the narrative.

He would briefly call to mind the sequence of events: how John baptized Jesus, but only after protesting that he wasn't worthy, how the Holy Spirit descended on Jesus, and how the Father said, "This is my beloved Son in whom I am well pleased." The exercitant might also recall the larger narrative. Jesus has been in Nazareth for 30 years and presumably left home to travel to the Jordan River. His public ministry is about to begin. Some exercitants may need to prepare for their meditation by reading the relevant Scripture passage ahead of time. Occasionally, as an aid to his memory, an exercitant may need to reread the Scripture passage at this point in the meditation.

It is important to keep in mind what the early Jesuits noted about the first prelude:

> What is intended in this first prelude is an overall and global view of the mystery in order to know the matter which will subsequently be reflected upon, so that the soul can begin to engage with it and be raised toward it. Later in the meditation itself, it will begin spending time on its individual parts, weighing and penetrating them. It is like when a person casts his eyes upon a painting which contains a great variety of objects: he firsts gets a hazy impression of the whole in a single glance, and then afterward focuses on the individual details of the painting, inspecting them more fully and accurately one by one.[92]

As we've noted before, making a meditation is different from a Scripture study or from a slow meditative reading of Scripture. If Scripture is used, it should be used as a memory aid.

There are several different ways he can organize his meditation. He can take the event from the life of Jesus as a whole and consider the people, what they say and what they do. This is the way the sample meditation on the Nativity is organized. He can also take the first point listed by Ignatius and consider the people, what they say and what they do, and then take the second point and consider the people, what they say and what they do, and so on. Several of the early directories recommend this way of organizing a meditation.[93] In this section of the meditation the exercitant isn't looking at the picture as a whole; rather, he's examining particular details, one by one, using his mind and his heart.

However he decides to organize his meditation, the exercitant should pause about three times along the way and "draw fruit" or "profit." When he speaks of drawing fruit or profit from a meditation, Ignatius means seeking the grace of the meditation and letting oneself be moved by the meditation. A heart inflamed can be the profit Ignatius has in mind. Drawing fruit can also include making resolutions for change. The exercitant does not, however, have to come up with a different resolution each time he pauses to draw profit from his meditation. He could, for instance, make the same resolution over and over. The exercitant could also make a resolution for the day or for the week. Finally, the exercitant closes the whole meditation with a colloquy and the Lord's Prayer.

The exercitant gradually becomes comfortable with the form and he settles into a routine. As we've seen, a typical day includes five meditations. The exercitant meditates on one episode in the life of Jesus, then another. As in the First Week, the third exercise of the day is a repetition of the first and second meditations. The exercitant makes the standard preparatory prayer and three preludes, and then goes back over his previous two meditations, paying special attention to the places where he experienced understanding, consolation or desolation. It makes intuitive sense to go back to the places where a light went on for the exercitant or where his heart was moved. The strategy here is for him to get as much from the grace as he can.

Why does one go back to moments of desolation? It certainly is not to experience more desolation. One goes back to win a victory. Ignatius is assuming that there is something there—some grace—for the exercitant to win.

The fourth exercise is another repetition. In the fifth exercise, the exercitant changes gears and applies his senses to the day's two episodes, seeing the people and the details of their surroundings, hearing what people say or the noise of the crowds, etc.

Although on a typical day the exercitant considers two episodes from the life of Jesus and makes a total of five meditations, there is some variation in the routine. When the exercitant is considering a decision, Ignatius recommends that he meditate on one mystery a day instead of two. He still makes five meditations a day, but he makes the meditation twice, repeats it twice and ends the day with the application of the senses. During the last week of the Exercises, when the exercitant is meditating on the resurrection mysteries, Ignatius recommends a less rigorous schedule. He still recommends covering two mysteries a day, but he suggests that the exercitant make four instead of five meditations a day. He recommends skipping one of the repetitions. Of course, as always, the director is free to change this routine, depending on the needs of the exercitant and his circumstances. For example, if the exercitant is tired or doesn't have the mental stamina needed to do five meditations a day, the director can have him do four, or even three. The *Spiritual Exercises* is a guidebook, not a law book.

Why does Ignatius have the exercitant spend all this time meditating on the life of Jesus? What is he trying to achieve? The exercitant embarks upon his contemplation of the life of Jesus after having considered the call of Christ the King. "It is my will to conquer the whole world and all my enemies . . ." (95). The exercitant is also looking at how a person inflamed with love responds to this call. Then he begins his contemplation of Jesus' life with an amazing meditation on the Incarnation. The event is the Annunciation, but Ignatius has the exercitant consider the wider context. He has the exercitant imagine the Trinity looking out upon the whole world, seeing everyone "going down to Hell" (102), and deciding together to do something about it. They decide that the "Second Person should become man to save the human race" (102). During the First Week, the exercitant is meditating on the consequences of sin. He is intimately aware that mankind has chosen a horrible destiny for itself. The world after Adam and Eve is barbaric, chaotic and despicable, and yet God acts to save us from that. In this meditation the exercitant comes face to face with God as Savior. What is Ignatius doing? He is always the fisher of men. He hopes to land some fish who will follow Jesus and join Him in His saving mission.

Ignatius's strategy for attracting people is simple. He has them meditate on the life of Jesus so that they can grow in the knowledge of the Lord. Knowledge isn't love, but it is the gateway to love. One can know a person without loving him, but one can't love a person without knowing him. Ignatius isn't aiming to give the exercitant a theological knowledge of Jesus or a historical knowledge of Jesus. He's not talking about the kind of knowledge one gets from reading biographies. He's talking about an intimate or interior knowledge of Jesus. He's talking about personal knowledge.

To understand the dynamics of the Second Week, the director should think about how one person comes to know another person. You can read about a person, but that's not really knowing the person. You have to experience the person, but how do you do that? It doesn't work to sit down opposite someone and try to perceive the full splendor of that person. You can only really experience someone's personal self through that person's words and deeds. A person says things, does things, walks a certain way, talks a certain way, laughs a certain way, relates to other people a certain way, makes choices, etc. Gradually, as you spend time with a person, you get to know that person. The person is more than what he says and does, and is more than the way he walks and the choices he makes, but the person is revealed in all his words, gestures, actions and choices, although never completely revealed. The person's actions, gestures and words reveal him gradually. For someone who has eyes to see and ears to hear, the experience of another person's words and deeds can eventually blossom into a personal encounter.

So Ignatius, filled with a holy wisdom, sends the exercitant to Jesus' words and deeds. Via the meditations, the exercitant examines, imagines and considers what Jesus says and does. He begins to know Jesus more personally, and sometimes his meditations blossom into a personal or semipersonal encounter. Jesus' actions or gestures reveal Him or shed light on Him as a person. Suddenly the exercitant catches a glimpse of the person. As he contemplates Jesus' words and deeds, his love for Him grows. It's not as if the exercitant meditates on the life of Jesus and gets to know Him and only after that begins to love Him. Rather, as he meditates on the life of Jesus, the exercitant comes to know Him a bit more personally and then loves Him more. That love enables him to know Him even more, which in turn stirs up more love. He's growing in interior knowledge and love concomitantly, not successively.

Meditating on the life of Jesus creates a setting in which love can grow. However, the director should be aware that growing in knowledge of the Lord doesn't always lead to increased love on the exercitant's part. He can sometimes end up observing Jesus from a distance, as an uninvolved spectator would. He gains insights from his meditations. Insights are fun and very satisfying. For example, he's meditating on the crucifixion, considering what the people around Jesus are saying. "You who would destroy the Temple and build it in three days, save yourself! If you are the Son of God, come down from the cross" (Mt. 27:40). He notices the phrase "if you are the Son of God" and remembers that this is how Satan began his temptations in the desert. He savors the insight, but he never moves from the insight to an affective response. His heart doesn't move him to say, Lord, I see how an old temptation returned at your weakest moment, and you still resisted. Yet another thing you endured! In other words, the exercitant is not moved by the Lord being tempted at His weakest moment, but he's delighted to know that it happened.

Because "it is not the abundance of knowledge which fills and satisfies the soul, but to feel and taste the matters interiorly,"[94] Ignatius has built into the Exercises several tools to help the exercitant move from knowledge to love. We've already touched on several of them. The meditations on the Two Standards and the Three Classes of Men along with the strategy of *agere contra* help the exercitant deal with the inordinate attachments that get in the way of his loving the Lord more. A person who has conflicting loves can't give his heart away. Also during the Second Week, the exercitant is beginning each of his meditations asking for the grace of "an intimate knowledge of our Lord, who has become man for me, that I may love Him more and follow Him more closely" (104). Included in this petition is a reminder of the Incarnation, which is a revelation of God as Savior. This, in turn, is a reminder of the whole First Week of the Exercises and how the exercitant has been saved from the consequences of his sin.

Another tool that helps the exercitant move from knowledge to love is the daily schedule. The repetitions of meditations and the application of the senses help create an opportunity for the heart to be stirred. The first time someone meditates on a mystery, his intellect is very active. He's turning the event over in his mind, looking at it from every angle. Perhaps he is meditating on Jesus calming the storm. The first point is, "While Christ our Lord was asleep in the boat on the sea, a great storm arose" (279). He might ask himself, What was Jesus doing that He was so tired?, and then recall that Jesus has just told an aspiring disciple, "Foxes have holes, and birds of the air have nests; but the Son of man has nowhere to lay his head" (Mt. 8:20). He remembers that Jesus didn't have a home. He might wonder whether a storm was brewing when they set out, or did it arise suddenly after setting sail? He might imagine the disciples struggling to keep control of the boat. He might marvel at how soundly He was sleeping, and so on. He brings to mind many things about each of the points.

Later in the day he returns to places in his meditation where he experienced understanding, consolation and desolation. He remembers Jesus asleep in the boat with "no place to lay His head." His heart was stirred there. He returns to that point. His intellect is not quite so active this time. It can rest a bit. It's already explored the event. Since his intellect isn't quite as active, there is room, so to speak, for his heart to respond. "He was probably so exhausted when He said that. Look how tired He was, laboring all the time. He gave up the comforts of home. He probably couldn't even stretch out in that boat." There is another repetition later in the day, and here the exercitant simply gazes at his exhausted Lord asleep on a rough seat in a boat with a heart full of compassion. Then he draws fruit or profit from what he sees and feels. He resolves not to be so mindful of getting enough sleep for himself when opportunities for charity arise, and in the colloquy he says, "Lord, I want to work that hard for you. I've never worked to the point of utter exhaustion for you," and so on with each of the points of the meditation.

Finally, at the end of the day, there is yet another opportunity for his heart to be moved. He applies his senses to the passage. He sees the dirty cushion on which His head rests and smells the fishy smell of the boat. He touches the rough-hewn surface on which He lies. He even hears the deep steady breathing of Jesus. Ignatius recommends that he smell "the infinite fragrance, and taste the infinite sweetness of the divinity, of the soul, of its virtues" (39, Mullan). He means that the exercitant is to savor the presence and the reality of the person he is meditating on—whether it is the Lord or some other Gospel character—with heartfelt love. After applying his senses to this scene, the exercitant might pray in his colloquy, "Lord, I want to be with you all the time, no matter how poor you are. If I were there as you got into the boat, I could have at least washed the seat before you lay down, and covered the stinking cushion with my cloak." By the end of the day, the exercitant isn't thinking about discovering and exploring the scene, he's experiencing it and responding to it with his heart.

Ignatius is, of course, relying on God to reveal Himself. He speaks of the Creator dealing directly with the creature and "the creature directly with his Creator and Lord" (15). The picture we've painted of an exercitant meditating isn't quite accurate, then. It's too one-sided. Perhaps an analogy will help here. When someone meditates on events in the life of Jesus, it's as if he's poring over a well-labeled photo album with his Friend at his side. He turns the pages slowly, even reverently, pausing at each picture. He leans over a picture to study it, and then his Friend says something. His Friend reveals something about the picture and about Himself. The contemplation of the photos turns into a personal encounter.

Not only is the Lord revealing Himself to the exercitant, but the exercitant is revealing himself to the Lord in the colloquies. Mutual intimate self-revelation fuels the growing love of the exercitant and his Lord. Relatively speaking, Ignatius has quite a lot to say about these colloquies. The exercitant enters into conversation with his Lord (71), pouring out his thoughts to Him (61). He tells the Lord what he is experiencing and asks according to what he feels in himself "in order more to follow and imitate our Lord so lately incarnate" (37, Mullan). This means, for example, that if the exercitant is feeling great compassion, he reveals that to the Lord and asks to serve his Lord in His suffering. If he has been restless throughout his meditation, he tells the Lord about that and tells Him that he will wait for Him forever if that would serve Him. He talks to the Lord about whatever is going on with him, especially how he's experiencing His life, and he's always straining forward, toward the grace of the meditation.

Even in the threefold colloquies that follow the exercise on the Two Standards, the exercitant speaks to the Lord about what he is experiencing as he contemplates the Lord's poverty and humiliations. He doesn't just formally ask to be received under the Lord's standard, using Ignatius's words and Ignatius's words alone. He might, for example, say, "Lord, I don't know if I could lay my head on an old filthy cushion." Then, using the *agere contra* strategy, he might pray to be received under the Lord's standard with no place to lay his head but an old filthy cushion.

Ignatius's longest instruction about the colloquies begins, "In the colloquy, one should talk over motives and present petitions according to circumstances" (199). He doesn't mean according to the content of the meditations. He means according to what the exercitant is experiencing in himself as he makes the meditations. Ignatius continues, "Thus he may be tempted or he may enjoy consolation, may desire to have this virtue or another, may want to dispose himself in this way or that, may seek to grieve or rejoice according to the matter he is contemplating" (199). All these things are matters of the heart, and the exercitant is talking to the Lord about them. He may even speak to Him about decisions he has to make if the meditation somehow brings them to mind. He is also asking the Lord for what he desires—to be received under His standard, for the courage to do what is right in a particular situation, and so on.

The colloquy is intimate and familiar, but the exercitant still shows respect for his Lord. As we've noted before, Ignatius counsels the exercitant, "As in all the following Spiritual Exercises, we use acts of the intellect in reasoning, and acts of the will in movements of the feelings: let us remark that, in the acts of the will, when we are speaking vocally or mentally with God our Lord, or with His Saints, greater reverence is required on our part than when we are using the intellect in understanding" (3, Mullan). The exercitant approaches the colloquy with some thought about what he is going to say. What can he say that will give his Lord an accurate picture of what is going on with him? At the close of the colloquy, he ends with a formal prayer.

The effects of all these colloquies add up. The exercitant speaks to his Lord about what he is experiencing five times a day for 30 days. Almost in spite of himself, by means of all these small self-revelations, he ends up welcoming and accepting Him into his life and his world. He lets his Lord become a part of his world. When he reveals what is going on with himself, he is able at the same time to give himself to his Lord. He ends up sharing his life with Him.

Ignatius was a brilliant student of human nature and personal relationships. The Exercises are crafted to stir up love, but what actually happens is up to the Lord and the exercitant. Typically, though, the exercitant grows in his knowledge and love of his Lord as he meditates on His actions, gestures, glances and touches. The Lord is revealing Himself, and the exercitant is revealing himself in the colloquies. These self-revelations also stir up love and lead to shared life. As the exercitant's love grows, he moves from an affection for the person of Jesus, to an affection for everything about Him: His preferences, His choices, His way of doing things, and His way of being in the world.[95] That's what happens when you love someone. The exercitant begins to love poverty and insults and contempt, not in themselves but because his Lord chose them.

As the exercitant grows in his love for Jesus and for Jesus' choices and priorities and ways of doing things, he typically experiences a desire to follow and imitate Him (109). He wants to join Him. He wants Him to succeed; he wants His mission to succeed, he wants to serve Him, but he wants more than that. He wants to share life with Him. When you love someone, you desire to be with that person, to share life with that person. For example, Ruth says to Naomi, "Entreat me not to leave you or return from following you; for where you go I will go, and where you lodge I will lodge; your people shall be my people, and your God my God; where you die I will die, and there I will be buried" (Ruth 1:16-17). Ruth doesn't just wish Naomi well or ask for her blessing, she wants to be with her and be like her.

Likewise, the exercitant experiences a desire to join Jesus and to do what He is doing. He doesn't just want to be with Him; he wants to adopt His ways. He wants to do things the way He does them. He wants to relate to the world the way Jesus does, so he prays for poverty. He wants to relate to people the way Jesus does, so he prays for insults and contempt. He wants to relate to his heavenly Father the way Jesus does, so he prays for opportunities to rely totally on

Him. He doesn't just grit his teeth and pray for poverty, insults and contempt. His heart is moved. He's growing in his love and is willing to take a risk. All love involves risk. He wants to share His life, and these are the ways Jesus has chosen to relate to material things, to other people and to His Father, so the exercitant says "Me, too!" He says yes to the life of Christ.

When the exercitant moves into the Third Week of the Exercises, he continues to meditate on the life of Jesus, but the form of the meditation changes slightly as he begins to consider the passion and death of Jesus. The meditations of the Third Week begin with the usual preparatory prayer and preludes. Now, however, the exercitant prays first for the grace to experience "sorrow, compassion, and shame because the Lord is going to His suffering for my sins" (193) and then in subsequent meditations for "sorrow with Christ in sorrow, anguish with Christ in anguish, tears and deep grief because of the great affliction Christ endures for me" (203). His petition changes according to the subject matter of the meditation, but he always begs God for an affective response to his meditations. In this case, as we'll see, he is asking for the grace to respond to Christ's passion as a friend would.

The meditations of the Third Week differ from those of the Second Week in that they have an additional three points for the exercitant to consider. As in the Second Week, the exercitant takes a mystery and considers the persons present, what they say and what they do. After that Ignatius has the exercitant "consider what Christ our Lord suffers" (195).

The exercitant is also "to begin with great effort to strive to grieve, be sad, and weep" (195). Mullan's more literal translation reads, "to commence with much vehemence and to force myself to grieve, be sad and weep." What's going on here? The exercitant asks for the grace of sorrow, but then he should do everything he can to get the grace. The dynamic here is a lot like what happens when a person prays for the gift of tongues. You don't pray for the gift of tongues and then wait tight-lipped for a miracle to happen—to speak in tongues in a way that is without your consent and outside of your control. No, you ask for the gift of tongues, and it's really a gift, but you need to open your mouth and start praying. Here, the exercitant doesn't pray for sorrow and then wait for a miracle. Rather, he prays for the grace and does what he can to grieve, be sad and weep.

It is possible for a person to do things and think things that will make him happy or sad. Sitting in a darkened room makes for sadness. Taking a walk on the first warm day of spring is a real pick-me-up. Listening to some music makes him sad; listening to other music makes him happy. Thinking sad thoughts makes him sad, and thinking happy thoughts helps create happiness. We're not recommending that the exercitant stop and listen to some sad music. The point here is that a person really can do some things to stir up sorrow and grief. Often there's a tendency to gloss over what really happened to Jesus and think things like, Jesus did that for me so that I can be happy with Him forever. In other words, there can be a tendency to drift into considering some joyful aspect of the episode in a meditation. It's difficult to grieve, be sad and weep. The exercitant may have to force himself to do so. Ignatius calls this "laboring." It's hard work and a big effort, so Ignatius instructs the exercitant to do it with all his strength and effort—with "much vehemence."

As he is grieving, the exercitant moves on "to consider how the divinity hides itself; for example, it could destroy its enemies and does not do so, but leaves the most sacred humanity to suffer so cruelly" (196). We often tell the exercitant to consider how the Lord chooses not to manifest His great power. For example, He could destroy His enemies but He doesn't. As a consequence, He suffers terribly. He's voluntarily undergoing this suffering. This is His choice.

Still grieving, the exercitant then moves on "to consider that Christ suffers all this for my sins, and what I ought to do and suffer for Him" (197). This last point echoes the colloquy of the first meditation of the First Week. There, after considering three sins, the exercitant imagines Christ present before him on the cross and asks, "What have I done for Christ? What am I doing for Christ? What ought I to do for Christ?" (53). We noted that the feel of that moment wasn't one of self-condemnation. Rather, it was more like standing beside the bed of a friend who has just been mortally injured while saving your life. The same is true here. The focus is on Christ, not the exercitant and his sins. In fact, the exercitant should be careful not to shift the focus from his Lord to himself. He's already considered his sin in the First Week. The Third Week is not a repeat of the First Week.

Here he's considering not his sin but what his Lord is enduring and why He's chosen to endure it. Jesus endures it for him. It's His choice. Jesus experiences and will experience the consequences of sin: pain and death. He wants to share the exercitant's life. In fact, He is sharing the exercitant's life—every aspect of it. Jesus is saying, "Where you die I will die, and there I will be buried." He loves the exercitant so much that He even wants to share his suffering. He wants to share his suffering not just to support him in some way and not just to lessen his suffering. He wants to be in union with the exercitant as completely as possible, sharing his life in every way. He wants them to have one life. And so the exercitant weeps. It's no wonder that exercitants are moved to do penance and take on some suffering. They don't want to be resting and enjoying life's pleasures while their friend is laboring and suffering.

Each meditation of the Third Week draws to a conclusion with the exercitant asking himself, What ought I to do and suffer for Him? (197). Ignatius doesn't want the exercitant merely to experience gratitude for all the Lord has done for him. He wants to help the exercitant bring that gratitude to completion through a mutual exchange of gifts. Jesus has done and suffered all this for him, so what can he do and suffer for Him? The sorrow the exercitant feels is like an engine which propels him to action. Of course, as always, the meditations of the Third Week close with a colloquy. The exercitant can choose between a free-form colloquy or he can use the threefold colloquy of the Second Week.

The exercitant experiences sorrow during the Third Week, but it doesn't arise from empathizing with Jesus. Empathy is a natural human reaction to another person's situation. If I'm empathizing with someone, I'm looking at his life as a spectator and then placing myself in his shoes and thinking, If I were in that situation, I'd be feeling. . . . Mothers often need to teach their children to empathize with others. It's a step in their development and it helps them become aware of others as persons. If an exercitant has trouble seeing Jesus as a man, he may find it helpful to empathize with Him. It may help him more fully realize His humanity. Some immature exercitants may never get past empathizing with Jesus, but empathy isn't what the Third Week is about.

The exercitant isn't asking for a grace of empathy. In fact, one can empathize with a stranger. It requires intuitive and imaginative power, but it doesn't require love. Webster's says that to empathize involves "an imaginative projection of one's own consciousness into another being." This is strange behavior for one who loves the Lord. It's as if the Lord himself need not be in the picture. The sorrow the exercitant is asking for is, on the other hand, the natural outcome of knowing, loving and following Jesus. For those who know each other, have revealed themselves to each other and love each other, there's so much more than empathy that happens when the beloved suffers and dies.

It happens all the time in human relationships that one person expresses sorrow for the sufferings of others. Sometimes one pities or commiserates with a person. Sometimes one can have a powerful feeling for another person who is undergoing severe suffering or misfortune and one is moved to do something to help him. That's called "compassion." The exercitant, however, isn't asking for the grace of pity, commiseration or compassion. The grace the exercitant asks for isn't even sympathy. He's not asking to feel the same thing Jesus was feeling. In fact, a person could experience all these sorrows even for a stranger. The sorrow the exercitant is asking for is a sorrow that arises out of his personal love and union with the Lord. He's not asking to respond to the Lord's suffering as a human being; he's asking to respond as a friend.[96] "Grief" is probably the best word to describe the grace of the Third Week because it has such profound interpersonal connotations.

What does it mean to respond to the Lord's suffering, ignominy and death as a friend would? The exercitant has been growing in knowledge and love of the Lord and has been experiencing a desire to follow and imitate Him. He wants to join Him and wants to be with Him and be like Him and do what He is doing. He wants to make Jesus' life his life and Jesus' ways his ways. He begins to experience Jesus' life as his own, just because it's His and he loves Him. Jesus' thoughts, affections and choices, His deeds, successes and failures, His joys and His sorrows become a part of the exercitant's life. They are integral to his life. In the Third Week, the exercitant experiences Jesus' sorrow, anguish and pain becoming part of his own life. He experiences as his own all the sorrows of his Lord. That's how friends are. For example, Naomi's shame as a childless widow was Ruth's. Naomi's poverty was Ruth's.

The exercitant identifies with Jesus. Jesus' life is his life; Jesus' ways are his ways; His sorrows and humiliations are to him as his own. The exercitant has joined Him. Jesus' fate is his fate. But there's more. Jesus is enduring all this for him. It's His choice. The exercitant is aware of his human condition. He knows that on account of sin his fate is pain and death. Now here is his Lord who has chosen to join him, and his fate becomes Jesus' fate: pain and death.

So when his Friend and his Lord suffers, the exercitant can experience and, by God's grace, does experience sorrow and anguish. He doesn't pray, Lord, let me love less, so I don't feel this anguish. No, a friend—not merely an acquaintance—prays for sorrow with Christ in sorrow, anguish with Christ in anguish. He prays, Let me be your friend and faithful servant, especially now. The exercitant wants to be in union with his Friend and Lord as much as possible, sharing his Lord's life in every way. The exercitant wants to have one life with Him, just as his Lord wants to have one life with him. So the sorrow he experiences isn't the sorrow of an empathetic therapist or a sympathetic supporter. Nor is it sorrow for sorrow's sake. It is a sorrow and a suffering which are really his but "in and through which" Christ makes him a sharer in His own sorrow and suffering.[97] It's not just his sorrow, and it's not just Jesus' sorrow; it's theirs together on account of their love.

The dynamic of the Fourth Week is similar to that of the Third Week. In the Fourth Week the exercitant is meditating on encounters that various Gospel characters have with the risen Lord. Ignatius calls them "apparitions." That sounds rather ghostlike to our ears, but that's not the connotation Ignatius intended. After all, the exercitant is meditating on the risen Christ, who does have a body, albeit a glorified body. The exercitant asks for the grace "to be glad and rejoice intensely because of the great joy and the glory of Christ our Lord" (221). Earlier in the *Spiritual Exercises* Ignatius is referring to this point and says, "in a contemplation on the Resurrection I will ask for joy with Christ in joy" (48). The exercitant isn't asking for an experience of "I'm so happy for you." Like the Third Week, he's responding to the Lord as a friend would. Jesus' victory is his victory. Jesus' joys are his joys, just because they are His.

As they make the meditations of the Fourth Week, exercitants frequently begin by identifying with the various Gospel characters who encounter the risen Lord. They can easily imagine Mary's fear, Peter's confusion, Thomas's unbelief and so on. Inadvertently, they end up praying for and pursuing an experience of Mary's or Peter's or Thomas's joy. They have, however, asked for the grace to share the Lord's joy and glory. Directors often have to gently redirect an exercitant's meditation and refocus him on the Lord.

Sometimes, as exercitants meditate on the risen Lord, they become puzzled. How do they share the life of the risen Lord? How do they relate to material things, to other people and to the Father the way He does? The best thing a director can do here is to encourage the exercitant to have faith. As St. Paul says, "It is no longer I who live, but Christ who lives in me, and the life I live now I live by the faith of the Son of God" (Gal. 2:20).[98] The director, of course, needs to believe that it is possible to share the life of the risen Lord. In this regard it's helpful for him to study Acts of the Apostles. Luke is pointing to the early Christians and saying, in effect, They are the risen Lord. Closed doors are no obstacles for them (Acts 5:23) and they show up on the road to explain the Scriptures (Acts 8:26ff), for example. The director, of course, doesn't explain all this to the exercitant, but he must at least be aware of and have faith in the possibilities for sharing in the Lord's resurrected life now. Even if he says very little about what he knows, the director will do a better job directing the exercitant if he has meditated often and humbly on these mysteries.

The meditations of the Fourth Week follow the same basic form as those of the Second Week, with a couple of adjustments. The exercitant begins with the usual preparatory prayer and the usual preludes. The first prelude, which is the history, makes subtle theological distinctions about the status of the body and soul of Jesus during the time between His death and His resurrection. We recommend simply instructing the exercitant in a way that echoes the Creed. So, for example, the director might say, "The first prelude is the history. Here it is good to consider how, after Jesus suffered, died and was buried, he descended into hell. There he sets free the just, then on the third day he rises from the dead and appears to His mother."

After considering the people, what they say and what they do, the exercitant has two more things to consider which are unique to the Fourth Week. He considers "how the Divinity, which seemed to hide Itself in the Passion, now appears and shows Itself so marvelously in the most holy Resurrection" (223, Mullan). So the exercitant considers Jesus, who hid His divine sonship during the passion yet now manifests Himself so gloriously. After that the exercitant is to "consider the office of consoling which Christ our Lord bears, and to compare how friends are accustomed to console friends" (224, Mullan).

The exercises of the Fourth Week prepare the exercitant for life after the retreat is over. As he meditates on the risen Christ, he is becoming acquainted with the kind of life he will subsequently lead in the world. It's a totally new kind of life. He has consciously died with Christ, and now he is entering the risen life of Christ. You could say that the Exercises are a method for entering into the resurrected life of Christ and perhaps even an experience of living the resurrected life.

While each exercitant is different, one can, in a general way, say that the three weeks he spends meditating on the life of Christ are usually marked by the exercitant coming to know, love, follow and even befriend Him. The exercitant is also usually experiencing consolations and desolations. One of the things the director does during this time is to instruct the exercitant about Ignatius's second set of rules for discernment. Discerning the work of God and the work of the Enemy becomes more complicated. We'll discuss this in the next chapter.

Before moving on, there are a few more things to note about the mysteries as they are laid out by Ignatius (261-312). These are relatively minor details, but the director needs to be aware of them so that the exercitant can make the meditations well. If he knows this section of the text well, the director will be able to prevent the exercitant from stumbling unnecessarily.

One might not notice this right away, but the list of mysteries emphasizes Gospel events rather than the theological content of the events. For example, Ignatius points out that, when Mary visited Elizabeth, "Our Lady chants the Magnificat, saying, 'My soul doth magnify the Lord'" (263). Ignatius subtly draws the exercitant's attention to the fact that Mary chants the Magnificat. The exercitant could come away with a picture of Mary singing in exultation, with the words a blur. Or, to take another example, if the exercitant meditates on the Supper at Bethany (286), the first point is to consider that "Our Lord eats in the house of Simon the leper together with Lazarus" (286). From a textual standpoint, this isn't the central point of the story, but the exercitant savors the picture of Jesus eating with the friend He has just raised from the dead in the house of a social outcast. To take another example, when Ignatius has the exercitant consider Jesus casting the sellers from the Temple, he concentrates on Jesus' actions in the Temple and His words to the sellers and not His subsequent exchange with the Jews, where He alludes to His body being the new Temple.

Some of the mysteries might raise questions for an exercitant. For example, there are two mysteries that don't have a scriptural basis. The first is a meditation on how the Lord appeared to the Virgin Mary. There is also another meditation on how He appeared to Joseph of Arimathea. In addition, there are some details that modern readers might dispute. For instance, Ignatius identifies both the penitent woman of Luke 7 and the woman who anointed Jesus with expensive nard as Mary Magdalene. He also conflates Matthew's account of this anointing (Mt. 26:6-13) with John's (Jn. 12:1-8, see paragraph 286). Sometimes, too, a point might seem to contain a minor inaccuracy. For example, when Ignatius recounts the raising of Lazarus, it looks like Jesus said, "I am the resurrection and the life . . ." to both Martha and Mary (285), while John's account makes it look like Jesus said this to Martha alone.

Ignatius's chronology and compilation of the passion can be questioned by modern scriptural scholars or even by attentive readers of the Gospel texts. For example, there are three passages (Matthew 26, Luke 22, Mark 14) referenced for the mystery entitled "From the Garden to the House of Annas Inclusive" (291) but none of them mentions Annas at all. In fact, one of the points of this mystery has to do with Jesus being struck in the face because of His supposed disrespectful answer to the high priest, but none of the Scripture passages referenced contain this detail. John's Gospel is the only Gospel that mentions Jesus being taken to the house of Annas and being struck in the face, but that text is not referenced with this mystery. When the exercitant considers the mystery entitled "From the House of Annas to the House of Caiaphas Inclusive" (292), he contemplates Peter denying the Lord twice. He already considered Peter's first denial, because Ignatius locates it at the house of Annas. If, in preparing to make a meditation, the exercitant picks up Matthew, Mark or Luke's Gospel and reads it closely, he'll notice, however, that Peter denies Jesus three times in the courtyard of the house of Caiaphas.

There are other details included in the mysteries which aren't found in Scripture. Joseph goes from Nazareth to Bethlehem to profess his subjection to Caesar (264). There's a maid with Joseph and Mary at the Nativity (114). Jesus bids farewell to His mother before traveling to the Jordan River to be baptized by John (273). Peter and Andrew seem to have been called by Jesus three times.[99] Jesus casts out those who are selling in the Temple but he speaks kindly to the vendors of doves (277). Jesus washes the feet of Judas. After sweating blood in the Garden of Gethsemane, Jesus' garments were saturated with blood. Jesus was bound all night. The exercitant might hear any one of these details and respond, "I never thought of that, but that's plausible." Many, in fact, assume these details are the fruit of Ignatius's meditations on the episodes in question. In fact, though, many come from Ludolph of Saxony's life of Christ. Maybe they were the fruit of his meditation.

How does the director handle these nonscriptural details? Some might be stumbling blocks to an exercitant. The key is for the director to understand that the meditations of the Second, Third and Fourth Weeks are not meditations on Scripture. They are meditations on events in the life of Jesus. The exercitant isn't meditating on the text. He's meditating on events, using the text to remember the event. The text is a tool; it's not the topic. The goal is personal knowledge, not textual knowledge. There is a wisdom in Ignatius's way of proceeding. When we reflect on our lives in the presence of others, the reflection is usually event-driven. We remember key events and center our recollections around those events. The events are primary, not their chronology.

So, given modern historical sensibilities, the director needs some strategies as he presents the mysteries. If we were giving a 30-day retreat, we would probably skip the meditation on the resurrection appearance to Joseph of Arimathea, but we might include the meditation on Jesus' resurrection appearance to His mother. It has a certain plausibility and usually it's enough to introduce it by saying, "We don't have a scriptural account of this resurrection appearance, but there is an ancient Christian tradition which attests to it." Most exercitants accept this. If we thought this particular meditation would be too much of a stumbling block for someone, we wouldn't use it. Some of the nonscriptural details which might easily be assumed to be the fruit of someone's meditation we would leave as is.

What about the discrepancies between the points in a particular mystery and the referenced Scripture passages? Clearly the director needs to have a strategy for dealing with them. First, he has to know where they are so he doesn't look ignorant and unwittingly undermine the exercitant's confidence in him or in the Exercises. We recommend that the director work with Ignatius's version of the mysteries as a starting point. He needs to take each mystery and read each of the referenced Scripture passages. He should compare the scriptural narratives with the points of the mystery and note any conflations, discrepancies and details that come from unmentioned Scripture passages.[100] After doing his homework, the director should figure out a way to present the mystery that will help the exercitant not to stumble over unexpected or surprising details. The director should not explain to the exercitant how to get around these problems; rather, the director himself should get around the problems for the exercitant, so that the exercitant is free to encounter the Lord in the meditation. For example, he might say to an exercitant meditating on the supper at Bethany, "Imagine Jesus at the house of Simon the leper. There is an episode in John's Gospel very similar to this one. He says Lazarus was there. After all, it was in Bethany, Lazarus's hometown. So think of Lazarus being there too." The director can then instruct the exercitant to use Matthew's text to prepare for his meditation. In the case of Jesus going from the garden to the house of Annas, the points rely primarily on John 18, but there are three details from other Gospels: Judas betraying Jesus with a kiss, Jesus saying, "Have you come out as against a robber, with swords and clubs to capture me?" (Mt. 26:55), and Jesus healing the servant of the high priest. If he has done his homework, the director can give the points as is and then say something like, "Most of this is in John 18:1-8, but with a few added details from other Gospels. To prepare for this meditation, you could read John 18:1-8, but don't waste your prayer time flipping through the Gospels looking for the missing details. They are in the other Gospels."

The director should make sure that exercitants take to heart Ignatius's advice to organize their meditations ahead of time. They should read the relevant Scripture passages ahead of time. After all, the important thing in the meditations is to be present to the Lord in new ways and to speak to Him.

CHAPTER 10

DISCERNMENT OF SPIRITS, SECOND WEEK

During the course of the Spiritual Exercises the exercitant encounters God. Many, if not most, exercitants hope for encounters with God that are marked by warm affective feelings of love. In other words, many exercitants hope for consolations. However, it is important to remember that consolations are not the only kind of encounter with God that happens on the retreat. Some people encounter God and grow in their knowledge of Him. They might not experience a lot of warm affective feelings on the retreat, but their love for Him grows more and more truthful. Some encounter God and experience the will to overcome an inordinate attachment. Some encounter God as they examine their conscience. Some people experience very few consolations, but on account of their "judgment and reason will offer their entire selves" (96) to the work of Christ the King. Each exercitant is different and each retreat is different.

The Official Directory of 1599 offers some sagacious advice about how the exercitant can pray well, even when he isn't experiencing much devotion or consolation:

> He [the director] should also remind the exercitant that the best way to obtain devotion from God is to humble himself under his mighty hand, subjecting and resigning himself to his divine will. Often the despondency and bitterness he feels come not so much from fervor as from an unspoken pride by which he places reliance on his own efforts, or from ambition to excel, or from a self-love that is avid for consolation. Hence it is important to remember that when a person has done his best he should leave everything else to

the will and charity of God, trusting that the very aridity from which he suffers is permitted by God for his best. This affection of humility and subjection of oneself to God is often the surest way to win the grace of praying well.[101]

The exercitant can pray well, even without feelings of affection for his Lord. Throughout the ages, Christ's disciples have often testified that nothing is more pleasing to Him than the humility described above.

Typically, though, as the exercitant meditates on the life of Jesus, he experiences quite a few consolations. It is, after all, "characteristic of God and His Angels, when they act upon the soul, to give true happiness and spiritual joy" (329). After the exercitant learns, using Ignatius's first set of rules for discernment, to successfully recognize and fight the Enemy's desolations, he might think that he has vanquished his opponent. The Enemy is, however, still active. When he sees that his desolations won't sideline someone or cause him to turn back, the Enemy tries a different, more subtle strategy.

It turns out that sometimes the Enemy can be the cause of an exercitant's consolation. One might think that every movement toward more faith, more hope and more love in one's soul is a consolation from God, but that's not always the case. For the person who is headed toward God, a spiritual desolation is always from the Enemy. Spiritual consolations, on the other hand, can be either from God or from the Enemy. The Enemy is the father of lies. He has no scruples about giving the exercitant consolations when it suits his purposes. When the Enemy can't turn the exercitant back or sidetrack him by means of a desolation, he will seek to imitate the Lord's way of speaking and acting, in order to get a person to listen to him and to follow him.

Since both God and Satan are willing to give consolations, discernment gets more complicated. Let's assume that the exercitant experiences a genuine spiritual event. As a consequence, he feels full of love, faith, hope and zeal. The exercitant ought not to assume that he has just encountered God. Ordinarily, he needs to use discernment. He must learn to ask, Did I just encounter the Lord or the Enemy? Ignatius's second set of rules for discernment (328-336) help the director teach the exercitant how to answer this question. They provide good counsel for recognizing consolations from the Enemy.

Before looking at how to tell whether a consolation is from God or from the Enemy, it's necessary to say a few more things about the consolations that are actually encounters with God. Usually, at the end of the First Week, the exercitant is acutely aware of all the Lord has done for him. He knows the Lord as his Savior and King. During the Second, Third and Fourth Weeks, the exercitant spends a lot of time looking at his Lord's words and deeds. He becomes aware of and then focuses on all the Lord's wonderful qualities: his compassion, wisdom and faithfulness, for example. As he comes to know the Lord more, he loves Him more. Typically, then, during the course of the Exercises, a person experiences a lot of semipersonal love for the Lord. These experiences are consolations to the exercitant. The exercitant is encountering God, and it's real love that he experiences, but it's not yet the fullness of personal love.

Sometimes, however, an encounter between the Lord and the exercitant becomes personal. The exercitant catches a glimpse not of the Lord's wonderful qualities but of the Lord Himself. He catches a glimpse of the splendor of His personal reality, revealed but not fully revealed in what just happened. He has a personal encounter with the Lord and is profoundly moved with love. He's loving the Lord not on account of what He does for him and not on account of the kind of person He is, but simply because He is who He is. He experiences a moment of personal love. These personal encounters between the exercitant and his Lord are profoundly intimate and very difficult to talk about. Words don't do justice to the experience. After all, it's impossible to put someone's personal reality into words. We can talk endlessly about a person, but everyone knows words can't substitute for meeting the person.

Every encounter with God is a gift, a grace. Even so, when the exercitant encounters God and is moved with love for Him on account of the Lord's mercy, His generous self-gift or His faith, usually he's been working hard to awaken his love. The exercitant has been examining the Lord's words and deeds with great care and diligence. Even when he's not making a meditation, he's pursuing the Lord, thinking about

Him, begging for graces and so on. He's working hard at making the retreat. It's as if he's going to a well with a pail and a rope (as St. Teresa of Avila pointed out long ago). The exercitant has to work hard to draw the water. It's slow going and laborious.

Occasionally, something out of the ordinary happens. The exercitant doesn't have to awaken his love. His love seems to leap forth, unbidden. When this happens, he's had a personal encounter with the Lord. This encounter with the Lord seems qualitatively different from previous encounters. The exercitant's many attempts to meditate on his Lord now seem like puny reflections. The sorrow or the joy he had experienced earlier seems like nothing compared with the true sorrow or the true joy he experiences then. Tears flow freely and it feels like he has done nothing to induce them or encourage them. Sometimes it feels like his heart is expanding. He's hardly working at all; his prayer is not at all wearisome. The exercitant doesn't need to travel to a well and then work to draw water. The water he's seeking wells up from within.

In our opinion, when Ignatius talks about consolations "through which the soul comes to be inflamed with love of its Creator and Lord; and when it can in consequence love no created thing on the face of the earth in itself, but in the Creator of them all" (316, Mullan), he's talking about these fully personal encounters with God. In one sense, the exercitant feels, at least for the moment, without constraint because he isn't caught between conflicting loves. The love the exercitant experiences during such encounters is pure, free from the admixture of any inordinate loves. He loves his Creator first, and all else through Him and with Him and in Him. In another sense, he feels like a willing captive. There seems to be no "possibility of resistance on our part, even should we wish to resist."[102]

These personal encounters with God are experienced by a surprising number of people. They vary in frequency and duration, but they are experiences of loving God Himself for Himself. If the exercitant is making a meditation and experiences such a personal encounter, he should lay aside the meditation and speak simple words of love to his Lord. In other words, he should follow the Lord's lead and respond personally. These personal encounters bring great benefit to the retreatant and often produce permanent good effects. They are notoriously difficult to write about, but despite the difficulty they are intelligible and can be understood to a great degree, if not completely.

Ignatius doesn't actually describe consolations in terms of semipersonal and personal love. However, he describes two kinds of consolations: consolations with a preceding cause and consolations without a preceding cause. Over the centuries, commentators have disagreed in their understanding of consolations with and without preceding causes, but we believe that Ignatius is describing what we are calling semipersonal and personal encounters with God. What we call personal encounters correspond to what Ignatius calls consolations without a preceding cause. They can happen out of the blue, even when the exercitant isn't praying or thinking about the Lord. If the exercitant is praying or thinking about the Lord, what he experiences seems disproportionate to what he was doing. The consolation will be experienced "as breaking into" his prayer, "not as a natural development of it" says one commentator.[103] "In relation with anything that might have been already happening, it is discontinuous and disproportionate."[104]

Satan can give consolations with a preceding cause but he cannot give consolations without a preceding cause. He can "assume the appearance of an angel of light" (332) and feign patience or compassion or mercy, but he cannot give the exercitant an experience of God Himself. It is, then, important to determine whether the exercitant's consolation is with or without previous cause. If it is without previous cause, he can be sure that he just encountered God personally. If the consolation had a previous cause, it could be from God or it could be from Satan. Maybe the exercitant was encountering God, but maybe he was encountering Satan.

It is, then, important for the director to listen closely when the exercitant is describing the consolations he's experienced. Did the exercitant experience semipersonal love for God or personal love? Exercitants can, in fact, use the same words to describe very different experiences. For example, one exercitant might tell the director, "I realized that I really matter to God." When the director asks for more details, the exercitant tells him what happened. As he was taking a walk, he was calling to mind "the mysteries of the life of Christ our

Lord" (130), beginning with the Incarnation. The exercitant was deeply moved by the Lord's labors on his behalf. The moment was important to the exercitant. He wrote it down in order to tell his director about it. Another exercitant comes to his director and says, "I really matter to God." He gets choked up as he speaks and has difficulty holding back the tears. When the director asks for more details, the exercitant recounts a similar story, but now he has tears streaming down his face. The tears seem to come from a well deeper than the tear ducts. "I just can't explain it," he says. "It wasn't anything I was thinking or reading, but something happened. I know I matter to Him." The two exercitants' words are similar, but the experiences they are describing are qualitatively different. Because the second exercitant experienced a personal encounter, that exercitant can be sure he was encountering God. The first exercitant, however, has at least to consider the possibility that he might have encountered the Enemy disguised as God.

It's a mistake to assume that every movement toward more faith, hope and love in the exercitant's soul is a consolation from God. The director and, eventually, the exercitant have to realize that encounters with Satan can result in an increase of faith, hope and love. Why would Satan inspire the exercitant to have greater faith, greater hope or greater love? It sounds counterproductive. It may be counterproductive in the short term, but not in the long term. If Satan can get the exercitant to pay attention to him and to enjoy his company, he's got a toehold in the exercitant's life. Ultimately he wants to become the exercitant's spiritual director, so at first he gives the exercitant genuinely good things in order that the exercitant becomes accustomed to listening to and trusting his voice. The voice brings delight and consolation, so when it eventually leads the exercitant to less faith, hope and love, he might not even notice. Later Satan might successfully "inspire" the exercitant to do something really evil. Thus, Satan is willing to give genuinely good things in order that the exercitant might want to befriend him.

In one of his letters, Ignatius describes this strategy of the Enemy: "He enters through the other's door and comes out his own. He enters with the other by not opposing his ways but by praising them. He acts familiarly with the soul, suggesting good and holy thoughts which bring peace to the good soul. Later he tries, little by little, to come out his own door, always suggesting some error or illusion under the appearance of good, but which will always be evil."[105] In his Rules for Discernment of Spirits, he describes the Enemy's strategy this way: "He begins by suggesting thoughts that are suited to a devout soul, and ends by suggesting his own. For example, he will suggest holy and pious thoughts that are wholly in conformity with the sanctity of the soul. Afterward, he will endeavor little by little to end by drawing the soul into his hidden snares and evil designs" (332).

Sometimes the Enemy will tempt a person under the appearance of good. He makes something that is evil, or even less good, look very good. But the wrapping belies the contents. When he gives consolations, he's using a different strategy. As a result of his action, the exercitant experiences something genuinely good. The exercitant is moved with love. He feels more faith and more hope. He could be filled with zeal and be fired up to do great things. The exercitant can have such experiences as a response to Satan. They are good experiences, but they are from Satan. The problem with such consolations from the Enemy is not the experience itself; it's the possible attachment to the source of the experience.

Generally speaking, the director should tell a person what he needs to know when he needs to know it. While the exercitant is being tempted openly or being assailed by desolations, he needs to understand and put into practice what Ignatius says in his first set of rules for discernment of spirits. Even if he's experiencing some consolations, he doesn't need to hear right away that some consolations might be from the Enemy. Typically, as the exercitant makes the exercises of the Second Week, he has more need of the teachings from the second set of rules. Although the director should be careful not to overwhelm someone with too much information, he does need to spend some time making sure the exercitant understands that to reject a consolation from the Enemy is to reject an experience which may be good in itself. This is a difficult concept for some people to grasp.

Often a few analogies help communicate this difficult concept. We use two examples—one about a ride in the rain and another about a preacher—to help communicate that one ought not to accept consolations from the Enemy. Imagine, we say, that Susan walks home from school every day. Each time it rains, a man stops and gives her a ride home. A ride home in the rain is a good thing. The man who offers the ride seems to be very kind and very polite. Evil people can, after all, be quite charming. The ride is a good thing, but Susan shouldn't take it. There are some rides a person just ought not to take. The man is offering to help Susan. He hasn't harmed her. Still, Susan shouldn't conclude that he is a good person. She ought to be asking herself, Who is he and why is he doing this? This ride could be the beginning of something really evil. If Susan accepted this ride, she's not a very discerning person.

The second example we use is more complicated, but more illustrative. Imagine, we say, that Evelyn goes to hear a preacher who is quite eloquent and inspiring. In fact, as Evelyn listens to him she is quite moved. She is filled with more faith and more zeal. She is inspired to go out and do more during the coming week: serve her neighbor more, pray with the sick for healing, speak to people about her Lord and so on. Evelyn wants to go back to hear more. She really likes this preacher and what he has to say. There's no doubt that Evelyn experienced something really good—more faith—as she listened to this preacher. There was, however, a moment in his sermon when the preacher was railing against the pagans on account of their fornication. In the same breath he went on to say how all things are lawful for Christians and they can do whatever they want. The clear implication was that fornication is lawful for Christians. The preacher revealed himself in that one line.

The preacher had all sorts of good qualities and attributes—his eloquence, the stories of mighty works he had done in the name of the Lord and so on—but then he was revealed. Evelyn's sister, who went with her to hear this preacher, says, "He's a wolf in sheep's clothing." Evelyn says, "I liked the service. It was great. I had a great experience." Evelyn is missing the point. She has been duped. Yes, she did have a good experience and she was moved to more faith, but where did that movement of her soul come from? Who was the cause?

Evelyn shouldn't go back to hear the preacher again. She says she liked him and enjoyed listening to him. The preacher did, after all, stir up her faith and her zeal. But look what happened to Evelyn. At least to some degree, she united herself with that preacher in spirit, but he is an evil man. She's just corrupted her soul. She is tempted to accept the greater faith and zeal and then to be indebted to the giver. In fact, that's just what the preacher wants. He wants women to come back again and again and again. A year later, Evelyn's sister reads in the paper an exposé showing that this fellow had seduced numerous women.

Of course, directors don't have to use these morality tales, but they do need to impress upon exercitants the importance of knowing the source of their consolations. In the Garden of Eden, the fruit was a really good thing. "The woman saw that the tree was good for food, and that it was a delight to the eyes, and that the tree was to be desired to make one wise. She took of its fruit and ate" (Gen. 3:6). It was good food. It was beautiful. Wisdom is a good thing, a really good thing. Unfortunately, Eve did not stop to ask, Who is giving me this good thing? She knew the difference between the serpent and God, but she preferred Satan to God on account of what he offered. The fruit was a good thing, but was it from the Lord? No.

Satan can take the form of an angel of light. When the exercitant encounters him in this form, he can come away with more faith in God, more hope in God and more love of God. What the exercitant experiences in his soul isn't bad. It's the origin of this experience in the soul which is evil, not the movement of the soul itself. The exercitant can even be moved by Satan to genuinely heroic things—to give away all that he has or to deliver his body to be burned for the sake of the Gospel or to speak with great eloquence about the Lord—but in the end he should reject this experience if he has discerned that it is not from God.

In Ignatius's account of his own life (where he refers to himself in the third person), he tells several stories about consolations from the Enemy. The first has to do with consolations he experienced as he was studying:

> Returning to Barcelona, he began his studies with great diligence. But there was one thing that stood very much in his way, and that is that when he began to learn by heart, as has to be done in the beginning of grammar, he received new light on spiritual things

and new delights. So strong were these delights that he could memorize nothing, nor could he get rid of them however much he tried.

Thinking this over at various times, he said to himself: "Even when I go to prayer or attend Mass these lights do not come to me so vividly." Thus, step by step, he came to recognize that it was a temptation. After making his meditation, he went to the Church of Santa Maria del Mar, near the house of his teacher, having asked him to have the kindness to hear him for a moment in the church. Seated there, the pilgrim gave his teacher a faithful account of what had taken place in his soul, and how little progress he had made until then for the reason already mentioned. And he made a promise to his master, with these words: "I promise you never to fail to attend your class these two years, as long as I can find bread and water for my support here in Barcelona." He made this promise with such effect that he never again suffered from those temptations.[106]

Ignatius was experiencing good things: great insight into the things of God and great spiritual delight. Nevertheless, he said no to these spiritual things.

Another time, Ignatius experienced consolations that he eventually rejected because he wasn't sure they were from God:

> Besides his seven hours of prayer, he busied himself with certain souls who came looking for him to discuss their spiritual interests. All the rest of the day he spent thinking of divine things, those especially which he had either read or meditated on that day. But when he went to bed he received great illuminations and spiritual consolations which made him lose much of the time he had set aside for sleep, and that was not much. He looked into this matter a number of times and gave it some thought. Having set aside so much time for dealing with God, and besides that even all the rest of the day, he began to doubt whether these illuminations came from the good spirit. He concluded

that he had better not have anything to do with them, and give the time determined on to sleep. And this he did.[107]

Again, Ignatius turned aside from great illuminations and spiritual consolations. Even though what he was experiencing was good, it didn't mean the giver was God.

During the course of making the Exercises, the exercitant learns how to tell whether a consolation is from God or from Satan. First, he has to ask whether the consolation was a genuinely spiritual event. One can mistakenly think that a natural movement of one's soul is a spiritual consolation. If the consolation is a spiritual one, the exercitant has to determine whether it was a consolation with or without a preceding cause. Usually, a consolation without a preceding cause is easy to recognize because it leaves no room for doubt. If it is without a preceding cause, it is from God. If, however, the consolation is with a preceding cause, the exercitant has to ask whether it is from God or from Satan.

How does the exercitant know that a spiritual consolation with a preceding cause is from God? He can look at the beginning, middle and end of the consolation. If the whole experience is unalloyed—if it is pure from beginning to end—then this is a sign that it's from God. "If the beginning and middle and end of the course of thoughts are wholly good and directed to what is entirely right, it is a sign that they are from the good angel" (333). So the exercitant has to reflect upon his experience and ask himself how the consolation began. Was the exercitant in the right place doing the right thing with the right motive? If the consolation began well, the exercitant then looks at whether it continued in the middle to be genuinely holy, righteous and true. Was it free from obvious evil such as envy or rash judgment? If so, the exercitant looks at the end of the experience. Was the end wholly good? If the consolation was a real spiritual event, but it had a bad beginning or a bad middle or a bad end, the exercitant can be sure it's not from God. In fact, it's from the Enemy.

Although they are not nearly as rich and nuanced as real life, a few simplified examples will help illustrate Ignatius's point. Let's say the director and the exercitant agree to meet at 4:30. The exercitant is out taking a walk. He sees a church and decides to stop in for a moment to pray, even though it will make him late for his meeting. While he's in the church a homeless man walks in. He's very bedraggled and so sad-looking. The exercitant experiences his heart burning with compassion for this homeless man and with love for God, who so loves this homeless man. He feels moved to give $10,000 to the local homeless shelter.

Was the experience really from God? It seems to have been a genuine spiritual event. Although perhaps it's hard to determine from such a brief telling, it is also a consolation with a preceding cause. The exercitant has then to look at the beginning, middle and end. There's nothing wrong with giving money to a homeless shelter. The middle seems acceptable also. The exercitant is praying and moved with compassion. But the beginning isn't totally pure. How did it happen that the exercitant was in the church praying? He was supposed to be meeting with his director. His choice to stop in the church was also a choice to make his director wait for him. The consolation had a bad beginning. One cannot be certain it was from God. It could have been from the Enemy. The exercitant certainly cannot say that he knows God moved him to donate to the local homeless shelter.

Perhaps another exercitant is out for a walk and stops at a church for a moment to pray. No one is waiting for this exercitant. While he is in the church a bedraggled homeless man walks in. This exercitant experiences his heart burning with compassion for the homeless man and with love for God, who so loves this homeless man. With disdain, he thinks, People in this town don't care about the homeless, and is moved to give $10,000 to the local homeless shelter. The beginning and the end of this consolation are acceptable, but the middle is polluted. Why is the exercitant passing judgment on his fellow citizens? Obviously this consolation cannot be attributed to God. In fact, the course of his thoughts, in particular the middle part, "is a clear sign that it proceeds from the evil spirit" (333, Mullan)

A third exercitant is out for a walk and stops at a church for a moment to pray. No one is waiting for this exercitant. While he is in the church, a bedraggled homeless man walks in. This exercitant experiences his heart burning with compassion for the homeless man and with love for God, who so loves this homeless man. He's so moved he decides to give $10,000 to the local homeless shelter. He had deliberately promised his wife that they would spend the money on renovating a bathroom in their home, but he doesn't care about that anymore. Was the consolation from God? No. It had a bad end. Unilaterally breaking a well-made promise isn't a good end.

It should be clear by now that the exercitant needs to develop the habit of reflecting upon his consolations. This reflection should take place after the consolation, not during it. In other words, he should not constantly examine what is happening in his soul as it is happening. That's no way to relate to a person and to build a relationship. At the end of an exercise in which he has been moved, the exercitant can take a few moments and examine what happened. He can look at the beginning, middle and end of the consolation, but while the consolation is happening he should just let it happen.

The exercitant should be sober and alert, but he doesn't need to be afraid. The Enemy can be discerned. He always leaves a telltale trail. If, after he examines the beginning, middle and end of an experience, the exercitant determines that the consolation was from the Enemy, he ought to learn from the experience. If he can see how the Enemy was working, a person "may be able to guard for the future against his usual deceits" (334, Mullan). Experiencing a consolation from the Enemy isn't the end of the world. The exercitant does, however, need to reject it once he realizes what is going on.

As an exercitant talks about a consolation, the director also needs to ask about the beginning, middle and end of the consolation. Some directors can make the mistake of asking too few questions. In fact, the director's questions can be a lesson in how to examine a consolation. For example, one time an exercitant came to his director saying, "I just had the most amazing experience today." He went on to tell his director about how he had a very sweet experience of God's love. Before the exercitant got too invested in describing the experience, the director asked, "How did this begin? What were you doing?" The exercitant responded, "I started to think about how to amend my life, as you directed me to do, but I just didn't feel like doing that. The whole topic was so overwhelming, so I started thinking about how much God loved me." The director didn't need any more information.

The consolation had a bad beginning. He cannot trust that the consolation was from the Lord. In fact, it looked like it was from the Enemy.

Some directors might get caught up in the exercitant's emotion and forget to ask questions. Imagine a situation in which a devout and generous nun is misunderstood and criticized.[108] Despite her good intention, her superior and her sisters misread her motives and criticized her work. This would be painful to any normal human being, and she felt hurt and frustrated. Then she began to wonder if perhaps she was deceived and was deceiving others. In her misery and distress she prayed. As she began to pray, suddenly she seemed to hear the Lord saying, You came to this life for me and not for these people. All that matters is what I think of you.

If such a person went to her director and recounted her consolation, the director would have to ask her more questions, even though the exercitant was feeling quite obvious relief from her distress at being misunderstood. The director wouldn't yet have enough information to help her discern the consolation. The director knows the beginning and the middle but not the end of the consolation. Did this woman feel better toward anyone—her superior or her sisters? Maybe, but as it stands the woman is just a hairsbreadth away from thoughts like: What do you care about those people? Those other people don't matter. If the consolation had ended in anything like those thoughts, she could conclude that it wasn't from God. If, on the other hand, the woman was moved to go back and love her sisters freely and openly because she had been freed from her vainglory, then it looks like the consolation was from God. Open-ended questions from the director could have helped her discern this consolation. For example, the director could have asked her, "Tell me more about what happened after you heard those words."

If a consolation is from the Enemy, the exercitant should reject the whole experience. Initially, exercitants often don't want to do this. They want to keep the good parts of the experience and just reject the questionable parts. For example, someone might say, "I was wrong to stop in the church and pray, even though someone was waiting for me, but I'll always cherish the love I felt for that homeless man."

Or, "I regret not following my director's instructions, but I'll hold on to the experience of God's love." It's very important for the exercitant to understand that if the consolation was from the Enemy he should reject the whole thing: beginning, middle and end. To do otherwise is to drink from a polluted stream.

Of course, if the exercitant experiences what we are calling an "act of personal love of God," which is what Ignatius calls a "consolation without a preceding cause," the exercitant doesn't need to examine the beginning, middle and end. He can be sure the consolation is from God. "When consolation is without previous cause, as was said, there can be no deception in it, since it can proceed from God our Lord only" (336). Even so, the exercitant needs to be careful. In the time immediately following the consolation, which some people call the "afterglow," the exercitant could come to certain conclusions or make certain resolutions to do things that aren't from God. For example, an exercitant could have a personal encounter with God and be very moved to proclaim His glory for all the world to see. Then, as he is savoring the experience, he decides to write a book. The exercitant can be sure the consolation is from God, but he can't be sure the resolution to write a book is from God. He was moved to proclaim God's glory, not to write a book. Writing a book was the exercitant's idea in the afterglow. That resolution needs to be examined more carefully. Directors need to teach exercitants to "cautiously distinguish the actual time of the consolation from the period which follows it" (336). In the time just after a consolation, "the soul frequently forms various resolutions and plans which are not granted directly by God our Lord. They may come from our own reasoning on the relations of our concepts and on the consequences of our judgments" (336). In other words, the exercitant has to be careful not to jump to conclusions on the basis of a consolation without a preceding cause.

The exercitant also needs to be aware that the Enemy can suggest something to him in the afterglow of a consolation without a preceding cause. In his letter to Teresa Rejadell, Ignatius puts it this way:

> But we can frequently be deceived, however, because after such consolation or inspiration, when the soul is

> still abiding in its joy, the enemy tries under the impetus of this joy to make us innocently add to what we have received from God our Lord. His only purpose is to disturb and confuse us in everything. At other times he makes us lessen the import of the message we have received and confronts us with obstacles and difficulties, so as to prevent us from carrying out completely what had been made known to us."[109]

God can reveal Himself to an exercitant but, as the exercitant savors the experience, the Enemy can get a foothold and trick him into adding to or subtracting from the revelation.

In the Garden of Eden God said, "You may freely eat of every tree of the garden; but of the tree of the knowledge of good and evil you shall not eat, for in that day that you eat of it you shall die" (Gen. 2:16). But Eve, in the presence of Satan, adds to what God said: "We may eat of the fruit of the trees of the garden, but God said, 'You shall not eat of the fruit of the tree which is in the midst of the garden, neither shall you touch it, lest you die'" (Gen. 3:2-3). Temptations to add to what God has said are always a possibility. After a consolation, the exercitant can also be tempted to subtract from what has transpired. Say the exercitant has been consoled and is moved to go out and spread His word anywhere, anytime. After the experience, he could be tempted to subtract from it, thinking, I wasn't moved to go just anywhere. I wasn't moved to quit my job and leave town. That's not possible. I couldn't give up my job. He would be jumping to conclusions if he thought, on the basis of that one consolation, that he was being moved to quit his job. However, it would be illogical to say that he was not being moved to consider the possibility.

So, in the time after a consolation without a preceding cause, "the soul frequently forms various resolutions and plans which are not granted directly by God our Lord" (336). These may come from the exercitant's own reasoning or from the evil spirit. The same thing can happen in the afterglow of a consolation with a preceding cause. Of course, sometimes the various resolutions and plans which the soul forms in the afterglow of a consolation are from God.

Ignatius has a few more comments about the work of God and the Enemy in the exercitant's soul, but first it might be helpful to stop and summarize what we've said about consolations and desolations. In order to discern the action of God and of the Enemy, the director has to ask a series of questions. If the exercitant was moved, was it a spiritual experience? Many things can move a person: physiology, wants and desires, things in one's environment and so on. If it seems to be a spiritual experience, then he has to ask, was the exercitant moved by God or Satan? In order to answer this question the director must ask, What is the general trajectory of this person's life? Is he moving "from one mortal sin to another" or does he fall into the category of those "who go on earnestly striving to cleanse their souls from sin and who seek to rise in the service of God our Lord to greater perfection" (315)? If the former, God bites the conscience and stings the soul with remorse, and the Enemy proposes apparent pleasures that encourage vices and sins. If the latter, and the person experiences a spiritual desolation, it's from the Enemy. God does not give desolations to those earnestly seeking greater perfection in Christ. If it's a consolation, the director should ask, Is the exercitant experiencing semipersonal love for God or personal love? If it's an experience of personal love (a consolation without a preceding cause), then the consolation was from God. If it's an experience of semipersonal love for God, what about its beginning, middle and end? If all three are pure, it's a sign that the consolation is from God. If something's wrong with the beginning or the middle or the end, then the consolation is from the Enemy. A person doesn't have to wait years, months, weeks or even days to see where a consolation takes him in order to figure out whether it was from God or not.[110] The consolation itself can be discerned.

Although Ignatius has a lot to say about consolations and desolations, it's important to remember that consolations are not the only grace God gives an exercitant. Likewise, desolations are not the only work of the Enemy. In the second set of rules for the discernment of spirits, Ignatius makes some general comments about the actions of God and of the Enemy. These more general comments are very helpful for the exercitant.

Ignatius says that for those who "are progressing to greater perfection" God's action is "delicate, gentle and delightful" (335). He goes on to say that "it may be compared to a drop of water penetrating a sponge" (335). God's action in such people is not flashy or noisy. The Enemy's action in the soul of someone progressing to greater perfection is just the opposite. His action is "violent, noisy and disturbing" and "may be compared to a drop of water falling on a stone" (335). The situation is just the reverse in "souls that are going from bad to worse" (335). God's action is violent, noisy and disturbing, while the Enemy's action is delicate, gentle and delightful. "The reason for this," says Ignatius, "is to be sought in the opposition or similarity of these souls to the different kinds of spirits. When the disposition is contrary to that of the spirits, they enter with noise and commotion that are easily perceived. When the disposition is similar to that of the spirits, they enter silently, as one coming into his own house when the doors are open" (335).

These observations about God's activity and the Enemy's activity are rules of thumb, not laws. For example, sometimes God's action in the soul of someone progressing to greater perfection in Christ is spectacular, if not noisy and splashy. Nevertheless, this description of God's and the Enemy's actions is often illuminating for the exercitant. Some may come to the Exercises having experienced a powerful conversion. Or they may experience a conversion during the First Week. In other words, at one time they were going from bad to worse but they changed course. Often their histories include stories of God's splashy or noisy actions. When their lives change and they begin pursuing the Lord and His ways, God's action in their souls changes. It becomes quieter and is especially easy to miss if the exercitants are looking for something noisy and splashy. Other exercitants come to the Exercises having pursued the Lord from their youth. If they've heard conversion stories in which the Lord enters a person's life with some commotion, they can mistakenly expect some spiritual fireworks in their own lives and therefore may not pay attention to God's quiet action in their souls.

All this might seem complicated, but it's important to remember that discernment is an art, not a science. The art is built on faith in our Father's loving providence. "What father among you, if his son asks for a fish, will instead of a fish give him a serpent; or if he asks for an egg, will give him a scorpion? If you then, who are evil, know how to give good gifts to your children, how much more will the heavenly

Father give the Holy Spirit to those who ask him!" (Lk. 11:11-12).

Ignatius's Rules for Discernment of Spirits are not a coherent exposition of everything there is to say about God's and the Enemy's actions in the human soul. They are more like tools thrown into a toolbox. It's up to the director and the exercitant to find the right tool for the right occasion. By reflecting on their experience, studying Scripture and reading about the lives of holy men and women, they might even discover other tools that Ignatius doesn't mention.

IV

DECISION-MAKING

CHAPTER 11

DISPOSITIONS FOR DECISION-MAKING

In the last two chapters we've been describing some of what happens affectively in a person as he meditates on events from the life of Jesus. The exercitant begins to love and admire his Lord more and more. Often his implemental love of the Lord develops into semipersonal love, and sometimes genuine personal love is enkindled. The exercitant can even begin to identify with the Lord, experiencing sorrow with Christ in sorrow, and joy with Christ in joy. Often, however, the exercitant is experiencing not only consolations but also desolations. Much is happening affectively in the exercitant, but Ignatius certainly doesn't want the exercitant to settle for sentiment alone. He believes "that love ought to find its expression in deeds rather than in words" (230, Ivens, emphasis removed). Love is generative. It issues in action, and decisions are the father of acts. Therefore, it's not surprising to find decision-making playing a central role in the Exercises.

In the second chapter we described in broad strokes Ignatius's strategy for decision-making: Be one with your Lord in whatever way you can and then act out of that union. During the Exercises, exercitants learn how their love for God can enable them to decide any issue they face. When making a decision, the exercitant isn't simply reasoning from general principles, pursuing the universally best course of action or receiving his superior's directions. Ignatian decision-making is more personal and collaborative.

It's time now to turn our attention to the particulars of Ignatius's method. In this chapter we'll focus on affective and intellectual dispositions for decision-making and we'll explain how the Second Week's exercises cultivate these dispositions. In subsequent chapters we'll describe the actual process of decision-making and the union which this process makes possible.

If an exercitant wants to make a decision, it's not uncommon for him to make it during the Second Week. The exercitant enters the Second Week with an awareness of sin's magnitude and with a firm determination to avoid sin, even venial sin. He's beginning to see his inordinate attachments and has been introduced to a method for ridding himself of them. He's also reflected on the goal of the Christian life and learned how indifference is an effective aid for reaching that goal. One could say that the exercitant has been working very hard at getting his own house in order.

The Second Week begins on quite a different note. The week opens with the exercitant considering how Christ the King calls everyone and each person in particular to join Him in His mission to conquer the whole world. The exercitant then considers how someone inflamed with love responds to that call. After meditating on Christ the King, he begins meditating on the life of Jesus. In the first of these meditations, on the Incarnation, the exercitant begins by noting "how the Three Divine Persons look down upon the whole expanse or circuit of all the earth, filled with human beings. Since They see that all are going down to hell, They decree in Their eternity that the Second Person should become man to save the human race" (102). The Second Week begins on a decidedly apostolic note. The exercitant is no longer looking at himself, but at Jesus and His burning desire to rescue those who are lost and headed toward the eternal death of hell.

The meditations on the life of Jesus are divided into two groups. First the exercitant considers events from the infancy and childhood of Jesus. Then he meditates on various events from the public ministry of Jesus. On or about the fourth day of the Second Week, as a kind of interlude between the two groups of meditations, he spends the day making the meditations on the Two Standards and the Three Classes of Men. The exercitant makes the Two Standards meditation twice and repeats it twice. The day closes with him meditating on the Three Classes of Men. Both these meditations are valuable in and of themselves, but they also are positioned as a preparation for decision-making.

The Two Standards meditation opens up new possibilities for choice and makes them attractive. The contrast between Satan's camp and the Lord's camp is eye-opening for the exercitant. As he contemplates Satan's strategy, he often begins to see that he has made many decisions and choices out of love for riches or honors. Then, when he turns to considering the Lord's strategy, he glimpses a whole new way of doing things—the Lord's way. The Lord's strategy for victory involves embracing poverty, insults and contempt, and humble, obedient love. As he prays the threefold colloquy, begging to be received under the Lord's standard, the exercitant begins to awaken to radical new possibilities for his life. He could choose to join his Lord, sharing His poverty and humiliations.

The Three Classes of Men provides the exercitant with the opportunity and the motivation "to crush" (157, Mullan) his inordinate attachments. Unless the exercitant is free of his inordinate attachments, he can't be really sure that love for God is inspiring his choice. If he's not detached, there's a good chance that his other loves are inspiring his choice. The desires of people who cling to their own plans and intentions are like "a moth which consumes the precious robe of their true vocation and utterly prevents them from discovering the truth."[111] If the exercitant isn't indifferent, desiring neither riches nor poverty, honor nor dishonor, sickness nor health, he can't enter into the reality of being united with God in his decision-making. He must enter that reality through the narrow gate of detachment.

The director does not, of course, explain to the exercitant the role these two meditations play as a preparation for decision-making. However, he does need to introduce the two meditations, and he uses the introduction to briefly mention the topic of decision-making. When we introduce these exercises, we say something similar to what Ignatius says (135), but in slightly updated language. The director could say something like this:

> You've been praying for the grace to know the Lord more so that you can love Him more and follow Him more closely. Don't be surprised if you find yourself inspired to do new or even radically different things. In fact, as you continue to contemplate the life of

Jesus, you should begin to think about your own life and how the Lord wants to use you. As an introduction to this, we'll consider the Lord's intention and, on the other hand, Satan's intention. We'll also see how we can prepare ourselves to be one with God in whatever choices we make.

In this brief introduction to the meditations of the fourth day, the director plants an important seed that will germinate in the days to come. The director hopes that the exercitant will be asking himself, more and more often, what more can I do?

After making the meditations on the Two Standards and Three Classes of Men, the exercitant returns to meditating on the life of Jesus, only now he is often using the threefold colloquy of the Two Standards. As the exercitant is awakening to the possibility of a radically different kind of life, Ignatius has him make several meditations which aid him. First, he has the exercitant meditate on Jesus' choice to leave His mother and His occupation in Nazareth (273). Then he has him meditate on Jesus' experience in the desert, where He decisively renounces all that the Enemy has to offer: riches, honor and pride. Then the exercitant contemplates Jesus calling the Apostles to change the way they live and the Apostles choosing to leave their possessions, their jobs and their families to become fishers of men with Jesus. And then he considers the radical vision of ordinary everyday life that Jesus lays out in the Sermon on the Mount. As the exercitant is making these meditations, the director begins to talk to him about decision-making.

Often, people come to the Exercises with specific decisions on their mind. For instance, they want to decide whether to take a certain job or whether they should pursue marriage or a life of dedicated celibacy. Some exercitants don't have a specific decision in mind, but they are at a turning point in their lives and are asking, What next? Others are simply asking, What more can I do?

The exercises of the Second Week, especially the meditations on the Kingdom of Christ and the Two Standards, raise a more fundamental question. Each person must ask himself, Is Jesus calling me to be actually poor for the sake of the Gospel? Am I called to go out, preaching, healing and delivering people, the way Jesus did, without any "gold, nor silver, nor copper in your belts, no bag for your journey, nor two tunics, nor sandals, nor a staff" (Mt. 10:9-10)? In other words, am I called to leave home, family and job to become a fisher of men? Typically, most exercitants have never actually considered such a life as a real possibility for themselves. The meditations on the Kingdom of Christ and the Two Standards put this question on the table.

The decision to sell what one has and follow Jesus is not a decision to have the same interior dispositions as Jesus did, such as kindness, courage, boldness and faith, as important as those are. It's not a decision to imitate Jesus' virtues; it's a decision to do what He did, in the way that He did it. He walked out of His retreat in the desert without any visible means of support, trusting His Father for His daily bread. He was sent into the world, "that the world might be saved through him" (Jn. 3:17), but He didn't use money and the things that money can buy to win His victory. He saved us by enduring insults and contempt and by being utterly obedient to His Father—not calling anything His own, even His life.

Jesus chose not to go forth into the world as a cultured, noble or wealthy man. He didn't depend on money to win victories for His Father. He didn't go out as a salesman selling His spiritual wares, or a holy man standing on a corner. He wasn't a benefactor handing out money, or a zealot out to overthrow evil structures, or a legal expert. He didn't come out of the desert as an eloquent philosopher or a trained public speaker. Money, the Mosaic Law, just political and economic structures, eloquent wisdom—Jesus knew that these things couldn't save a single person. All He offered was Himself, filled with the Holy Spirit, trusting in His Father.

The exercitant who decides to be actually poor is deciding to go out into the world, as Jesus did. This particular call isn't a call to go out as a salesman, or a social worker, or a philanthropist, or an educator, or a medical professional, or a politician. It's a call to go out in Christ, as Christ, filled with the Holy Spirit. Those who go out this way have only themselves to offer, alive in Christ. Like St. Paul, they say, "For the sake of Christ, then, I am content with weaknesses, insults, hardships, persecutions, and calamities; for when I am weak, then I am strong" (2 Cor. 12:10).

It goes without saying that no one should embark on a life of actual poverty in the name of the Lord without a call from God. In other words, one should not make such a choice unilaterally. Although the Lord does call people to actual poverty, He doesn't call everyone. He didn't, for instance, call His dear friends Mary, Martha and Lazarus to such a life. Normally the Lord wants people to have money, but to say that one is called to the normal Christian life is not a self-serving excuse for doing what everybody else is doing and calling it godly. In fact, the Lord has definite opinions about how to use and not use money. The Gospels are full of His advice about money and possessions.[112]

As the prologue of John's Gospel makes clear, the life of Jesus is the beginning of a new creation. In the beginning of all time and space, God created Adam to be His intelligent, loving and free co-worker, telling him to "be fruitful and multiply, and fill the earth and subdue it; and have dominion over the fish of the sea and over the birds of the air and over every living thing that moves upon the earth" (Gen. 1:28). Of course, we know that God's plan for His creation went awry with the first sin. Although God originally intended Adam to rule creation, with all things in subjection under his feet (Ps. 8), that place is now taken by Christ (1 Cor. 15:27, Eph. 1:22 and Heb. 2:6-9). It is no longer Adam who is to be God's agent in His creation; it is Christ, Christians united with one another and with their head, the risen Jesus. Christ must reign—not by force—until He has put all things under His feet and then God will be all in all. As Paul says, "For he has made known to us in all wisdom and insight the mystery of his will, according to his purpose which he set forth in Christ as a plan for the fulness of time, to unite all things in him, things in heaven and things on earth (Eph. 1:9-10)."[113]

The call to a normal Christian life is not a call to multiply religious activities. It's not even a call to fix up Adam. It's a call to leave behind the life of Adam and to live a new life, the life of Christ. It is a call to bring all things under Christ's reign, so that the Father's will may be done in every home, every business, every school, every neighborhood and every political, cultural and economic interaction. "Thy will be done on earth as it is in heaven." It's a call to create places where life, work and worship are united in Christ. It's a call to be a light to the nations and bread for the world.

What such a life looks like varies according to place and time, but three things are certain. First, Christ cares very much about all of His Father's creation. He has, after all, become one with it through the Incarnation. Second, living the life of Christ means being at the center of storms of controversy and conflict. Third, life in Christ is life together.

What role does money play in the normal Christian life? Money becomes a thing that can be used to tie Christians (and indeed all people) together, rather than a thing that divides them from one another and from God. It becomes a tool for unity, not for independence.

Conversations between the director and the exercitant about decision-making vary a great deal, depending on the exercitant and the choices he has already made in his life. Some exercitants, for example, may have already made choices about their way of life. If it was a well-made choice, they shouldn't make it again. Nevertheless, the director should briefly describe the choice between the life of actual poverty and the normal Christian life. Often such a description gives clarity to what exercitants have already chosen and equips them to make further good choices.

For those who have already made a choice about their way of life, particularly those who have chosen the normal Christian life, Ignatius offers some instructions on how to "amend and reform one's own life and state" (189, Mullan) or, as another translation puts it, "Directions for the Amendment and Reformation of One's Way of Living His State of Life" (189). It's helpful to note that "to amend" and "to reform" have different meanings.[114] "Amend" means to correct what is defective. Often, as exercitants make the Exercises, they begin to see that there are some things about their current life they could and should do differently. They've made fundamentally good choices about their lives, but there are corrections and additions they can make to better "praise, reverence, and serve God our Lord, and by this means to save his soul" (23). On the other hand, "reform" means "to reshape." Sometimes during the Exercises God calls people not only to amend their lives but to reshape them. They are not called to actual poverty, but they come out of the Exercises having decided to reshape their lives in a radical way.

Ignatius gives some examples of the kinds of things the exercitant might consider if he is amending or reforming his life:

> [During] the Exercises and during the consideration of the ways of making a choice as explained above, he will have to examine and weigh in all its details how large a household he should maintain, how he ought to rule and govern it, how he ought to teach its members by word and example. So too he should consider what part of his means should be used for his family and household and how much should be set aside for distribution to the poor and other pious purposes[115] (189).

Some changes the exercitant makes as a result of this kind of deliberation can be rather small, relatively speaking. For example, someone could decide to amend his life by inaugurating household prayer or a regular household fast day. Small decisions can, however, be enormously important. A three-degree change in course can have significant effects in the long run. Other decisions could substantially change the exercitant's life immediately. For example, someone could reshape his life by choosing to give away a substantial portion of his money, thereby lowering his standard of living.

Many people who make the Exercises have already made a choice about their way of life, so the decisions they make during the Exercises most often fall into the categories of amending or reforming their lives. The director, however, must not forget that Ignatius is putting a fundamental question on the table: Am I called to be actually poor for the sake of the Gospel? If a person is free to undertake a life of actual poverty, he should, normally, deliberate about whether the Lord is calling him to actual poverty or to the normal Christian life.

Sometimes an exercitant can have a big decision to make and yet not show much desire to go forward and make the decision. In this case the director shouldn't lead him through the decision-making process. As the 1599 Directory says, "The nature of this task is such that unless undertaken with fervor of spirit it cannot turn out well. It demands a large, courageous, and persevering spirit arising from heightened devotion."[116] The director has to be careful not to force any election upon someone who has no desire for it. The director should, however, go ahead and teach such an exercitant about decision-making. Such exercitants often leave the retreat and, using the knowledge they have gained, make good choices at riper moments.

At this point in the Exercises, usually about the fifth day of the Second Week, the conversations the director has with the exercitant about decision-making serve a preparatory function. As we've already noted, these conversations take different forms, depending on the exercitant's circumstances, his questions and his experience of God during the retreat. In general, though, the director has several goals for these conversations.

First, the director wants to help the exercitant clarify the matter about which he will be deliberating. Second, the director wants to begin to educate the exercitant about decision-making. Third, the director should be aware of and take advantage of opportunities to teach the exercitant about the second set of rules for discernment of spirits. Talk of decision-making and the specter of real change in the exercitant's life often triggers spiritual activity.

Being clear about the matter for deliberation is an important part of the decision-making process. On the director's part, it's helpful for him to know whether he's dealing with 1) a fundamental election about money and one's way of life, 2) a deliberation about an amendment of life or 3) a deliberation about a reformation of life. On the exercitant's part, it's important for him to be thinking clearly and specifically about the matter to be decided. Initially, the exercitants will often propose a matter for election that is too broad or they will propose several matters at once. By the end of these preliminary conversations, the director and the exercitant should have determined the exact matter about which the exercitant is going to deliberate. At this time, more than any other, the director should listen carefully to what exercitants are trying to say.

Some situations might seem complex and confusing until the director and the exercitant reach some clarity about the matter for deliberation. Suppose, for example, a 60-year-old woman (Mary) wants to deliberate about retiring. She's been a nurse for 35 years. She wants to retire but wonders if she can afford it. She's been volunteering at a local medical clinic for the poor and wants to get more involved there, because they need a nurse. There are several issues involved in this small scenario: retirement, finances and involvement with the poor at the medical clinic. Should Mary retire? Is that the issue? What should Mary do to secure her future financially? Is that something the Lord wants her to think about? It's a big issue. The third issue involves her service at the medical clinic. Is the Lord calling her to do more there? Mary's deliberation will look very different, depending on her starting point.

If Mary begins deliberating about her retirement and looks at her involvement with the medical clinic in light of her finances, the issues surrounding her retirement will sort themselves out one way. If she begins deliberating about whether the Lord is calling her to serve at the medical clinic and looks at her retirement in light of her participation at the medical clinic, the issues might sort out another way. Mary and her director need to talk about where to begin.

Let's say Mary begins deliberating about whether to volunteer more at the clinic. If money keeps coming up as a complicating factor in the decision—if she lets it be a complicating factor—she's making her financial security a higher priority than her involvement at the clinic. Is that a problem? Not necessarily. It may be that God is leading her this way. She might need to lay aside the deliberation about more involvement with the clinic and deliberate first about her financial future. She might say, "I shouldn't be so concerned about money," in which case the director might say, "It could very well be that God wants you to take care of your financial security first."

Sometimes a director might be disappointed in what a person puts on the table to decide. Perhaps the exercitant is free and able to do just about anything for the Lord, but he doesn't want to consider embarking on anything essentially different. Instead of considering how he could change his circumstances, the exercitant thinks only about how to be a better person in his present circumstances. The director, on the other hand, can see radical possibilities for the person and for the Lord.

Ignatius's instructions to directors are very helpful at this point. He tells them not to exert undue pressure on the exercitant and reminds them that they too must be detached:

> The one giving the Exercises must not encourage the exercitant more toward poverty or to the promise of it rather than to the contrary, nor to one state or way of life than to another. Outside the Exercises it can indeed be lawful and meritorious for us to encourage all who seem suitable, to choose . . . every form of evangelical perfection; but during these Spiritual Exercises, it is more opportune and much better that in the search for the divine will the Creator and Lord communicate himself to the faithful soul, inflaming that soul in his love and praise, and disposing her toward the way in which she will be better able to serve him in the future. Hence the giver of the Exercises should not be swayed or show a preference for one side of a choice rather than the other, but remaining in the center like the pointer of a balance should leave the Creator to deal with the creature, and the creature with the Creator and Lord (15, Ivens).

It is the exercitant's choice, not the director's. The director must, at all times, be creating a climate in which the exercitant realizes he is free.

Some directors might be surprised by and dismissive of the things an exercitant wants to consider. Perhaps the exercitant is zealous and wants to leave college or a well-paying job to serve the Lord in a different way, but he is also young and inexperienced. If the director does not take the exercitant seriously, he would be doing him a grave disservice. The director should listen to what the person says about what he is experiencing and be open to God calling someone to do something out of the ordinary.

As the director talks about decision-making with the exercitant, he should emphasize that a choice made during the Exercises is only the first of many. Sometimes a person can be focused on the end product—a decision about something that is looming large on his horizon—but the director knows that each decision only opens the door to more decisions. For this reason, it's helpful for the director to speak of the exercitant's election as the first of other such elections. In fact, usually a person can only make one or two choices during the Exercises themselves. In the above example, Mary might discern that the Lord is calling her to serve more at the medical clinic, so she then decides that she should retire in order to enable this to happen. Later, after the retreat, she will have even more decisions to make. For example, she might consider how much time she should spend at the clinic and whether she should adjust her standard of living in view of the fact that she's now retired. She might want to consider taking a part-time job to supplement her income, and so on. Fortunately, an exercitant can learn not only how to make one good decision but also how to make every decision in union with God.

The director also has to help the exercitant think about his decision-making in the context of friendship. Although the director shouldn't explain a theory of Christian decision-making or try to repeat the whole second chapter of this book, he should watch for misunderstandings on the exercitant's part and forthrightly correct them. For example, if someone seems to be thinking that God is going to make him do something he doesn't want to do, the director might say, "God isn't going to make you do something you don't want to do, but sometimes during the Exercises you discover a desire you didn't know you had, and sometimes a new desire is born."

In these conversations, the director not only helps the exercitant clarify the matter for deliberation, but he also educates the exercitant about decision-making. The whole process of decision-making is a learning experience, but here at the beginning of the process the director wants to make sure a person understands two things in particular. First, he wants to make it clear that the matters about which the exercitant will be deliberating are means to an end, not ends in themselves. This usually entails a review of the Principle and Foundation. Second, he wants to give the exercitant some further instruction concerning "matters about which a choice should be made" (170).

In many ways, the process of decision-making is a laboratory for understanding and implementing the Principle and Foundation. Although the director is, of course, very familiar with the Principle and Foundation and all its implications, he shouldn't gloss over this review too quickly. It's been quite a few days since the exercitant last considered it.

In the section entitled Preamble for Making an Election (169, Ivens), Ignatius provides an example of what this review of the Principle and Foundation should look like. He instructs the exercitant to remember the end for which he is created. Then comes the punch line: "Hence whatever I choose must help me to this end for which I am created. I must not subject and fit the end to the means, but the means to the end" (169). Ignatius goes on to give several examples of what it looks like to confuse means and ends:

> Many first choose marriage, which is a means, and secondarily the service of God our Lord in marriage, though the service of God is the end. So also others first choose to have benefices,[117] and afterward to serve God in them. Such persons do not go directly to God, but want God to conform wholly to their inordinate attachments. Consequently, they make of the end a means, and of the means an end. As a result, what they ought to seek first, they seek last (169).

The language here echoes Ignatius's description of the second class of men, who try to get God "to come to what they desire" (154).

As we've seen, the second class of men choose, for example, the normal Christian life and then choose to serve God in that life, or they choose to pursue music and then choose to serve God with the music. Such people are in effect first choosing to have money and the things that money can buy and then, only second, choosing to serve God with their money and things. Or they are choosing beauty first and the service and praise of God second. So, just before the exercitant starts deliberating about a matter to be decided, the director reminds the exercitant not to mix up the means and the end. He is seeking to serve God first. Everything else is a means to that end. He shouldn't be choosing something and then trying to serve God in and through the thing he has chosen. The exercitant needs to be constantly on guard against making such a mistake.

This review of the Principle and Foundation is especially important for those who are facing a choice between a life of actual poverty and a life of normal Christianity. Often, people are tempted to compare the two ways of life in order to determine which life is better. Such comparisons are not helpful. Both ways of life can lead to deep and abiding friendship with God. After all, in Christ he's rescuing sinners by his life of poverty, humiliations and humility, and in Christ he's reigning, putting all things under His feet by the power of the Holy Spirit. Both ways of life have their temptations, too. Those who live the normal Christian life face temptations to use money for their own benefit, to despise poverty, to avoid insults and contempt and, generally speaking, to live the life of Adam, not the life of Christ. Those who choose actual poverty face temptations to think they are better than other Christians, to love penance too much, to despise the things of the world, and so on.

Exercitants can forget or not understand that both ways of life are means to an end. The issue is not which way of life is better. The issue is which way of life is a more efficacious means for this particular exercitant. The better way of life is the one which will best help a particular exercitant to "praise, reverence, and serve God our Lord, and by this means to save his soul."

Besides making sure that the exercitant understands his decision in light of the Principle and Foundation, the director also needs to give the exercitant some basic instruction regarding "Matters About Which A Choice Should Be Made" (170). As they are talking about decision-making, the director should take a few moments to distinguish between things which one can legitimately make choices about and things one cannot. Thinking clearly about the choices one is making is an essential element of Ignatian decision-making.

First, it is important for the exercitant to understand that he must choose between things which are either "indifferent or good in themselves" (170). So, of course, a person can't make an Ignatian discernment to do something against the laws of God and His Church. For example, he couldn't make an election about whether or not to move in with his girlfriend or embezzle a lot of money. Usually this is fairly obvious to the exercitant. However, exercitants will often speak about their options as if one of them is "the right thing to do" and the other is "the wrong thing to do." Of course, everyday speech is imprecise, but the director should make sure that the exercitant understands that he is choosing between two goods. Sometimes, during the election itself, the director may need to remind someone that he's confronted with a difficult choice precisely because he's choosing between two good things.

Second, it's important for the exercitant to understand that he is deliberating only about those things which are real possibilities for him to do. Some examples will often help make this clear. Let's say an exercitant wants to deliberate about whether or not to join a missionary company. He can decide to offer himself for a particular missionary company, but he can't unilaterally decide to join it. He has to be accepted by the head of the missionary company. Joining it is outside his control. An exercitant may want to decide whether or not to go graduate school, but actually all he can decide is whether to apply to graduate school with the intention of actually going if accepted. He doesn't have control over whether or not he is accepted. In fact, it's not his responsibility to decide who will be in a missionary company or who will be accepted by a particular graduate school. The exercitant should only be deciding about matters for which he is responsible. In these examples, he's deciding to apply for admission.

Often, exercitants and directors will speak as if the exercitant has decided to join a missionary company or to go to graduate school. They are speaking colloquially. The exercitant is actually deciding, for example, to choose to intend to go to graduate school. His intention is to do everything within his power to gain admittance to graduate school. Likewise, a person might choose to intend to join a missionary company. As we'll see in a moment, if the exercitant is not admitted to graduate school or can't join a missionary company, that doesn't mean he has made a poor discernment. It just means that he has another decision to make.

Third, the exercitant is choosing about a present moment. He is not deciding what will happen in the future. Making a choice together with the Lord does not give a person prophetic knowledge of the future. So, for example, an exercitant could decide to choose to intend to sell his antique car and give the money to the poor. Maybe the day after the retreat he drives the car for one last time and gets in an accident, lowering the car's value. Did the exercitant make a poor choice? No. The exercitant decided to choose to intend to sell his car. He wasn't deciding what would happen after he made his choice. Another common example centers around the choice to be married. Actually, a person may choose to intend to be open to marriage. He has no doubt that this is what he should do. He leaves the retreat intending to do what he can to pursue marriage, such as to begin dating. The exercitant makes this decision together with the Lord, for the Lord, in real freedom, but 20 years later he isn't married. Did he make a poor discernment? No. What happened wasn't what he expected, but he made a good choice at the time.

When someone makes a choice and the results are not what he expected, he can be tempted to doubt his choice. He could even begin to doubt whether it is possible to make a choice together with the Lord. Choosing in union with the Lord does not change the nature of life. Life is a series of choices. Even though the Lord is with us, we are like explorers going west without much of a map. At each new fork in the road we have to make a choice, even though we don't know exactly where the roads will lead. We don't know what obstacles lie ahead, nor do we know what beautiful vistas are just around the corner. Occasionally we may find ourselves in what seems to be a box canyon, and then we have to find our way out. We'd like a superior vantage point. We might think that because the Lord is with us and in us we have access to such a vantage point, but He does not give us a map of the future. We could think we can't decide anything because we don't have a map. However, it's a mistake to think we can't decide anything without knowing everything. The reality is quite different. At each fork we can make a decision in union with the Lord. Making a choice or choices during the Exercises is only the beginning. Ignatius is laying the foundation for a lifetime of loving choices made in union with the Lord.

The exercitant also needs to understand that he is not discerning what another person should do.[118] He can only know with certainty what he himself should choose to intend to do. He is not responsible for other people's choices. In fact, other people may decide, in union with the Lord, to oppose the exercitant's intention and they may be successful in doing so.

There's a wonderful illustration of this principle in one of Ignatius's letters to a fellow Jesuit, Francis Borgia. Ignatius did not want Jesuits to become bishops and cardinals. In fact, Jesuits normally made a vow not to accept any such ecclesiastical dignities. In 1552, before Borgia made such a vow, the Emperor Charles V asked the pope to make Borgia a cardinal. When Ignatius heard about it, his first inclination was "to prevent it in any way I could."[119] However, he wasn't at all sure whether this intention was the Lord's. Ignatius didn't yet know what they together thought about what he should do in this situation. Eventually he decided with a "judgment [that] was so conclusive" and a "will so tranquil" to choose to intend to oppose the appointment.[120]

Ignatius knew that he and the Lord were united in the intention to oppose the appointment. He also knew that the pope and the Lord could be united, deciding to choose to intend to make Borgia a cardinal. Ignatius tells Borgia about his choice:

> Consequently, I held and now hold that it is the divine will for me to oppose this [appointment], even though others might think otherwise and bestow this dignity on you. There would be no contradiction at all involved; for the same Divine Spirit is able to move me to that action for certain reasons, and for other reasons to move others to the contrary action and to bring about the result to which the emperor was pointing.[121]

Ignatius wasn't making any claims about whether or not God wanted Borgia to be a cardinal. He also wasn't making any claims about what the pope should do. Nevertheless, he had real certainty that he and God were of one mind and heart about what Ignatius should choose to intend to do.

If the pope made Borgia a cardinal, did that mean that Ignatius was wrong in opposing the appointment? No. If Ignatius correctly discerned that he should oppose the appointment and the pope made Borgia a cardinal, was the pope somehow wrong? No. In such a situation, the question isn't who is right and who is wrong. The question is simply, What next? Life is full of choices, each of which can be made in union with the Lord.

When the director describes "matters about which a choice should be made" (170), he doesn't need to go into as much detail as we have. He should, however, make sure the exercitant knows he is choosing between goods and that he can only make choices about things for which he is responsible. The exercitant should understand the phrase "choose to intend to do" and he should know that he is not making choices about what will happen in the future or about what other people should do. Several well-told examples are a great help in making these points.

Typically, the director initiates an election some time between the fifth and the seventh days of the Second Week. The exercitant has been meditating on Jesus leaving His life in Nazareth and the Apostles leaving their occupations to follow Jesus. He's often using the threefold colloquy of the Two Standards and he's following Ignatius's advice about crushing his inordinate attachments (157, Mullan). The director, for his part, has been talking to and educating the exercitant about decision-making. The director decides to allow an election to begin when he judges the exercitant is sufficiently free from his inordinate attachments. Freedom from inordinate attachments is the necessary prerequisite for beginning an election.

If the director doesn't think someone is sufficiently free from his inordinate attachments, he should not take the exercitant through the decision-making process. If the exercitant is attached to something—riches or honor or health or marriage or education or any other thing—he'll come up with godly reasons for choosing what he wants. Then he'll proceed with his life, in the name of God. Ignatius is adamant that such a person not foist his choice upon God by calling it a divine vocation. "Such an election does not appear, however, to be a divine vocation, since it is disordered and biased. In this many deceive themselves, making a divine vocation out of a biased and wrong election" (172, Ivens). It may seem as if Ignatius is intent on protecting his friend's good name but, in fact, he does not want God being blamed for a choice He had nothing to do with.

If someone isn't free of his inordinate attachments, what should the director do? There are several options, depending on the circumstances. The director can postpone the election for a few days. The director can then keep the exercitant making meditations for two or three more days "so that, partly by his own efforts and partly by asking it of God with fervent prayers, he may gradually be brought to this equilibrium of mind."[122] The director might postpone the election until a future date and continue the Exercises without the election. The director could also simply decide not to lead this particular exercitant through the decision-making process.

Although a director should be careful about starting the election, an overly zealous director could end up never starting an election with anyone. After all, who is ever perfectly free of inordinate attachments? In order to avoid this trap, it's important to realize a couple of things. Some inordinate attachments have no bearing on the decision at hand. For example, an exercitant may have an inordinate attachment to watching movies, but that seems to have little or no bearing on his deliberation about where to live upon retirement. Also, most people (perhaps all, but especially beginners in the spiritual life) are not totally free of inordinate attachments. They can, however, gain sufficient freedom in the secluded environment of the retreat to make a good choice. The director certainly doesn't want inadvertently to teach the exercitant that he has to be perfectly virtuous before he can make decisions for the Lord or together with the Lord. Things have gone awry if the exercitant thinks he can't have union with God until he perfects himself. When in doubt, the director should give the exercitant the benefit of the doubt and go ahead with the election.

Before actually starting an election, the director has one last preparatory exercise to give the exercitant, The Three Kinds of Humility. This isn't a meditation per se. In fact, it's a kind of summary of the Exercises so far. In particular, Ignatius is describing the humility of those in the Lord's camp. He has, after all, said nothing about it so far. In some ways, then, this exercise is a continuation of the Two Standards meditation. As the exercitant deliberates about his decision, these three kinds of humility "should be thought over from time to time during the whole day" (164). As he is considering these three kinds of humility, the exercitant can, whenever he wants, pause and make the threefold colloquy of the Two Standards. His consideration of these kinds of humility is meant to pervade the decision-making process.

In our discussion of the Two Standards, we've already noted how humility in the Lord's camp is manifested in obedience and looks like love. Ignatius himself occasionally called these three kinds of humility, "three kinds of love." In 1538 he gave the Spiritual Exercises to Pedro Ortiz, an ambassador to the papal court, at the famous monastery of Monte Casino. Remarkably, we have the notes Ortiz took during his retreat. Ortiz refers to this section of the Exercises as "Three kinds and degrees of love of God and desire to obey and imitate and serve His Divine Majesty."[123]

Ignatius's sense of timing is impeccable. A person making a decision must make it in the context of a living relationship of love. The whole retreat is aimed at creating such an atmosphere, but just before the election Ignatius has the director do one more thing to heighten the atmosphere. The director asks the exercitant to "consider attentively" (164) what are essentially three ways of loving. It makes sense that Ignatius has something to say about love at this point in the retreat. The person who is free from inordinate attachments is a person who is free to love. His "one desire and choice" (23) is for whatever will more serve and glorify his Lord and King. In other words, he prefers whatever will make his Lord louder, brighter and firmer in the world. Of course, his Lord is at the same time desiring whatever will make him louder, brighter and firmer in the world. At this point in the Exercises there is a remarkable convergence of freedom (no inordinate attachments), obedience (humility) and love.

We began our study of the Exercises by describing three different types of love: implemental love, semipersonal love and personal love. It turns out that Ignatius's presentation of the three kinds of humility maps onto our discussion of three types of love. Implemental love manifests itself in the first kind of humility: "I so subject and humble myself as to obey the law of God our Lord in all things" (165). Semipersonal love manifests itself in the second kind of humility, which is perfect indifference. The exercitant has only "one desire and choice." Personal love manifests itself in the third kind of humility: "I desire and choose poverty with Christ poor, rather than riches; insults with Christ loaded with them, rather than honors; I desire to be accounted as worthless and a fool for Christ, rather than to be esteemed as wise and prudent in this world" (167).

One way to love God is to love Him implementally. That is, I love Him because He is in some way useful or pleasurable. So, for example, I might love Him because He saves me from my sins. I deserve hell, but He gives me heaven. In other words, I love Him as my Savior. Or I might love Him because I find life among His people, in His realm, so much better than life outside the gates, so to speak. He's in charge and He's created a good place for me to live. I love Him as my King. Or I might love Him because He is constantly doing me good. He gives me life, health and strength. He gives my life meaning. I love Him as my Helper. Sometimes I might even love Him because it's a delight and a thrill for me to be associated with someone so powerful and it's a privilege to love someone so perfect. Loving Him is good for me and I am profoundly grateful for all the good He has done for me.

This kind of love is generative. It results in choosing to live in such a way that I don't violate any of the commandments. (This kind of love is integral to the First Week.) I see that my relationship with God brings me great benefits. I don't want to cut myself off from Him. He is King and I want to live in His kingdom, so I'm going to obey His laws and the laws of His church. I'm willing to respect and honor Him in that way. I humble myself and submit to the boundaries He has established. I'll do what is necessary to save my soul. I don't, however, really have any interest in being like Jesus. I'm not at all attracted to His personal life. For example, He was constantly laboring to the point of exhaustion, but I'm motivated by rest and relaxation. I don't want to work that hard, but I'm going to obey at all times, not just when He is watching or when it's convenient or easy. "[N]ot even were I made Lord of all creation, or to save my life here on earth, would I consent to violate a commandment, whether divine or human, that binds me under pain of mortal sin" (165).

The director will go on to talk about more perfect ways of loving God, with the hope that the exercitant will aspire to these more perfect ways of loving. Nevertheless, he must be able to speak of this first kind of love with respect, having the mind and heart of God about it. This way of loving God and relating to Him is literally the difference between heaven and hell for a person. This kind of love is also really good for the world. What a paradise the world would be if everyone obeyed the Ten Commandments, for instance. Besides, God loves the righteous and devout keepers of the Mosaic Law—the Simeons and the Josephs of Arimathea of this world. This way of loving God can even result in martyrdom. The church has many martyrs in her ranks who would not consent to violate a commandment in order to save their lives.

There is another way to love God which is more personal than simply obeying God's laws. We've called this way of loving God "semipersonal love." When I love Him in this way, I begin to see the Lord and relate to Him as someone who is really admirable. As I move closer to Him, pay more attention to Him and get to know Him better, I begin to love Him because of the kind of person He is. (This kind of love is integral to the Second Week.) I admire how merciful He is, how patient He is, how He trusts His Father unconditionally and so on. I'm dazzled by Him personally, but I'm still relating to Him as an interested observer.

This kind of love is also generative. Not only do I want to live in a way that will save my soul, but I also want to live for the praise of His glory. To do this effectively, I strive to be an expert at living out the Principle and Foundation. "I neither desire nor am I inclined to have riches rather than poverty, to seek honor rather than dishonor, to desire a long life rather than a short life" (166). My one "desire and choice" is whatever will better serve and praise my Lord. As we've already seen, in order to live out the Principle and Foundation effectively, I have to get a grip on my inordinate attachments. Again, as we've already seen, inordinate attachments are usually the root causes of the many small or venial sins a person commits. So it turns out that when I love God with a semi-personal love and live out the Principle and Foundation by getting a grip on my inordinate attachments, "not for all creation, nor to save my life, would I consent to commit a venial sin" (166). There's no need to commit a venial sin because I have only one desire and choice.

When someone loves God with this second kind of love, he ends up leading a holy and virtuous life. He avoids committing even small sins. He prays well every day. He fasts and gives alms. He uses his time well. He humbles himself, serving his brothers and sisters gladly and generously. He is careful in his speech and dress and in the way he runs his house so that everything he does pleases the Lord. In fact, he becomes increasingly able to live the Sermon on the Mount and is able to exemplify the detachment of heart that the Lord revealed in the Beatitudes. All this is the fruit of living out the Principle and Foundation.

There is yet a third way of loving God, which is, according to Ignatius, the most perfect way of loving God. Someone might astutely ask, "What could be more perfect than a love which manifests itself in the declaration, 'not for all creation, nor to save my life, would I consent to commit a venial sin'?" There is, however, a love which is "higher and better" (168). It can be quite a shock to an exercitant to discover that his personal holiness isn't the end of the story. Discovering that something so good is a subplot of a much larger story can be very disorienting, especially if the exercitant has devoted much of his life to the pursuit of this kind of perfection. Nevertheless, there is a larger story. After all, the call of Christ the King isn't simply a call to holiness. His call is a call to join Him in conquering the whole world. Some exercitants may be very much surprised to discover that they can actually join Christ in His mission.

This third way of loving the Lord involves more than simply admiring the kind of person He is and all His wonderful qualities. In other words, my love for Him can be more personal. I catch a glimpse of HIM—the splendor of His personal reality—and begin to love Him for His own sake. I love Him because He is who He is; He is the reason I love Him. I don't just want to be like Jesus. I want to be with Him. When I love the Lord in this way, I want to be with Him; but I also want to make His ways my ways. I want to do things the way He does them. I want to make His life my life. I identify with His life and I am eager to participate in it. The Third and Fourth Weeks of the Exercises seem designed to stir up this kind of love. It's possible for me not only to admire Jesus' personal life of poverty, insults and contempt but to want it as my own. He's already loving me in this way—identifying and participating in my life. When I begin to love Him with this third type of love, the door to friendship opens.

How does this kind of love manifest itself? The person who loves the Lord in this way responds like the man in the Kingdom of Christ meditation, who professes that it is his "earnest desire and deliberate choice" to join the Lord "in bearing all wrongs and all abuse and all poverty" (98). In his notes on this third way of loving, Ignatius puts it this way: "whenever the praise and glory of the Divine Majesty would be equally served . . . I want and choose poverty with Christ poor, rather than riches; insults with Christ loaded with them, rather than honors; I desire to be accounted as worthless and a fool for Christ, rather than to be esteemed as wise and prudent in this world" (167). At this point the exercitant is actually very familiar with the second way of loving God. If he's gotten this far, he wants to be able to choose poverty if it were for the greater glory of God. Here, however, the exercitant is confronted with a new possibility, although it's been foreshadowed in the meditation on the Kingdom of Christ. Ignatius is saying that if poverty and riches both equally serve God's glory, the exercitant could, on his own initiative, choose poverty. Why? Just to be with his Lord as much as possible, to share His life in every way.

After presenting the Three Kinds of Love, the director tells the exercitant that he can pray and indeed beg God for the grace to love Him with this third kind of love. If the exercitant wants to love God in this way, "it will help very much" (168) to use the threefold colloquy of the Two Standards. Once again the exercitant can pray for the grace to be with the Lord under His standard "first in the highest spiritual poverty, and should the Divine Majesty be pleased thereby, and deign to choose and accept me, even in actual poverty; secondly, in bearing insults and wrongs" (147). It should be clear by now that Ignatius knows this threefold colloquy is a powerful tool for the exercitant.

The exercitant can, however, make his petition more pointed. He can "petition imploringly (if this pleases the Divine Benevolence) to be led to such an Election."[124] In other words, the exercitant can beg not only to be with the Lord under His standard, but also to have the chance to choose poverty or insults. For this to happen, he has to be in one of two situations. In order to choose, for example, poverty, the exercitant has to be in a situation where the choice of poverty is clearly for God's greater glory. He might also be able to make such a choice if he is choosing between two alternatives, both of which would glorify God to the same degree, and one of which is a life of poverty. Then he would be free to declare his love by choosing poverty.

The responses of exercitants to the Three Kinds of Love can vary greatly. Some exercitants seem to be deaf to the Third Kind of Love. The director presents all three kinds of love, but the third kind may seem to make no impression on the exercitant. When this happens, the director might be tempted to think he didn't make himself clear. He might then repeat himself or say more about the third kind of love, even though this isn't what is needed. When it seems as if the third kind of love doesn't even register with the exercitant, the director should take this as a sign that the exercitant is choosing, at least for the moment, to aspire to no more than the second kind of love. The director should respect the exercitant's choice, even if it seems like a semiconscious choice, and do what he can to secure the exercitant in his resolve to live out the Principle and Foundation.

Sometimes, however, an exercitant's choice to aspire only to the second kind of love can look more like a deliberate rejection of the third kind of love. Often this takes the form of a false humility: "Oh, I'm not worthy of such a love. My sins are so many that I don't dare aspire to such a perfect love. That's for people who are holy, and I certainly can't say I am holy. Join Christ in His saving work? Be Christ? Not me. I'm a sinner." Again, the director should do what he can to help the exercitant live out the Principle and Foundation. This is, however, a more precarious spot for the exercitant. He's in danger of criticizing those who want to live the life of Christ poor. The director should do what he can to help the exercitant admire and support those who aspire to such a love.

Some exercitants have very realistic self-assessments. One exercitant said to us, "I'd like to say I love the Lord the way you described. I've thought about myself and I think I can say that I won't commit a mortal sin, not even to save my life. But I am ashamed to admit that I probably would lie or commit some other venial sin to save my skin or even just my good name." The director should encourage such a person to go ahead and pray for the grace to love the Lord with the third kind of love. The exercitant doesn't have to wait until he is totally free from venial sin before loving the Lord in this personal way.

Some exercitants hear about the possibility of identifying and participating in the Lord's life and say simply, "I want that." Such a declaration provides a great opportunity for the director to confirm them in their aspirations. It is realistic for these exercitants to hope to love the Lord in this way. Some hear about the third kind of love and are aflame with zeal and desire to love the Lord in the best possible way. They are like race horses at the starting gate. The director should encourage them, too, but he may also need to remind them to desire first of all whatever will glorify and serve their King.

Some exercitants are inordinately attached to whatever they believe to be "the best," and this comes to light when they realize that the third way of loving God is better than the second. They hear the word "better" and their freedom seems to vanish. They can feel as if they are somehow obliged to love with this third kind of love. They are in the habit of thinking something like, Only the best for me. This is especially problematic for those who are not at all attracted to Jesus' personal life of poverty and humiliations. Perhaps for the first time in their lives, they aren't attracted to the best. Some exercitants even seem to think that anything less than the best is morally deficient. The director has some tough decisions to make in this case. He might decide to postpone the election and have the exercitant work on his inordinate attachment to being the best. He might also decide to forego the election.

At this point, it's important to note that a person can love the Lord with this third kind of love without necessarily choosing to be actually poor. Great lovers always want to be with their beloved, especially in an hour of trial, but they cannot always do so. A woman might desperately want to be with her husband as he suffers in a distant place, but she doesn't join him. Either the circumstances won't allow it or she chooses to stay where she is and take care of their children and his aging mother, knowing that this is what her husband wants. Another person might want to join Jesus, preaching the Good News, going from place to place without anywhere to lay his head. He doesn't do this, however, because he's too sick or because the Lord has asked him to do something else.

Exercitants can, in fact, earnestly desire and choose "insults with Christ loaded with them, rather than honors" and "to be accounted as worthless and a fool for Christ, rather than to be esteemed as wise and prudent in this world" without having the chance to choose poverty with Christ poor. In Ignatius's Autograph Directory he remarks that an exercitant can choose two things in this regard:

> The first is, where it is equally for God's service and without scandal or harm to the neighbor, to desire injuries, opprobrium, and abasement in all things with Christ, in order to be clothed in his livery and imitate him in this aspect of his cross. The other is to be willing to suffer patiently anything of this kind whenever it should befall him for love of Christ our Lord."[125]

The director presents the Three Kinds of Love so that the exercitant is aware of all the possibilities for love. To put it succinctly, the exercitant can aspire to be good, to be very good, or to be a friend of Jesus. A person can be a friend of Jesus in any circumstance. The person who loves the Lord with this kind of personal love may not be poor, but he does have eyes to see the Lord. He is able to recognize Him alive in the world today even when He has "no form or comeliness that we should look at him, and no beauty that we should desire him" (Is. 53:2).

After considering the Three Kinds of Humility, the exercitant is usually ready to begin the decision-making process. He and his director have determined the matter about which he is going to deliberate. The exercitant is learning to recognize and to fight the Enemy's desolations and consolations. He's also becoming more skilled at identifying and cooperating with the Lord's consolations. He has been prepared both intellectually and affectively. Intellectually, he's been educated about decision-making. He's thought about the Principle and Foundation again and he knows what he can and cannot make choices about. Affectively, he's crushed his inordinate attachments, and his meditations on the life of Jesus and the Three Kinds of Humility have enkindled love for the Lord. The next step is to begin the election.

CHAPTER 12

THREE TIMES TO MAKE A DECISION

Writing about the Spiritual Exercises is like trying to describe a piece of music with the written word. Like a symphony, the Exercises contain several motifs: overcoming one's inordinate attachments, growing in love of Jesus, saving the world, recognizing and overcoming the work of the Enemy, and recognizing and cooperating with consolations from the Lord. At the election these motifs come together in a rich, harmonious way.

As he begins the decision-making process, the exercitant is, ideally, aware of his inordinate attachments. In fact, he should have reached the point of indifference, standing before the alternatives like a balance at equilibrium. Some exercitants will have come to the point of preferring to "choose poverty with Christ poor rather than riches, opprobrium with Christ replete with it rather than honors; and to desire to be treated as worthless and a fool for Christ, Who first was held as such, rather than wise or prudent in this world," provided "the praise and glory of the Divine Majesty being equal" (167). As Ignatius's close associate Juan Alfonso de Polanco pointed out, "The reason for this is the same one that leads us (as the Philosopher says) to straighten a stick by bending it in the opposite direction."[126] We'd prefer to say "a reason" instead of "the reason," but the point remains.

The exercitant enters the election free from the influence of his inordinate attachments, though sometimes bloody from the fight. Because his "one desire and choice" are whatever will most "praise, reverence and serve God our Lord," he's free to make a decision out of love for the Lord. What does it look like for a person to choose something out of love for the Lord? Ignatius gives us three pictures of what it can look like. He describes them as "three times for making, in any one of them, a sound and good election" (175, Mullan).

It's important to remember that, while the exercitant is considering his choices, he continues to make meditations on the life of Jesus. Ignatius does, however, recommend that the director lighten the exercitant's schedule to allow more time and energy for the election. Instead of meditating on two mysteries a day, the exercitant meditates on one a day. Generally speaking, he still makes two repetitions and an application of the senses. This results in four meditation periods a day instead of the usual five. This might amount to an hour with the director and four hours praying the meditations: a total of five hours, leaving about nine hours to pray about the election each day. If need be, the director could reduce it to three meditation periods a day.

Although the director might reduce the number of meditations, he doesn't normally want to eliminate them altogether. They are integral to the decision-making process. As the early Jesuits noted, "The nature of this task is such that unless undertaken with fervor of spirit it cannot turn out well. It demands a large, courageous and persevering spirit arising from heightened devotion."[127] In fact, "if the mind is exclusively occupied with the thoughts of the election, its juice and flower of devotion might easily be sucked dry and exhausted and the soul enfeebled."[128] The exercitant wants to make a decision out of love for the Lord. The meditations stir up that love.

FIRST-TIME DECISIONS

What does it look like for the exercitant's love of God to determine his choice? Occasionally, "God our Lord so moves and attracts the will, that without doubting, or being able to doubt, such devout soul follows what is shown it as St. Paul and St. Matthew did in following Christ our Lord" (175, Mullan). Occasionally, the exercitant's election doesn't seem to involve any deliberation. The exercitant has some kind of encounter with God, at His initiative, which results in a decision. The exercitant has no doubt about what he wants to do, and he is sure that his newfound desire is from God. These kinds of decisions are what Ignatius calls "first-time" decisions.

Ignatius himself recounts what appears to be a first-time decision in his autobiography. He had decided to abstain from meat and then, at God's instigation, he decided to eat meat on a regular basis:

> While he was carrying out his abstinence from meat, without any thought of changing it, one morning as he got up, a dish of meat appeared before him as though he actually saw it with his eyes. But he had no antecedent desire for it. At the same time he felt within himself a great movement of the will to eat it in the future. Although he remembered his former resolve, he could not hesitate to make up his mind that he ought to eat meat. Relating this to his confessor later, the confessor told him that he ought to have found out whether this was a temptation. But he, examine it as he would, could never have any doubt about it.[129]

It's important to note that, even though Ignatius was willing to examine the experience to see if it was a temptation, he simply "could not have any doubt about it." In fact, Ignatius finally concluded that "any doubt about it would be an offense against His Divine Majesty."[130]

Ignatius's picture of this kind of decision-making is a bit blurry, to say the least. Judging from the three examples we have, the experience varies. St. Paul seems to have had an intensely personal encounter with God. As Saul, the Pharisee, he loved God. He carefully observed the Mosaic Law and was blameless according to it (Phil. 3:6). Eventually, though, his love became personal. On the road to Damascus he saw and accepted God's revelation of Himself. "I am Jesus whom you are persecuting." Ignatius's encounter, however, doesn't seem as intimate. We don't know very much about Matthew's experience, other than that he heard Jesus say, "Follow me." Immediately, Matthew "rose and followed him," freely consenting to leave everything and accept the call (Mt. 9:9). It's not the experience itself that Ignatius emphasizes, however. It's the outcome of the experience that's significant. The exercitant knows, seemingly without deliberating, what he wants to do with and for the Lord. The exercitant has no doubt about what to do.

Outside the Exercises, small first-time decisions seem to happen fairly often for someone with the second or third kind of love. The matter may be small, but the person knows without a doubt and without deliberation what he and the Lord desire to do. It's just obvious. First-time decisions are not as frequent with matters of great import, however. During the Exercises, the director must be alert to the possibility of a first-time decision even if the majority of exercitants will probably make what Ignatius calls a "second-time" decision or a "third-time" decision.

Sometimes, then, when an exercitant makes a choice, he "follows what has been manifested" to him without "doubting or being able to doubt" (175, Puhl and Mullan), but this is not the only way he can make a choice out of love for God. An exercitant can also make a second-time choice. This happens "when enough light and understanding is received by experience of consolations and desolations, and by the experience of the discernment of various spirits" (176, Mullan). If the exercitant isn't experiencing consolations and desolations, he can make a third-time decision. For pedagogical reasons, we'll first explain third-time decisions, followed by second-time decisions.

THIRD-TIME DECISIONS

Experientially, the difference between a second-time decision and a third-time decision has to do with the state of the exercitant's feelings. During a second-time decision the exercitant experiences consolations and desolations. As we've seen, consolations are marked by warm, affective feelings of love. Desolations are marked by a loss of relish for spiritual things and feelings of sadness, dejection, confusion and so on. In other words, the exercitant experiences many emotions, sometimes strong emotions, during the course of a second-time decision. In a third-time decision, the exercitant is experiencing a time of emotional tranquility. It's a "time of quiet, when the soul is not acted on by various spirits, and uses its natural powers freely and tranquilly" (177, Mullan).

If an exercitant is not experiencing a lot of warm sentiments of affection for God, how does he make a choice? Briefly put, he thinks clearly and rationally about his alternatives and then judges which alternative would be more for God's praise, reverence and service and the salvation of his soul. He measures his alternatives in light of the Principle and Foundation and then chooses. Although the calm use of the exercitant's rational faculties plays a big role in this kind of decision-making, it's a mistake to think that love isn't involved. Just because a person isn't experiencing consolations doesn't mean he isn't loving God. The exercitant's love can be strong, committed and firm, even though feelings of love are, for all practical purposes, absent.

A third-time decision is quite common for beginners in the spiritual life as well as for those well advanced in the spiritual life. Although most exercitants would prefer their love to be suffused with warm affection—and rightly so—they are, in fact, making a choice out of love for God when they make a third-time decision. God is the reason the exercitant chooses to do what he does—not the exercitant's own happiness, financial well-being or reputation. The exercitant chooses a course of action so that the Lord may shine more brightly into the world.

Most exercitants would rather be making a second-time decision than a third-time decision. That is to say, they would rather be experiencing consolations as they make a decision. After all, "the affective act of love without the appropriate feelings of love is not a full human response to the loved one."[131] Of course, whether the exercitant experiences consolations is beyond the director's control, but, according to Ignatius, there are several things the director can do to help dispose the exercitant to consolations:

> When he who is giving the Exercises sees that no spiritual movements, such as consolations or desolations, come to the soul of him who is exercising himself, and that he is not moved by different spirits, he ought to inquire carefully of him about the Exercises, whether he does them at their appointed times, and how. So too of the Additions, whether he observes them with diligence. Let him ask in detail about each of these things (6, Mullan).

The director can also recommend that a person do some penance. Ignatius says that one reason to do penance is "to seek and find some grace or gift which the person wants and desires" such as "tears, consolations, etc." (87, 89, Mullan).

If, however, the exercitant is in a state of tranquility, how does he make a third-time decision? Ignatius actually lays out two ways an exercitant can make a sound and good election in a time of tranquility. The first way to make a third-time decision involves six steps. Briefly, Ignatius recommends, first, that the exercitant get the matter for choice clearly in his mind's eye; second, that he keep his end clearly before him, being indifferent to all else; third, that he ask the Lord to guide him to a good decision; fourth, that he make lists of pros and cons; fifth, that he deliberate and make a decision; and sixth, that he go before the Lord, offering him his decision and asking for confirmation. Ignatius lays out this method, in what is for him quite a lot of detail, in paragraphs 178-183.

In order to examine this decision-making method in more detail, it's helpful to have an example in mind. David is a lawyer in his late 30s. He graduated from law school six years ago. He's married with four children. Law school and the long hours it entailed were hard on his family. Currently his family seems to be prospering. He became a lawyer because he saw it as a way of serving God and His people. In particular, he knows he's been called by God to be a minister of justice. He's a member of a small but growing firm of 10 lawyers. He sees his law firm as filling a real need for affordable legal counsel in his local area. He's been able to form good Christian relationships in the firm and to help make the corporate environment a good place for dedicated Christians to work. He says his present salary is adequate, even generous. He wasn't looking for a new job, but unexpectedly he has received a job offer from a large law firm. The firm employs 200 lawyers, with 40 lawyers in the local office. He's acquainted with a few of the firm's lawyers, but doesn't have any real relationship with them. David is being offered twice as much money as he's making presently.

The offer is attractive to David for three reasons: 1) He suspects his call from God to be a minister of justice might eventually include serving Him as a judge and thinks that working in this larger firm would position him for a judgeship. 2) If he took this higher-paying job, he could give the increase in net income to the work of the Lord. 3)

Working at the larger firm would give him more contact with the people who influence things in town. He thinks it is very much to the advantage of God's people to have some allies in the local halls of power.

David has a choice of working in the local office or in the firm's office in the state capitol. He quickly decides only to consider working in the firm's local office. He's a member of the People of Praise, and the People of Praise doesn't have a branch in the state capitol. He's confident of the decision he made to be a member of the People of Praise and he sees no reason to change it. In fact, one thing he appreciates about his current situation is that his participation in the community and the work he does there have been appreciated and accepted by his colleagues. Of course, there are still many factors to consider about the decision. David knows the new job would entail longer hours. How will the longer hours affect his family? Will he continue to have time and energy to devote to the work of the Lord in the People of Praise?

With this example clearly in mind, we can now take a closer look at the first way to make a third-time decision. Ignatius recommends that a person first "put before me the thing on which I want to make election" (178, Mullan). As much as possible, the exercitant ought to have his alternatives clearly before his mind's eye. In David's case, he ought to consider what his life would look like if he worked for the larger firm. For example, how would his daily, weekly and monthly schedules change? He might picture himself in an office where he doesn't know very many people and so on. He isn't making a theoretical decision; his decision will impact almost every area of his life. David also needs to keep his choice clearly defined. He's not deciding whether or not to become a judge. A judgeship is not on the table. No one has appointed or elected him. He's simply deciding whether to accept a job offer from a law firm.

As the exercitant makes a third-time decision, he needs to exercise a twofold vigilance. First, he has "to keep as aim the end for which I am created" (179, Mullan). He ought to be asking himself how a particular option will be more for the glory and praise of God. It is, however, very easy for the exercitant's deliberations to degenerate into a consideration of how a particular option will be good for him personally. For example, David could begin deliberating about which job situation would best serve God, and end up deliberating about which job situation would make the best use of his talents. He needs to keep his primary goal ever before him.

An exercitant also has to be on guard against inordinate attachments in order to maintain his indifference. Although he may enter the deliberation indifferent, the act of deliberating about something very real in his life can bring an unsuspected inordinate attachment to the surface. For example, as David is considering life in a big law firm, he might discover that he abhors the thought of being a small fish in a big pond. In his current situation he's a big fish in a small pond and he loves that. Unless he takes action against this inordinate attachment, David will end up finding reasons to stay in his small firm, and it won't be a decision he made with and for the Lord. He'll end up trying to negotiate with God in order to keep what he desires, just as the second class of men do.

If he exercises this twofold vigilance, the exercitant will be able to "be not more inclined or disposed to take the thing proposed than to leave it, nor more to leave it than to take it, but find myself as in the middle of a balance, to follow what I feel to be more for the glory and praise of God our Lord and the salvation of my soul" (179, Mullan). As he thinks about his alternatives, the exercitant isn't inclined one way or the other. The alternatives leave the exercitant cold, so to speak. Some exercitants may find this state of indifference disconcerting. It's not what they expected that choosing for God's glory would feel like. The director's encouragement can be especially helpful here. The exercitant actually may be in a great place to make a third-time decision.

Once the exercitant has the matter for choice and his purpose in life clearly in his mind's eye, he asks the Lord, even begs the Lord, to guide him to a good decision, in order to "promote more His praise and glory" (180, Mullan). He asks for a clear mind and a pure heart. This prayer and faith in its efficacy are crucial to the whole process. The exercitant should not omit it or make it halfheartedly.

How, then, does a person choose what would be more for the glory and praise of God? He considers his options in light of his purpose in life by making what we call a "pros and cons list." Ignatius says that the exercitant considers a course of action's "advantages and utilities" and its "disadvantages and dangers" (181, Mullan). Frequently, an exercitant has one particular choice to make. For example, David is deliberating about accepting a job offer. His pros and cons list has four columns. He considers the advantages and disadvantages of accepting the job offer, and he also considers the advantages and disadvantages of not accepting the offer. In David's case, the latter meant he had to consider the advantages and disadvantages of remaining in his present situation. If necessary, an exercitant can spend several days working on his pros and cons list. The list is worth a lot of thought, and sleeping on it is often a big help. Talking about the list with the director is also very helpful. In fact, the exercitant should actually show his list to his director. Doing this will enable the director to guide him better. Again, it's important to note that a person is considering how a particular course of action is to God's advantage.

Although the director has to be careful not to push the exercitant toward any particular alternative, he can still make some helpful contributions to the third-time deliberation process. He can point out poor reasoning on the exercitant's part. For example, if the list of advantages for accepting the new job includes, "I'll be able to be a better husband and father because I'll be able to buy my wife and children nicer things," the director can and should initiate a conversation about this. More buying power does not make a man a better husband and father. In addition to correcting faulty reasoning, the director can also make sure the exercitant is considering all the facts. For example, if David says that accepting the job offer will enable him to give an additional X dollars to the work of the Lord, the director might ask whether there are any hidden costs in working for this law firm. After considering the hidden costs—more lunches out, a longer commute, better clothing, perhaps a newer, more reliable car and so on—David can better estimate what more he can give to the work of the Lord.

As the exercitant considers how and to what degree a particular course of action will make God louder, brighter and firmer in the world, he should also consider whether he has the personal wherewithal to accomplish it. In other words, the exercitant should ask himself, What's the probability that I can actually do this? For example, David thinks that accepting the job offer from the larger firm will enable him to be an ambassador for God's people in the local halls of power. He should ask himself, Is that attainable, or is it wishful thinking? David might conclude that he's not likely to be such an ambassador because he knows he doesn't have a diplomatic or political bone in his body. He might think that God will provide for what he lacks, but exercitants ought not to count on such miracles in a third-time election.

Some exercitants find it helpful to assign numerical values to their lists of advantages and disadvantages. For example, David could take each of his listed advantages and assign it a number between 0 and 10, depending on how much he thought it contributed to his goal of serving God. David might assign a 6 to "give the increase in net income to the work of the Lord." Next David would take each of his listed advantages and assign it another number between 0 and 1, indicating the probability that David would actually do the thing in question. David might assign "give the increase in net income to the work of the Lord" a 0.3 probability. Then David would multiply the two numbers, arriving at an overall score for each advantage. "Giving the increase in net income to the work of the Lord" would get an overall score of 1.8 (6 x 0.3). An exercitant could, using negative numbers from 0 to 10, do the same with his disadvantages. Then, totaling all the plusses and minuses, he arrives at a number which indicates the weight and worth of an option. Exercitants should not be bound by these numbers, but this exercise does help some of them focus and clarify their thinking. It also gives the director a window into their thinking.

After weighing his alternatives, using a pros and cons list, the exercitant decides which alternative would be more for God's praise, reverence and service and the well-being of his soul. As always, he should be on guard against inordinate attachments interfering with his deliberation. Also the exercitant must have a clear idea of what makes something more for the glory of God. He's deciding in which alternative he, personally, can best serve God's purposes. Two exercitants with identical choices and identical pros and cons lists could very well decide two different things. David might decide that it's more for God's glory to remain where he is. Another exercitant in the same circumstances might decide to accept the job offer. A third exercitant might decide, rather unexpectedly, to turn down the job offer but to look for a better way to position himself for a judicial career. Making a choice is a highly personal moment.

If, in a time of tranquility, an exercitant is unable to come to a decision, he can use Ignatius's second way of making a third-time choice (184-187). This way of decision-making seems to be less analytical than the first way. It begins with the exercitant checking himself to make sure that it is the love of God which is moving him. Ignatius puts it this way: "The first is that that love which moves me and makes me choose such a thing should descend from above, from the love of God, so that he who chooses feel first in himself that that love, more or less, which he has for the thing which he chooses, is only for his Creator and Lord" (184, Mullan). Although the exercitant is in a time of tranquility and therefore not experiencing a lot of warm affection for God, Ignatius assumes that he can make his choice out of love for God.

When using the second way of making a third-time decision, the exercitant considers three scenarios. First, he asks himself what advice he would give to someone else in a similar position, someone who wanted above all else to praise, reverence and serve the Lord. In the Spanish edition of the *Spiritual Exercises*, Ignatius directs the exercitant to consider a man whom he has never seen or known. In the later, more polished Latin version, he directs the exercitant to consider a friend. In our experience, this particular exercise often works better if the exercitant considers someone he knows and has some affection for.

After considering what advice he'd give to a friend, the exercitant considers himself on his deathbed, and then before the Lord on the day of his judgment. An exercitant might expect to ask himself: What decision would I wish to have made? Although that's a good question and it can trigger a good decision, Ignatius's advice to the exercitant is slightly different. The exercitant asks himself how he would "want to have deliberated about the present matter" (187, Mullan) and what procedure and norm of action he would "wish to have followed in making the present choice" (186). Ignatius seems to be emphasizing not the content of the decision but the manner of making it. As he considers himself on his deathbed, David might conclude, I wish I'd done more research about the larger firm and consulted some wise lawyers about my choice. After imagining himself giving an account of his choice to God, David might conclude, even though disappointing his earthly father was not on his pros and cons list, I'd hate to have to say to my Lord, "Well, I made that decision because I didn't want to disappoint my father."

The first way of making a decision in a time of tranquility and the second way both end identically. The exercitant has been thinking a lot. Eventually he gets to the place where he knows for sure what he wants to do out of love for God. The exercitant makes a decision on account of Him. In other words, God is the cause of the decision. Once the exercitant makes his decision, he should then offer it to God as a kind of gift. "Such election, or deliberation, made, the person who has made it ought to go with much diligence to prayer before God our Lord and offer Him such election, that His Divine Majesty may be pleased to receive and confirm it" (183, Mullan). Of course, as always, when the exercitant asks something of His Divine Majesty, he does so respectfully, not presuming to tell his King what to do, but humbly submitting his request.

What does it mean to ask in this way for confirmation? Ignatian scholars differ on this point, as do directors. We recommend that the exercitant ask the Lord to "confirm me," not to "confirm my decision." The exercitant has just made a decision in a state of tranquility. He hasn't experienced much desire or inclination for any particular alternative. Now that the choice is made, he's asking the Lord to affirm him, the choice-maker. He's asking the Lord to give him some heart for his choice and for the zeal and energy that come from a heart enkindled. He's asking for the joy that comes from a good decision. He's asking for strength and encouragement. In short, he's asking for a consolation, a felt experience of loving God in and through the thing he has chosen. Sometimes the exercitant experiences the answer to his prayer right away, but often the confirming consolation comes at some point in the next two weeks of the Exercises. If, however, the exercitant is not moved by a consolation, he should still act on his decision. Lack of consolation doesn't mean his election wasn't sound.

We don't recommend that the exercitant pray for proof that he's made the right decision. For one thing, there's the danger of an infinite regress here. The exercitant makes a decision and then asks for proof. He gets confirmation, but then he asks, Is that really from the Lord? Is that proof? So then he prays for confirmation of the confirmation, and so on. More importantly, when the exercitant makes a choice he should be confident that he's made a good and sound election. If he lacks such confidence, he should keep deliberating. Once the exercitant makes a decision, he shouldn't then put the decision into question by praying for proof. Making a decision and then asking, Did I get this right?, is like having a tooth filled and then pulling out the filling to see if it fits correctly.

SECOND-TIME DECISIONS

Some people think that the best time to make a decision is when they are experiencing a time of emotional tranquility. After all, don't strong emotions cloud their vision? Some people even say that a person ought not make a decision unless he has "free and peaceful use" of his soul's natural powers. They ask, "Isn't the human heart too fickle to trust?" We all can think of people who have followed their hearts and ended up mired in sin. Some loves—inordinate ones—do cloud people's vision and lead them off track.

If, however, a person is experiencing a lot of consolations and desolations—which means his heart is far from tranquil—Ignatius says that person can make "a sound and good election." In fact, if the exercitant is experiencing a lot of consolations and desolations, it's an ideal time to make a decision. During this time, "much light and understanding are derived through experience of desolations and consolations and discernment of diverse spirits" (176).

At first glance, it looks as if Ignatius says very little about these second-time decisions. In fact, he says a great deal about the experience of consolations and desolations in his Rules for Discernment of Spirits. The director needs to be intimately acquainted with these rules, always on the lookout not only for true consolations but also for all the graces God is giving an exercitant. Likewise, he always has to be alert not only to the Enemy's desolations but also to all the other ways he tries to harass, derail, tempt or trick the exercitant.

It's especially important to remember two things about consolations and desolations. First, they are spiritual events in which a person encounters either God or Satan. Such encounters are marked by very human emotions: joy, hope, zeal, ardor, love, faith, discouragement, listlessness, dejection, hopelessness and so on. Often, the exercitant is acutely aware of his own feelings (i.e., movements of the soul) and only vaguely aware of the person he's just encountered; hence the need for discernment. Second, a person can experience joy, hope, zeal, ardor, discouragement, listlessness, hopelessness, etc., because of many things, not just because of encounters with God or Satan.

As we've seen, in a first-time decision, "God our Lord so moves and attracts the will that without doubting or being able to doubt such a devout soul follows what is shown to it" (175). In a second-time decision God is also moving and attracting the exercitant's will, but the exercitant is not able to respond immediately "without doubting or being able to doubt." He isn't certain, at least initially, where his love for God is leading him. The exercitant is experiencing consolations from God but no one consolation has taken away all doubt as to what he should choose to intend to do. The Enemy is also active during this time, muddying the waters, so to speak.

How, then, does someone make a second-time decision? He keeps thinking and praying about his decision until he can respond to God without doubt. It takes time, but he can get to a point where he knows, without a doubt, what he wants to do out of love for God. The exercitant reaches this point on account of a preponderance of consolations from God. Also, being able to correctly discern the Enemy is integral to the exercitant's ability to know without a doubt how to respond to God.

Second-time decisions are difficult to describe because each exercitant's experience of God and the Enemy is unique. Nevertheless, there are some observations we can make about these decisions. Typically, in a second-time decision, the exercitant is making meditations and having colloquies with the Lord. While making meditations he should focus on the meditation, not on the decision before him, but in his colloquy he's free to talk with the Lord about the choice before him. If, however, he experienced consolation during the meditation, it's helpful for him to first talk to the Lord about what moved him in the consolation. After his prayer, he should reflect on his experience, especially his consolations. At other times during the retreat, the exercitant is thinking and praying about his decision.

Often the exercitant notices a pattern in his consolations. For example, he might notice that every time he thinks of a particular option he's filled with more faith, more hope and more love. He's consoled. With the thought of doing this particular thing comes a consolation. He may then come to the conclusion that this particular option has more potential for him loving and serving God. It has the greater love-of-God payoff, so to speak. Or the process may be reversed: the exercitant might notice that, when he is consoled, he's attracted to a particular course of action. With the consolation comes a desire to do a particular thing. Again, the exercitant doesn't make his decision on account of one consolation. Rather, by reflecting on his experience, he notices a pattern in the consolations. Eventually, by using the preponderance of consolations as evidence, the exercitant concludes that God is leading him to a particular course of action.

Occasionally, an exercitant will try to pray about two alternatives at the same time. He is consoled, but doesn't get any light from his consolations. In such a case, it's helpful for the exercitant to take a period of time and pray about one alternative and then to take another period of time and pray about a second alternative, noticing if and how he is moved in his prayer.

Normally, an exercitant should not make a decision on the basis of a single consolation. If he knows, without doubt, what he wants to do after a single consolation, it's probably a first-time decision. Second-time decisions take time. The decision emerges as if out of a fog.

When praying about a decision, the exercitant is, of course, very focused on that particular decision. Sometimes, though, God wants to broaden the conversation. He's not so interested in the decision at hand. One time, we were directing an exercitant who had previously made a good decision not to pursue marriage. On his retreat he was reexamining this issue and praying about whether he should be open to marriage. After one consolation, he sensed that God "didn't want him to be alone." It would have been easy for him to jump to a decision to begin dating. Upon further prayer and discussion with his director, he realized that he needed to look at his whole life. He had been making a long series of decisions that isolated him from other Christians. He left the retreat having made several good second-time decisions to reshape his life and having decided to postpone dating for another year.

Sometimes an exercitant enters the retreat hoping to make a particular decision, and leaves the retreat having made the expected decision. Sometimes, though, the experience of consolations and desolations is like a matrix out of which an unexpected decision is born. The exercitant is praying and revealing himself more and more to his Lord. God is also revealing Himself. The exercitant is coming to know Him more and love Him more. As he experiences these consolations, the exercitant sees something that he could do for and with the Lord. A decision is born out of their relationship. It's their mutual decision.

If all someone had to do to make a second-time decision was pray and pay attention to his consolations, his decision would be relatively easy to make. However, during a second-time decision, the exercitant is not only encountering God, he's also frequently encountering the Enemy of his soul. Satan's activity during this time makes the process more complicated. It takes time for the exercitant to recognize and filter out the noise caused by the Enemy.

It's quite common for a person to experience desolation coming on the heels of consolation. For example, during one prayer period, as he thinks about choosing actual poverty, an exercitant feels drawn to love God more, seemingly inexplicably. He feels great enthusiasm for a life of poverty. In his next prayer period, maybe just a couple of hours later, as he prays about poverty he feels dread, as if a cold wind is blowing through his soul.

The experience of consolation followed by desolation can be disorienting and confusing. The exercitant asks himself things like: What's going on? Am I double-minded? Is there some kind of inordinate attachment involved? Was I really drawn to love God in the first place? Was that first consolation from God or was it just my imagination? Of course, the answers to his questions are more complicated. The exercitant needs to examine his experiences. The first experience was real. If it had a good beginning, middle and end, it was probably a consolation from God. The second experience was also real, but it too needs to be examined. Let's say that, upon reflection, the exercitant remembers having thought that God will surely abandon him if he steps out in faith. Then he felt a cold dread. If that's the case, he wasn't experiencing God in that second prayer period. He was encountering the Enemy. What should the exercitant do? Among other things, he should make acts of faith, in order to counterpunch. He should also keep praying, until he's sure about how his love for God is moving him.

It's possible that, as an exercitant savors a genuine consolation, the Enemy enters into the afterglow and suggests something. For example, in a consolation, an exercitant senses that God doesn't want him to be alone, and then in the afterglow the Enemy suggests that God doesn't want the exercitant to be celibate. Of course, it's also possible that on his own an exercitant could, upon sensing that God doesn't want him to be alone, rashly jump to the conclusion that God doesn't want him to be celibate. The surety that God doesn't want him to be alone could be from God, but the conclusion about celibacy is something the exercitant comes to on his own. It's his own idea, not God's and not Satan's. Exercitants (and directors) need to pay attention to the actual consolation and be wary about what follows in the afterglow.

Some exercitants also experience consolations from the Enemy. Suppose, for example, an exercitant is praying about a life of actual poverty. Each time he thinks about a life of actual poverty, his heart is moved with delight and fervor at the thought of how such a life would glorify God. After a while, however, he begins to notice that such considerations eventually leave him dry, dissatisfied and sad. Although he is moved with love for God, he ends up wanting to flee God's presence because he thinks he can't live such a life. The exercitant and his director eventually conclude that the delight and fervor the exercitant experienced were a consolation from the Enemy. The consolation began well, but it ended with the exercitant wanting to flee God's presence.

If consolations from the Enemy go unnoticed, they create confusion and delay the decision-making process. If discerned, they can also wreak havoc because an inexperienced exercitant can begin to doubt all his consolations. While it's necessary to examine the beginning, middle and end of consolations, it's not necessary to doubt them all. In fact, if the exercitant's consolation is without a previous cause, he can be sure he just encountered God personally.

Because they are afraid of being deceived, some exercitants might even want to abandon the second-time decision-making process and opt for a third-time decision, which is of course always a possibility, but it's important to remember that the Enemy can be discerned and that at least some of the time the exercitant is being moved by God. It's not good for the exercitant to close his heart to God's consolations out of fear. A good director can be a great help in such situations. He should above all exude confidence that the Enemy can be discerned.

The Enemy can be discerned, but the exercitant can't simply look at what the Enemy is doing and then use that to figure out what God is doing. If, for example, an exercitant experiences desolation when he thinks about actual poverty, it doesn't mean God is calling him to be actually poor. Likewise, if an exercitant is moved to desire actual poverty in a consolation from the Enemy, it doesn't mean that God wants him to embrace the ordinary Christian life. Sometimes, for instance, the Enemy may move an exercitant to desire exactly what God wants, but in the process he insinuates a selfish or disordered motive.

Although the exercitant experiences many—sometimes strong—emotions during a second-time decision, reason still has a role to play in the process. For one thing, as in a third-time decision, the exercitant needs to be thinking clearly and realistically about the matter for choice. For example, if he is considering a life of actual poverty in order to preach the Gospel, he should understand that this might very well mean he'll often be hungry and he'll spend a lot of time with strangers, talking with them about the Lord and so on.

Furthermore, during a second-time decision the exercitant should be weighing the choices before him, in the same way he does during a third-time decision. He thinks about what is the best way to praise, reverence and serve his Lord. He asks himself the same kinds of questions he asks in a third-time decision: How will this course of action help me achieve my goal as it is elucidated in the Principle and Foundation? What's the long-term benefit of this course of action for God's glory? The short term benefit, and so on? He may very well make a list of pros and cons. He does not, however, make a third-time decision. His evidence for the decision is different. In a second-time decision his criterion is his consolations—the movements of his soul that are from God. In a third-time decision the exercitant doesn't have the movements of his soul to guide him, so he uses his reason to figure out what is more for God's glory.

Second-time decisions are difficult to describe because each one is unique. Fortunately, we have Ignatius's account of two of his own second-time decisions. Each is illuminating in its own way, but neither is a textbook case of decision-making. In the end, that might be what is most helpful about them. Christian decision-making is an art, not a science, more like medicine than mathematics.

In his autobiography, Ignatius describes a decision that arose out of the matrix of spiritual activity in his life. At the dawn of his new life in Christ, as he was convalescing from his cannonball wound, Ignatius read a life of Christ and a book on the lives of the saints. Often, "pausing in his reading, he gave himself up to thinking over what he had read" (6). Frequently he found himself thinking, "Suppose that I should do what St. Francis did, what St. Dominic did?" (7). At other times he would spend two, three or even four hours "fancying what he would do in the service of a certain lady. . . . He was so enamored with all this that he did not see how impossible it would all be, because the lady was of no ordinary rank; neither countess, nor duchess, but of a nobility much higher than any of these" (6).

Gradually, Ignatius began to notice something. "When he was thinking of the things of the world he was filled with delight, but when afterward he dismissed them from weariness, he was dry and dissatisfied" (8). On the other hand, Ignatius noticed that when he thought about imitating the saints and their penances "he was consoled, not only when he entertained these thoughts, but even after dismissing them he remained cheerful and satisfied" (8). At first he paid no attention to this, but one day "his eyes were opened a little" and he began to seriously consider the fact that "one kind of thought left him sad and the other cheerful" (8). Ignatius then came to the conclusion that he was being moved by the Enemy when he was thinking of pursuing "a certain lady" and that he was being moved by God when he was thinking of imitating the saints. After this he seems to have resolved to undertake a life of penance, and as soon as he was able he set out on a penitential pilgrimage to Jerusalem.

It is somewhat difficult to apply Ignatius's rules for discernment to this particular experience. It's important, however, to remember that Ignatius's notes in the Exercises on discernment of spirits are "rules for perceiving and knowing *in some manner* the different movements which are caused in the soul" (313, Mullan, emphasis added). Ignatius seems to have been experiencing consolation as he thought about imitating the saints. It's much harder to locate the other half of his experience in the rules for discernment. It's not clear that he was experiencing desolations as he daydreamed about the lady, nor that he was experiencing consolations from the Enemy, but he was surely right in saying that he was moved by the "evil spirit." Perhaps the most we can say is that he was being tempted by the Enemy to return to his worldly life.

It's also difficult to apply some of Ignatius's advice on decision-making in the Exercises to this particular choice. After all, it doesn't seem likely that Ignatius was free from inordinate attachments as he made his choice to embark on a penitential life. Nevertheless, it does look like a second-time choice and it certainly seems that God was in his choice. Can one then conclude that an exercitant need not be free from inordinate attachments to embark on an election? No. It's not a good idea to embark on an election in the grip of an inordinate attachment. Does it happen that exercitants sometimes make good and sound elections without having adequately dealt with their inordinate attachments? Yes.

Ignatius left a much longer and more detailed account of another second-time decision he made. It was the first major decision he made as he began to work on the Constitutions. He was deciding whether the sacristies of churches belonging to the Jesuits should be allowed to possess income. In other words, would the Jesuits' poverty be complete or partial? Just after they were canonically instituted as an order, the first Jesuits had decided to allow incomes for their churches. In his new role as superior general, Ignatius was reconsidering this decision. Eventually he decided to revoke the earlier policy, opting for complete poverty.

Ignatius kept a diary—or, as one translator aptly named it, "a discernment log-book"—as he prayed about his decision.[132] In this logbook, there's an unfiltered account of spiritual activity. Although Ignatius may have reflected on and analyzed his experiences, those reflections aren't recorded in the logbook until the very end. The logbook is full of the kind of raw data that a person has to deal with as he makes a second-time decision. Examining the logbook provides the student of Ignatian decision-making an opportunity to apply what he's been learning.

It took Ignatius a long time to make the decision—40 days. He did, eventually, make a sound and good election, praying until he had no doubt about what to do. As is typical of a second-time decision, he seems to have been pushed and pulled in contrary directions for most of the decision-making process. As he was praying about the decision, he had many extraordinary mystical visions and consolations, but he also encountered the Enemy. He experienced temptation, desolation and perhaps consolation from the Enemy. He was even goaded by the Enemy to "feel anger with the Blessed Trinity" (Feb. 18, 50). The 40 days were a time of intense spiritual activity.

Ignatius's logbook is bewildering to read. On the next page is a short timetable for what he records for this period. Even if we pay no attention to his extraordinary experiences in prayer, the logbook would still be bewildering. He says over and over again that the decision is done, that his resolution is fixed, that the matter is settled and so on, but he keeps praying about it, day after day. Each time he says the decision is done, he chooses to reopen it. Ten days into the election, on February 11, he speaks quite definitively of the election being over, saying, "I no longer sought or desired to seek for anything, considering the matter finished, except for thanksgiving, also out of devotion to the Father and to the mass of the Blessed Trinity which I had already proposed to say tomorrow" (19). He says a mass of the Trinity the next day, but goes on to say 15 more masses of the Trinity, which in his mind were somehow necessary to end the election. The attentive reader can't help but ask, What's going on? The experience of reading the logbook is like the experience of making a second-time decision: it's bewildering until it becomes clear what God and the Enemy are doing.

EXCERPTS FROM DISCERNMENT LOGBOOK

February 2:	The election begins.
February 2 to 10:	Much devotion and growing inclination to choose complete poverty.
February 11:	Finishes the election except for thanksgiving.
February 12:	Arises, gives thanks, hears noise, leaves prayer and is tempted to reconsider the election. Says mass, feels coldness.
February 13:	Decides to keep away from the Divine Persons.
February 14:	Writes about the previous three days in the evening.
February 16:	Reopens his deliberation, remakes the election and considers the matter finished except for thanksgiving.
February 18:	Desolation. "Confirm me" prayer. Feels indignant with the Blessed Trinity.
February 19:	Intuitions of the Blessed Trinity and decides to say six or more masses of the Blessed Trinity.
February 20 to March 11:	Great graces in prayer.
March 6:	Suspects an inordinate attachment.
March 8:	*Agere contra* prayer.
March 9:	Content, hopeful for a resolution.
March 12:	Decides to end the election, tempted to prolong the election, rebukes the Enemy, ends the election with much clarity.

We cannot do a complete analysis of the logbook here, but there are several things we'd like to point out, things that shed light on second-time decisions. First, however, we have to give a brief account of Ignatius's experience. Oddly enough, the place to begin is at the end, at the point when things became clear for Ignatius. He reached this point of clarity on March 12, the final day of the election.

Ignatius was stuck saying mass after mass of the Blessed Trinity, not knowing for sure how to bring the election to an end. On March 12 he says mass and then experiences a desolation. "I felt as remote and separated from them as if I had never felt their influence in the past, or was ever to feel any of it in the future." He was "beset with thoughts" against Jesus and the other Divine Persons (145). As he thinks about his situation, he says, "I seemed to be wanting too many signs" (146). He is, however, worried that, if he ends his election feeling so distant from God, he would eventually become discontented with the choice.

In order to determine what to do, Ignatius decides to make an election within an election. He wants to make a judgment about whether "it would please God Our Lord more were I to conclude now without waiting and searching for further proofs, or whether I should say more masses for them" (147). Ignatius decides to conclude the election because he thinks it would be more pleasing to God. Then it occurs to him to say three masses of the Trinity in thanksgiving. He decides that this is a suggestion of the Enemy. Then, after praying, he thinks about waiting till evening to conclude the election, but decides to conclude the election at once. Again, as he has done so many times before, he offers his choice to the Lord.

That very afternoon, "the Tempter" tried to make him have doubts. At this point, Ignatius does something decisive. "Suddenly, yet calmly—as if to a beaten enemy—I said to him, 'Get to your place'" (151). He tells the Enemy to go to hell. About 15 minutes later, "I awakened to a new fact" (152). Ignatius "saw clearly that when the Tempter suggested thoughts against the Divine Persons and Mediators, he was putting, or trying to put, doubts into my mind on the subject; and on the contrary, when I experienced visitations from, and visions of the Divine Persons and Mediators, all was firmness and confirmation on the matter" (152). Once Ignatius rebukes the Enemy, he can see clearly what to do. Thus, when "enough light and knowledge is received by experience of consolations and desolations, and by the experience of the discernment of various spirits" (Puhl 176), Ignatius is able to bring his deliberation to an end.

Firmly rebuking the Enemy paved the way for Ignatius's election. There is another moment, close to the end of the deliberation, which is also important. About a week before he finally makes his election, Ignatius begins to suspect that some inordinate attachment might be operative. On March 6, he notes, "I wondered to myself and thought perhaps the Blessed Trinity wanted to make me content without visitations of tears, with my not being avid for them nor inordinately attached" (119). On March 8, he makes an *agere contra* prayer, "imploring that if it were equally to God's glory He would not visit me with tears" (136). The prayer works. On the next day Ignatius notes, "I was more content without tears than I had been at times with many tears. I seemed to understand that although I experienced no intuitions, no visions and no tears, in some way God Our Lord wanted to show me a way or manner of proceeding" (139). Three days later, on the last day of the election, Ignatius admits to himself, "I wanted to put an end to the affair with my soul in a state of consolation and complete satisfaction" (145). He goes on to say, "I seemed to be wanting too many signs, and wanting them during certain periods or during masses ending in my own satisfaction; the question itself was clear; I was looking not for more certainty, but for a finishing touch that would be to my taste" (146). He is then able to let go of this desire and end the election. The *agere contra* prayer was a decisive moment.

What was happening before March 12? The election began on February 2. For approximately the first week he seems to be doing what he recommends in the Autograph Directory, examining "when he finds himself in consolation, in which direction God is moving him."[133] For example, he notes, "Devotion, not without tears, before and during mass, and more inclined to complete poverty" (Feb. 6, 5). As the days pass, the consolations continue and his inclination to choose complete poverty grows stronger and stronger. By February 8 he begins to say his resolution is fixed on poverty. On Monday, February 11, he has an extraordinary experience of the Holy Spirit and feels confirmed in his desire to choose complete poverty. He is further strengthened when he remembers "that the Son first sent his Apostles to preach in poverty, and later the Holy Spirit, by granting his spirit and his gifts of tongues, confirmed them" (15). He offers God his choice and considers the matter settled.

Actually, Ignatius says he considered the matter settled "except for thanksgiving, also out of devotion to the Father and to the mass of the Blessed Trinity, which I had proposed to say tomorrow Tuesday" (19). The next day (Feb. 12), he arose, giving thanks "most earnestly to God our Lord" (21). As he was giving thanks, he heard a noise, left his prayer to investigate and at that moment experienced a temptation to reconsider his choice. At mass that morning, he feels disturbed by the people in the room and he seems to indicate that they caused a certain "coldness."[134] On March 12, Ignatius experienced a similar temptation and told the Enemy to go to hell, but he doesn't do that here. It looks as if he experienced the temptation at dawn, said mass, visited a man named Don Francisco and then "disposed" of the temptation that occurred at dawn.

At this point Ignatius's logbook becomes confused. Before the morning of Tuesday, February 12, the entries in the logbook are like the waters of a small creek—clear, with a small current. For at least a week after February 12, the entries are murky. It's as if someone stepped into the creek, stirring up the sediment. In fact, editors of the document claim that Ignatius didn't even write in his diary for almost three full days. He finished his deliberation on Monday the 11th, was tempted at dawn on Tuesday and didn't write anything until the evening of Thursday the 14th. At that point, he recapped the three days, beginning with a heading, "How the Persons Hid Themselves." It's the statement of a confused, perhaps desolate, person. If one reads the text, it's clear that the Divine Persons did no such thing. Ignatius describes how he knew he was at fault for leaving his prayer on Tuesday morning and so decides to "keep away from the Divine Persons" (24). It looks like some fallacious reasoning.

In the week after his fault and temptation, Ignatius continues praying. On Wednesday, Thursday and Friday, he notes that he had no doubts about his decision, but on Saturday he reopens his deliberations. Once again he remakes the election and considers the matter finished, "except for two days in which to give thanks" (36). He says mass on Sunday and experiences consolation. He hopes to bring the election to a close on Monday, with a mass of the Trinity.

On Monday morning (Feb. 18) he experiences another desolation. "I awoke . . . a little before daybreak and then afterward felt heavy-hearted and bereft of all spiritual things" (44). Later, as he is praying, he seems to experience at least some genuine consolation. Then, he experiences what we think is a consolation from the Enemy. While he is preparing the altar and vesting for mass, "there came to me: 'Eternal Father, confirm me'; 'Eternal Son, con<firm me>'; 'Eternal Holy Spirit, con<firm me>'; 'Holy Trinity, con<firm me>'; 'My One Sole God, con<firm me>'" (48).[135] Ignatius comments, "very deeply did I feel it" (48). This movement of his soul seems rather innocuous, but it has, as we shall see, a bad ending. Then he prays, "Eternal Father, will you not confirm me?" He's petulant. The consolation has a bad ending; it's from the Enemy.

At mass he experiences some devotion and a few tears. The thought comes to Ignatius, "pricking and preventing devotion," that his tears aren't as copious as they had been before (49). On the basis of this he decides that he hasn't received the confirmation he was looking for. After mass, he tries to humble himself, but eventually he ends up feeling angry (*indignándome*) with the Blessed Trinity (50). The next day he feels intense love for the Blessed Trinity and decides to say in succession six or more masses of the Blessed Trinity. He prays for 18 more days, until, after much struggle, he is finally able to bring his deliberation to an end.

During those 18 days, Ignatius experiences many extraordinary graces. For example, he has "intuitions" of the Trinity, claiming that "what I had then understood feeling and seeing I could not have learnt in a whole life of study" (52). On another occasion he says, "I so felt and saw Jesus, that it seemed that nothing could happen in the future capable of separating me from Him" (75). On yet another occasion he says, "I felt and saw, not obscurely but brightly, in full light, the very Being or Essence of God, appearing as a sphere" (120). During these days, however, Ignatius continues to struggle with the decision and the events of February 12 and 18. On March 12 he makes his final decision.

This document raises several questions about confirmation. First of all, one can't but help wonder what Ignatius means by the term. Early on in the document, it seems to mean "consolations" which strengthen and equip a person for what he has decided to do. For example, Ignatius speaks of the gift of the Holy Spirit (presumably at Pentecost) confirming the Apostles after Jesus sent them out to preach in poverty (15). At other points (147), he talks as if confirmation would give him some kind of proof that he's made the right decision. Second, did Ignatius think an exercitant should pray for confirmation after making a second-time decision? Ignatius doesn't recommend this in the *Spiritual Exercises*, but in his own second-time decision he does pray for confirmation. The answers to these questions are beyond our ken. Perhaps the questions, especially the second one, are unanswerable.

Each director, however, must decide whether or not to tell an exercitant to pray for confirmation of a second-time decision. We do not tell exercitants to pray for confirmation in a second-time decision. We simply recommend that an exercitant continue a second-time deliberation until he's sure about what he wants to do. Exercitants who make *third-time* decisions often are helped greatly by a confirming consolation. They have been unmoved throughout their deliberation. They don't need proof that they've made the right decision, but a heart enkindled is a great source of energy and zeal for what they have to do. Exercitants who make *second-time* decisions have already had a felt experience of loving God in and through the thing they are choosing. They don't need another consolation and they certainly shouldn't put their decision into question by praying for proofs. Our position is not totally inconsistent with the text. After all, one could conclude that God seems to have been showing Ignatius that he didn't need the confirmation he was looking for.

It's easy to get caught in the complexities of Ignatius's discernment logbook and miss the lessons it teaches about second-time decision-making. First, the experience of alternating consolations and desolations is confusing until an exercitant is able to discern what's going on. Second, the fact that someone is experiencing desolations, false consolations, fallacious reasoning and other temptations of the Enemy doesn't mean he can't or isn't also experiencing consolations at other times. In fact, even saints can encounter the Enemy and not immediately recognize him. Third, and perhaps most importantly, Ignatius's consolations did not contain a revelation about what he was to do about poverty in the order. Sometimes an exercitant can expect some kind of word or sign or sense from God telling him what to do. Although that can happen, it usually doesn't. Nevertheless, a person can reach a point where he knows without a doubt that he's moved by love of God to do something. He is able to act because he's confident that he and his Lord are united in their desires. We'll return to this topic in the next chapter.

CHAPTER 13

A TOOL FOR LOVE

We have come full circle. As we pointed out in the first chapter, the Spiritual Exercises are an opportunity for love. They provide exercitants an opportunity to grow in their knowledge of and affection for their Lord. Of course, this happens because God is eagerly responding to the exercitant's prayers for graces and consolations. The Exercises also provide exercitants an opportunity to do something for and with their Lord. The exercitant can, in fact, make a decision during the retreat. He learns to use his decisions and the actions which flow from his decisions to build his relationship with God.

The First and Second Weeks' exercises set a person free to make decisions out of love for the Lord. The exercitant then learns how to use that freedom to choose what will better "praise, reverence and serve God our Lord." As we saw in the last chapter, Ignatius offers the exercitant three ways in which he can make a choice because of his love of God. Occasionally, an exercitant has some kind of an encounter with God, at God's initiative, which results in a decision. He knows, seemingly without deliberating, what he wants to do with and for the Lord. Sometimes, while trying to make a decision, an exercitant experiences many emotions, some of which are very powerful and some of which may seem contradictory. He is, in fact, being moved both by God and by the Enemy. In such circumstances he can apply the rules for discernment to his experience and thereby gain enough "light and understanding" to make a choice out of love for the Lord. Often, however, an exercitant's soul is calm and tranquil as he makes a decision. He is then able to make a free choice entirely for God by considering which of his options will be more for God's glory. In each case, the exercitant's decision is the fruit of the love he has for the Lord.

Although the paths to a decision can vary, each decision ends in the same way. The exercitant reaches a point where he knows, without doubt, what he wants to do out of love for God. A sound election is marked by the exercitant's experience of being without doubt. For example, when deciding whether to oppose Francis Borgia's appointment as a cardinal, Ignatius eventually reached a point of certainty. He wavered for three days, "until finally, on the third day, I made my usual prayer with a determination so final, so peaceful and free, to do all I could with the people and the cardinals to prevent it. I felt sure at that time, and still feel so, that, if I did not act thus, I should not be able to give a good account of myself to God our Lord—indeed that I should give quite a bad one."[136]

Typically, as someone begins an election, he is wavering between two options. Often he seems double-minded, wanting one thing at one moment and another thing at another moment. Sometimes he feels at a loss, without a way forward. Eventually, though, he reaches a point where he's confident of the way forward. He's no longer tossed to and fro. He's single-minded, knowing what he wants to do out of love for God. When Ignatius finally made his decision about complete poverty for the Jesuits, he says he felt "in my soul a great sense of security."[137]

A sound and good election results in the exercitant being without doubt about what he chooses to intend to do. It is important to understand the nature of an exercitant's confidence. He does not, as a result of his election, experience the kind of certainty that reasoning syllogistically from true universal principles provides. After all, he isn't following a set of principles; he's relating to a person. Nor does he experience the kind of certainty that comes from receiving an order from a superior. God does give the Christian certain direct commands—Do not steal, Do not commit adultery, and so on—but He does not normally legislate the particulars of a person's life. The exercitant is not God's puppet any more than Jesus was His Father's puppet. Sometimes out of devotion and sometimes out of irresponsibility, an exercitant wants access to the mind of God Himself, but such a thing is impossible. After all, the only mind a person can know with absolute certainty is his own. It turns out that the surety the exercitant experiences is that of a lover, not that of a logician, an underling or a mind-reader.

The exercitant makes an election in the context of a living relationship of love. If he has reason to doubt his own heart, he won't have confidence that he's making his decision on account of love for God. Why would someone have reason to doubt his own heart? Most often, it's because he knows that he hasn't ordered his loves so as to have "one desire and choice." In other words, inordinate attachments give the exercitant reason to doubt his heart. How can he know for sure he's being moved by the love of God if he knows that in his heart there are other loves which are competing with his love of God? It's no wonder that Ignatius says early on that the Exercises "have as their purpose the conquest of self and the regulation of one's life in such a way that no decision is made under the influence of any inordinate attachment" (21). The Exercises set the exercitant free to love, not just in words but also in deeds.

It is important for the director to realize that a beginner, especially one who is making a third-time decision, will experience decision-making differently than someone who has a more mature relationship with the Lord. Both can reach a point of genuine certitude in their decision-making and both use the same methods to make a good decision. Even so, their experiences differ.

Decisions are declarations of love. In a young relationship, declarations of love may feel risky. All relationships of love experience moments of risk on the way to mutual, intimate shared life. A young man, for example, may be absolutely certain that he wants to propose marriage to his beloved, but he still experiences himself as taking a risk. He might even be confident of his intended's love, yet still wonder, Will she love me loving her in this way? So too, with an exercitant who is, perhaps for the first time, making a decision free from the influence of inordinate attachments.

Often a beginner loves the Lord with what we've been calling semipersonal love. He admires all the Lord's good qualities and loves Him on account of them. He experiences the Lord from the outside, as a spectator, so to speak. He studies and meditates on His actions and gestures and begins to see and admire the Lord's marvelous qualities: His courage, His faithfulness, His self-control, etc. There is not much intimate sharing or mutual self-revelation going on, although the love taking root in the exercitant's heart is very real. The self-aware exercitant might admit that he doesn't actually know much about his Lord's interior life and that he longs for encounters with his Lord of a more personal nature. The exercitant in this situation can get to a place where he knows for sure what he wants to do out of love for God. Nevertheless, he will still experience an element of risk in making his decision. It's as if the exercitant is climbing out on a limb. He's certain that this is the limb he wants to be on, but it feels risky. The exercitant is making a declaration of love. How will the Lord respond to his declaration? The exercitant might very well wonder, Will my Lord love me loving Him in this way? Of course, the exercitant has ample reason to believe in his Lord's love for him and commitment to him. Making a decision is, then, the exercitant's chance to respond audaciously.[138]

The person whose relationship with the Lord has grown into a friendship of mutual personal love experiences decision-making quite differently. Declarations of love don't feel risky. The exercitant and his Lord have "one life lived wholly by each and wholly by both together."[139] The decision isn't the exercitant's decision or the Lord's decision. It's their decision. It's not the exercitant's will or the Lord's will. It's their will. The person in this kind of relationship experiences deciding together with his Lord what to do next. He experiences the decision as "our decision" and the choice as "our will." He doesn't say to himself, This is what I am doing for the one I love. Rather, he often says to himself, This is what we are thinking and feeling and choosing to do. He and his Lord have reached a point in their friendship where "words of separation and distinction" are not adequate to describe the reality of the union and the decision-making.

Sometimes beginners can have difficulty reaching a point of certainty because their experience doesn't match their expectations. Often, for example, an exercitant who has never made a second-time decision before is surprised by the experience. Although most exercitants don't expect handwriting on the wall, they do expect God to communicate His will in or through consolations. In other words, they either look at consolations as God's way of voting on what they are proposing or they expect the consolations to contain directions about what they are to do. They expect some kind of word, sign or sense from God telling them what to do. Although that can happen, it usually doesn't. When, for example, Ignatius was making his decision about poverty in the order, his consolations did not contain God's directions about what to do.

What actually happens in a second-time decision is far more intimate and personal than receiving instructions via consolations, but it is surprising to the exercitant. His consolations are encounters with God in which his love is inflamed. Eventually, the exercitant comes to the conclusion that his desire for a particular thing is God's desire. It's not simply that God gives an exercitant a desire, where the giving is like the giving of a gift. Rather, the exercitant experiences God desiring in him. It often takes a leap of faith for someone to believe that his desire is also God's desire, but that's exactly what's happening in a second-time decision. The love that's present creates a union, and the exercitant is able to discern what God is willing in him. This can be surprising to the exercitant, because what he's experiencing is his own desire; it's not something external to him.

During the Exercises, exercitants learn how to make a choice in union with God, but the Exercises are about more than a single decision. They are a training ground for life, and life involves many decisions. The exercitant normally makes his decision in the Second Week, about halfway through the retreat. He spends the rest of the retreat meditating on the passion, death and resurrection of Jesus, growing in love and friendship with his Lord. The love that is forged there opens the door to a life of decision-making in union with the Lord. On account of their mutual love, the exercitant can at all times and in all circumstances live God's life and, in this sense, make God's decisions in the world. It's no wonder that the retreat ends with an exercise in which the exercitant prays for the grace to love and serve God in all things.

The Contemplation to Attain Love (230-237) is the last exercise of the retreat. It is a recapitulation of the retreat which serves to launch the exercitant back into normal life. The exercise is rather long, having four substantial points for the exercitant to consider. In our experience, sometimes it's helpful either to have the exercitant make the meditation several times or to divide the meditation in half.

Although long, the exercise itself is rather simple in conception. Ignatius has the exercitant look at God's loving action and then do the same. It's a very active contemplation, designed to occasion a mutual exchange of love in which the mutual responses are "so interdependent as to form one composite act of one composite agent."[140] The exercise is designed to occasion a communion of love. When such a communion becomes habitual, as it does in friendship, the exercitant loves and serves his friend in all things. That's what friends do.

The structure of this last exercise is similar to that of other exercises, but it begins in a unique way. The exercise opens with a note, "Before presenting this exercise it will be good to call attention to two points" (230). Ignatius wants the exercitant to think for a moment about how "love ought to manifest itself in deeds rather than in words" (230). The exercitant has been meditating on the life of Jesus, and in the last two weeks of the retreat he has been praying specifically for the grace to feel things, namely, sorrow and joy. Now, as the retreat is drawing to a close, Ignatius takes pains to remind him that love is more than sentiment. In fact, if one's feelings don't lead to some kind of action, they are empty. Love is generative.

Ignatius says, "love consists in interchange between the two parties; that is to say in the lover's giving and communicating to the beloved what he has or out of what he has or can; and vice versa, the beloved to the lover" (231, Mullan and Puhl). Love generates mutual giving. The last exercise is built around this fact.

Ignatius gives an example of the mutual giving that love generates. "So that if the one has knowledge, he gives to the one who has it not. The same of honors, of riches; and so the one to the other" (231). This example surprises some exercitants. After all, aren't honors and riches the tools Satan uses to entrap men (142)? Yes, but they are not evil in and of themselves. At this point in the retreat, inordinate attachments are off the table. In fact, this particular exercise is about one love, shared by two persons. The exercitant will, during the course of the exercise, become increasingly conscious of how God loves and serves him in all things and how he too can love and serve God in all things. Although it is not the main point of the exercise, Ignatius is signaling that the "all things" includes riches and honors.

To begin the exercise, Ignatius has the exercitant do two preparatory things. As usual, he begs "God our Lord for grace that all my intentions, actions, and operations may be directed purely to the praise and service of His Divine Majesty" (46). Then Ignatius has the exercitant imagine himself "standing in the presence of God our Lord and of His angels and saints, who intercede for me" (232). It is a solemn, important moment that is filled with hope and expectation.

In the second prelude Ignatius directs the exercitant to ask for "an intimate knowledge of all the many blessings received, that, filled with gratitude for all, I may in all things love and serve the Divine Majesty" (233). There are several things worth noting about this second prelude. The exercitant is asking for "an intimate knowledge of the many blessings received." He isn't asking for a speculative or merely philosophical knowledge. This is important to remember because several of Ignatius's points, especially the second one, are couched in philosophical language. As the exercitant makes the meditation, it's also helpful for him to remember the grace he's asking for. In this case, he's aiming for gratitude. It is, however, a gratitude of a certain type. He's not aiming at a gratitude that enables him to receive blessing and gifts graciously or politely. He's asking for a gratitude that desires to give in return, a gratitude that manifests itself not just in words, but in deeds. It's also worth pointing out that the second prelude resembles the preparatory prayer. In a way, this exercise revisits the Principle and Foundation, unveiling its inner glory. There are endless possibilities for the exercitant who has "one desire and choice."

In the first point of the exercise, Ignatius asks the exercitant to consider "all the blessings of creation and redemption, and the special favors I have received" (234). In the First Week of the Exercises, the exercitant considered and, more importantly, personally experienced the blessings of creation and redemption. At this point, the exercitant calls those blessings to mind, along with any particular graces for which he is especially grateful. The exercitant has to take a kind of panoramic view of all the blessings he's received, otherwise he won't be able to finish the exercise. Nevertheless, he is to ponder them "with great affection" (234). He is to think, especially, about "how much God our Lord has done for me, and how much He has given me of what He possesses, and finally, how much, as far as He can, the same Lord desires to give Himself to me" (234).

The astute exercitant will guess what is coming next. He is to love in the way that God Himself loves. He is to give God what he possesses and, as much as he can, give himself. So, after the exercitant has considered God's gifts and God's desire to give His very self, Ignatius directs him to say what is now a famous prayer: "Take, Lord, and receive . . ." (234). With the prayer, the exercitant has the opportunity to give to the Lord "all that I have and possess" and himself along with it: "all my liberty, my memory, my understanding, and my entire will." Some exercitants won't think of themselves in terms of memory, understanding and will. The important thing is that they give God everything they have, and themselves along with their gifts. If they prefer, they can think of themselves in terms of their mind and heart and perceptions and feelings and so on.

Ignatius recommends that the exercitant pray this prayer "as one would do who is moved by great feeling" (234). For various reasons, some people find this difficult to do. Sometimes they aren't moved by their consideration of the blessings of creation and redemption. Sometimes they are simply weary. Sometimes they are afraid. Whatever the reason, the director should encourage them to do whatever they can to arouse great feeling in themselves, just as they worked to arouse sorrow in themselves while meditating on the passion, and joy in themselves while meditating on the resurrection.

The director should be aware that to love in the way that God Himself loves involves both the giving of self and the giving of one's possessions. To some he needs to emphasize the importance of giving oneself. These exercitants may find it relatively easy to give what they possess, but they hold themselves—their opinions, their judgment, their perceptions, their feelings—very dear. To others he needs to emphasize the importance of sharing their possessions. Such exercitants find it easy to say a prayer offering themselves, but such an offering is hollow if they don't also offer the things they own.

Sometimes exercitants will be puzzled about how to give something they own, like a car, to God. They might say, "How can I give Him what I possess? He is, after all, pure spirit." They might also say, "God doesn't need anything I have." If this happens, the director might remind the exercitants of Jesus' words, "as you did it to one of the least of these my brethren, you did it to me" (Mt. 25:40). At the very least, the exercitants can give their money, their possessions, their time and even themselves to "one of the least of these my brethren."

After the exercitant offers himself and all that he possesses, Ignatius recommends that he continue his prayer, saying, "All is Thine, dispose of it wholly according to Thy will. Give me Thy love and Thy grace, for this is sufficient for me" (234). This part of the prayer can often be misunderstood by the exercitant. For one thing, "Give me Thy love" means "give me love for you, my God." Insecure or inexperienced exercitants sometimes mistakenly think that they are begging for God's love. The exercitant doesn't need to do that. He ought to believe and trust in God's love for him. The exercitant is, rather, praying for the grace to love as God loves.

Often, too, exercitants misunderstand "All is Thine, dispose of it wholly according to Thy will." In particular, they mistakenly think that giving themselves to God means denying their very personhood, as if they could actually somehow divest themselves of their memory, understanding and will. They think that giving themselves to God is like giving Him one of their possessions. When a person gives a possession—for instance, a treasured book—he first possesses the book, then he relinquishes possession by putting the book in another's hands. Giving God—or anyone, for that matter—one's self is not like giving a possession. Exercitants who think that giving God their selves means somehow ceasing to exist as themselves will have trouble making this prayer, and if they don't have trouble they ought to. Giving one's self is a giving which is also an accepting. In the very act of giving oneself, one accepts the beloved into one's heart. If the exercitant tries to have no life or self or person, he won't be able to accept his beloved into his life. Love is thwarted. Likewise, God does not want the exercitant to become as nothing. He loves the exercitant. He wants more of him, not less of him. He wants to make his existence, his very act of being, firm and sure and deeply rooted. He wants the exercitant to shine into the world. He loves the exercitant. "I am yours" does not mean "I am no longer a person and no longer want to be a person." In fact, the giving of self in love is not something that can be done once and for all. It is, rather, a giving in which the exercitant is constituted as gift, from the very first instance of loving and at every moment thereafter. This giving of self is never over and done with. The act of giving can continue and it can grow into greater love and into a fuller and more intense gift. It is neverending.[141]

If the director detects such a misunderstanding on the part of the exercitant, a few words should be sufficient to redirect him. The director does not need to explain all this to him. The important thing is for the exercitant to ponder God's giving and then to do likewise. During the rest of the exercise, Ignatius directs the exercitant to consider other facets of God's giving and then to respond appropriately.

In the second point of the exercise, Ignatius asks the exercitant first to consider how God dwells in His creatures and especially in man. One could say the second point is about presence as an act of love. Ignatius directs the exercitant to first consider how God dwells in all of creation: rocks, plants, animals and mankind. Then the exercitant is to consider himself and how God dwells in him, as in a temple. Although Ignatius doesn't use Scripture at this point, one can't help but think of Paul's declaration to the Corinthians, "you are God's temple" (1 Cor. 3:16) and John's insistent reminders to his brethren that God abides in them (2 Jn. 3:34, 4:13-16). Of course, Jesus' words also come to mind, "If a man loves me, he will keep my word and my Father will love him and we will come to him and make our home with him" (Jn. 14:23). God dwells in all of creation, but He dwells in the exercitant in a special way. He is making him His home.

Ignatius begins by asking the exercitant to consider something that is, generally speaking, intuitively accessible. Most exercitants have experienced God in His creation, even though they might describe that experience differently than Ignatius does. Although an exercitant ought to linger on a point if he is moved while considering it, the director needs to be aware that the consideration of God dwelling in creatures is propaedeutic to the "and so in me" (235, Mullan). Normally, an exercitant should spend a good portion of his time considering how God is dwelling in him as in a temple.

How, then, is the exercitant to respond? Ignatius says, "Then I will reflect upon myself again in the manner stated in the first point, or in some other way that may seem better" (235). In the first point, after considering how God gives what He possesses and Himself along with it, the exercitant considers what he ought to give to God: "all that I possess and myself with it." In this second point, after considering God dwelling in him, the exercitant ought to consider how he can dwell in God. In other words, he should do what he can to make himself more present in God. One way to do this is, of course, to repeat the *Suscipe* prayer, but, as Ignatius points out, there may be other ways that seem better to the exercitant. Of course, the exercitant's response depends on him believing that he can abide in God. Again, 1 John is helpful here. "So we know and believe the love God has in us. God is love and he who abides in love abides in God and God abides in him" (4:16, translation ours).

At this point it's helpful to remember that the exercitant has asked God for gratitude and is, therefore, aiming for gratitude. After considering how God dwells in him, false humility might tempt an exercitant to say, "Oh, no," but a better response is, "Oh, yes, Lord. I love you loving me in this way." Such a response will increase the mutual abiding between lover and beloved. Since the exercitant has just considered how God is participating in his life and making his thoughts, his affections, his choices, his deeds, his successes, his failures, his sorrows and his joys a part of His own life, the exercitant might tell the Lord about how he desires to do the same. He can tell God how he desires not just to be with Him, but to share His life, participate in His life in every way and make His thoughts, His affections, His choices, His deeds, His successes, His failures, His sorrows and His joys a part of his own life. The possibilities for a sweet communion of love are enormous here.

Next, Ignatius has the exercitant consider how "God works and labors for me in all creatures upon the face of the earth" (236). This point calls to mind earlier moments in the Exercises. In the First Week, after reflecting on his sin, the exercitant cries out in wonder (60) as he considers how God has been laboring for him "in all the creatures on the face of the earth." In the Second Week, the exercitant considers the call of Christ the King, "whoever would like to come with Me is to labor with Me, that following Me in the pain, he may also follow Me in the glory" (95, Mullan). Here again he considers how God "conducts Himself as one who labors" (236).

Exercitants generally find this point easy to consider. They think about how God is using all of creation to sustain them in life. They also think about all the labors Jesus endured in His public ministry and in His passion and death. They also, usually, have an instinct about how to respond. They can, of course, say the *Suscipe* prayer, but they often simply want to tell their Lord about how they intend to labor for Him in the coming days, weeks, months and years, using all of creation to do so. "Me, too!," they exclaim.

Finally, Ignatius directs the exercitant to consider "all blessings and gifts as descending from above. . . . as the rays of light descend from the sun, and as the waters flow from their fountains, etc." (237). The exercitant doesn't receive God's gifts as one receives a watch and puts it on. Ignatius is saying something more. In the previous points the exercitant has considered God giving, God dwelling in and God laboring. Now he is to consider God descending and sharing His very life and light with the exercitant.

Fortunately, Ignatius gives some examples of what he means. "Thus, my limited power comes from the supreme and infinite power above, and so, too, justice, goodness, mercy, etc., descend from above" (237). The exercitant's intellect, his will, his justice and his mercy are not just from God; they are God's. His being and his life are God's. He shines with God's light. He loves with God's love, and so on. It's as if Ignatius is saying to the exercitant: "You are His glory. You are His presence in the world. You are His light, His life, His being in the world. You are Christ."

How is the exercitant to respond? How can he love as God Himself is loving? His response mirrors God's action in a surprising way. God is descending. The exercitant is ascending, responding to "the upward call of God in Christ Jesus" (Phil. 3:14). As Paul says, God has "made us alive together with Christ . . . and raised us up with him and made us sit with him in the heavenly places in Christ Jesus" (Eph. 2: 5-6). Mirabile dictu! The exercitant is giving himself to God, and God doesn't receive his gift as one receives a watch.

Rather, God's being and life are his. God's love is his love. God's joy is his joy. God is shining with his light and his being. They have the life of each other in common. There is a co-being happening. His response is a shining, too, often taking the form of a simple prayer, "Abba, Father" or "O my God."

The exercitant ends the exercise as always, making a colloquy and saying the Lord's Prayer. The great Ignatian scholar Ignatius Iparraguirre, S.J., comments, "Through this 'exchange of loves' realized in mutual self-giving, a formal friendship with God is established, which later will be lived out in ordinary life."[142] The exercitant will have to tend the relationship, using all he has learned in the Exercises, but endless possibilities stretch out in front of him. The unity of two people who love each other with personal love is incredibly rich and multifaceted. When two people have the life of one another in common, they can each say, "Your ways are my ways. All that you have and possess, all that you are, all that you think and do—it's all mine in you." And each can say, "My ways are your ways. All that I have and possess, all that I am, all that I think and do—it's all yours in me." The exercitant may not be accustomed to thinking of his relationship with God in this way, but overcoming his inordinate attachments opens the door to union and to ever-increasing personal self-giving and acceptance.

Much of the experience and richness of shared life can be captured in the following two statements:

1. I experience my friend's life as my life in him.
2. I experience my life as my friend's life in me.[143]

One can, for example, imagine Jesus saying, "I experience my Father's life as my life in Him" and "I experience my life as my Father's life in me." Likewise, one can imagine Jesus' Father saying, "I experience my Son's life as my life in him" and "I experience my life as my Son's life in me." During the retreat, exercitants often catch a whiff of this kind of union with the Lord when they make a decision. After the retreat, as they make more and more free decisions out of love for the Lord, they enter more fully into the divine life and begin to taste this reality in their own lives.

After the retreat, as the exercitant and the Lord grow in their friendship, they experience more and more often having the will of each other in common. In order to catch a glimpse of what it means to have the will of each other in common, it's helpful to do a small thought experiment using the above description of friendship. Imagine both the exercitant and the Lord each describing the experience of shared life. We'll call the exercitant "Mary." To begin with, imagine Mary describing her experience of her will and the Lord describing His experience of Mary's will:

1. I, Mary, experience my will as my Lord's will in me.

2. I, the Lord, experience Mary's will as my will in her.

Both Mary and her Lord experience Mary's will as the Lord's will in her. Mary's will is God's will.

Next, imagine Mary describing her experience of the Lord's will and the Lord describing His experience of His will:

1. I, Mary, experience the Lord's will as my will in Him.

2. I, the Lord, experience my will as Mary's will in me.

Both Mary and the Lord experience the Lord's will as Mary's in Him. God's will is Mary's. We end up with: Mary's will is God's. And God's will is Mary's. They have one will.

This is, of course, only a thought experiment. Who can actually say what God experiences except God Himself? On the other hand, this is a good description of the union and shared life that friends can experience. Furthermore, it does describe the experience of some exercitants who make a decision in union with their Lord. They experience a union of wills. We have here an explanation of Augustine's oft-quoted maxim, "Love and do what you will." The exercitant who is free to love the Lord with his whole heart, soul, mind and strength is one in love with the Lord. He can then act out of that union, habitually if he so chooses.

Because he is a friend of God, the exercitant can in every place, in every circumstance and in all things make God's decisions in the world. "It is no longer I who live but Christ who lives in me," he exclaims, with Saint Paul. The exercitant becomes a partaker in the divine nature, and God is one step closer to becoming all in all. It is the "mystery hidden for ages and generations but now made manifest to his saints. . . . Christ in you, the hope of glory" (Col. 1:26,27).

APPENDIX

LETTER TO SISTER TERESA REJADELL

Venice, June 18, 1536

May the grace and love of Christ our Lord be our never-failing protection and help.

Your letter, which I received a few days ago, brought with it much joy in the Lord, whom you are serving and whom you desire to serve even more earnestly, and to whom we must attribute all of the good that we see in creatures.

You said that Caceres would inform me at length about your affairs. He has done so. And not only that, but he has given me an account of the direction he gave you in each particular. Reading over what he tells me, I do not find anything to add, although I should like further enlightenment from your letter because no one can give an account of another's experiences that will be as accurate as that given by the one undergoing them.

You ask me for the love of God our Lord to undertake the direction of your soul. It is many years now since His Divine Majesty, without any merit on my part, has given me the desire to give as much pleasure as I can to those men and women who walk in the way of His will and to be of help to those who labor as they should in His service. I have no doubt that you are of their number, and I am therefore very desirous of being in a position to practice what I preach.

You also are very earnest in asking me to tell you what our Lord may have to say to me and to tell you frankly what I think. I will be very glad to give you a frank opinion; and if at times I appear severe, it will be rather against him who is trying to upset you than against you yourself. The enemy is leading you into error in two things, but not in any way to make you fall into a sin that would separate you from God our Lord. He tries rather to upset you and to interfere with your service of God and your peace of mind. In the first place he proposes and leads you on to a false humility. And in the second, he gives you an exaggerated fear of God, with which you are altogether too much occupied.

In the first place, then, the enemy as a rule follows this course. He places obstacles and impediments in the way of those who love and begin to serve God our Lord, and this is the first weapon he uses in his efforts to wound them. He asks, for instance: "How can you continue a life of such great penance, deprived of all satisfaction from friends, relatives, possessions? How can you lead so lonely a life, with no rest, when you can save your soul in other ways and without such dangers?" He tries to bring us to understand that we must lead a life that is longer than it will actually be, by reason of the trials he places before us and which no man ever underwent. He fails to remind us of the great comfort and consolation which our Lord is wont to give to such souls, who, as new recruits in our Lord's service, surmount all these obstacles and choose to suffer with their Creator and Lord. The enemy will then try his second weapon, which is pride and vainglory. He will endeavor to make the individual see that there is a great deal of goodness and holiness in him, and puts him in a position high above his merits. If the servant of God is proof against these darts, humbling and abasing himself and refusing consent to the suggestions of the enemy, the enemy draws his third weapon, which is false humility. When he sees that the servant of the Lord is so good and humble and, obedient to all the Lord's commands, regards his own uselessness and weakness without any thought of self-glorification, he is ready with the suggestion that, should he happen to speak of the graces our Lord has bestowed upon him in actual deeds or merely in resolve or desire, he sins by another kind of vainglory in speaking favorably of himself. In this way he tries to prevent him from speaking of any of the blessings he has received. His purpose is to prevent him from producing fruit in others as well as in himself. For he knows that, when such a person recalls to mind what he has received, he is always helped in regard to greater things. One ought, however, to be very reserved, and speak only with the motive of helping others or himself: others if he sees that they are in the proper dispositions and likely to believe him and draw some profit from what he says. Thus, when the enemy of our salvation sees that we are humble, he tries to draw us on to a humility that is excessive and counterfeit.

What you say makes this very plain; for after you speak of weaknesses and fears, which are very much to the point, you continue: "I am a poor religious, and I think I have a desire of serving Christ our Lord." You don't venture to say "I have a desire of serving Christ our Lord," or "Our Lord gives me the desire to serve Him," but you say "I think I have a desire." And yet you see and you understand that these desires of serving Christ our Lord are not your own, but come to you from our Lord. If you were to say that our Lord gives you great desires of serving Him, you would be giving praise to the same Lord because you are making known His gift, and you glory in Him, not in yourself, because you do not attribute that grace to yourself.

Hence we must examine the matter closely; and if the enemy uplifts us, we must abase ourselves by recounting our sins and miseries. If he keeps us down and depresses us, we must raise ourselves up in true faith and hope in our Lord by recalling the blessings we have received and with how much love and affection He is waiting to save us. The enemy does not care whether he speaks the truth or whether he lies. His sole purpose is to overcome us.

Consider attentively how the martyrs declared that they were Christ's servants when they were arraigned before their pagan judges. Now, when you find yourself in the presence of the enemy of human nature who is tempting you, trying to rob you of the strength which our Lord gives you and to render you so weak and timid with his snares, won't you have the courage to say that you desire to serve our Lord? Rather, you must answer him by a forthright and courageous declaration that you are His follower and that you would rather die than fall away from His service. If he puts justice before my eyes, I will think of mercy. If he suggests mercy, I will think of justice. We must in this way keep to our road without perturbation, leaving the mocker to be mocked, and placing all our reliance on the authority of Holy Scripture: "Beware that thou be not deceived into folly and be humbled" (Ecclus. 13:10).

To come to the second point. The enemy, having instilled a fear in us that has some appearance of humility—a false humility—aims to prevent us from speaking of good, holy, and profitable things. He will then confront us with a much worse fear, the fear that we are separated and estranged from our Lord. To a great extent this is the result of what precedes. For, as the enemy was successful in his first attempt, he finds it easy to attack in this second stage. To explain this in some way I will point out another line of thought which the enemy follows. If he finds one whose conscience is easygoing and who falls into sins without a thought of their gravity, he does all he can to make venial sins appear no sins at all, and mortal venial, and a very serious mortal sin a mere trifle. In this way he takes advantage of the failing he perceives in us, I mean this excessively lax conscience. If on the other hand he comes upon one whose conscience is delicate (a delicate conscience being in itself nothing faulty, however) and sees that such a person avoids not only all mortal and all venial sin (as much as the latter is possible, for we cannot avoid them all) but even tries to keep from himself the very appearance of slight sin, imperfection, and defect, he tries to darken and confuse that good conscience by suggesting sin where there is none, changing perfection into defect, his only purpose being to harass and make one uneasy and miserable. When, as frequently happens, he cannot induce one to sin, or even hope to do so, he tries at least to vex him.

For a clearer understanding of this fear and its origin I will call your attention briefly to two lessons which our Lord usually gives, or permits. The one of them He gives, the other He permits. The first is an interior consolation which casts out all uneasiness and draws one to a complete love of our Lord. In this consolation He enlightens some, and to others He reveals many secrets as a preparation for later visits. In a word, when this divine consolation is present all trials are pleasant and all weariness rest. He who goes forward with this fervor, warmth, and interior consolation finds every burden light and sweetness in every penance or trial, however great. This consolation points out and opens up the way we are to follow and points out the way we are to avoid. It does not remain with us always, but it will always accompany us on the way at the times that God designates. All this is for our progress.

But when this consolation is absent the other lesson comes to light. Our ancient enemy sets up all possible obstacles to turn us aside from the way on which we have entered. He makes use of everything to vex us, and everything in the first lesson is reversed. We find ourselves sad without knowing why. We cannot pray with devotion, nor contemplate, nor even speak or hear of the things of God with any interior taste or relish. Not only this, but if he sees that we are weak and much humbled by these harmful thoughts, he goes on to suggest that we are entirely forgotten by God our Lord, and leads us to think that we are quite separated from Him and that all that we have done and all that we desire to do is entirely worthless. He thus endeavors to bring us to a state of general discouragement. We can thus see what causes our fear and weakness: it is a too-prolonged gaze at such times on our miseries. We allow ourselves to be laid low by his misleading suggestions. For this reason it is necessary for us to be aware of our opponent. If we are in consolation, we should abase and humble ourselves and reflect that soon the trial of temptation will come. And when temptation, darkness, or sadness comes upon us, we must go contrary to it without permitting ourselves to pay any attention to the unpleasant impressions caused in us, and hope patiently for the consolation of our Lord, which will cast out all our uneasiness and scatter all the clouds.

It remains for me to speak of how we ought to understand what we think is from our Lord and, understanding it, how we ought to use it for our advantage. For it frequently happens that our Lord moves and urges the soul to this or that activity. He begins by enlightening the soul; that is to say, by speaking interiorly to it without the din of words, lifting it up wholly to His divine love and ourselves to His meaning without any possibility of resistance on our part, even should we wish to resist. This thought of His which we take is of necessity in conformity with the commandments, the precepts of the Church, and obedience to our superiors. It will be full of humility because the same divine Spirit is present in all. But we can frequently be deceived, however, because after such consolation or inspiration, when the soul is still abiding in its joy, the enemy tries under the impetus of this joy to make us innocently add to what we have received from God our Lord. His only purpose is to disturb and confuse us in everything.

At other times he makes us lessen the import of the message we have received and confronts us with obstacles and difficulties, so as to prevent us from carrying out completely what had been made known to us. Right here there is more need of attention than anywhere else. We may often have to control the desire we feel and speak less of the things of God our Lord; at other times we may speak more than the satisfaction or movement we feel prompts us to. We act thus because in this matter we should give more heed to the good of others than to our own desires. When the enemy thus tries to magnify or diminish the communication received, we must proceed for the purpose of helping others, like a man who is crossing a ford. If I find a good footing—that is, some way or hope of profiting the neighbor—I will pass right on. But if the ford is muddied or disturbed and there is danger that scandal may be taken from what I say, I will rein in and seek an occasion more favorable to what I have to say.

We have touched on matter that can hardly be dealt with in a letter, at least without a much longer treatment. Even then there could be matters that could better be felt than put into words, let alone written down in a letter. If it please our Lord, I hope to see you there soon, and then we can come to a clearer understanding of some things. In the meantime, since Castro is close at hand, I think it would be good to communicate with him. No harm can come of it and possibly some good. Since you tell me to write what I think in the Lord, I will say that you are fortunate if you know how to keep what you have.

In closing I beg the most holy Trinity to bestow upon us all plentiful grace to know God's most holy will and perfectly to fulfill it.

Excerpt from *Letters of St. Ignatius of Loyola*,
translated by William J. Young, S.J.,
(Loyola Press, 1959).
Used with permission by Loyola Press,
www.loyolapress.com.

NOTES

1. In the famous exercise on the Two Standards, Christ addresses "His servants and friends" and recommends that they "seek to help all, first by attracting them to the highest spiritual poverty, and should it please the Divine Majesty, and should He deign to choose them for it, even to actual poverty. Secondly, they should lead them to a desire for insults and contempt, for from these springs humility." Louis J. Puhl, S.J., trans., *The Spiritual Exercises of St. Ignatius: Based on Studies in the Language of the Autograph* (Chicago: Loyola University Press, 1951), paragraph 146. Unless otherwise noted, all quotations from the *Spiritual Exercises* will be taken from Puhl's translation and all references will refer to the paragraph number rather than the page number.

2. Ignatius makes this point in a letter to a man who had asked for a copy of the *Spiritual Exercises*: "I am sending you a book of the Exercises that it may be useful to you. . . . The fact is that the power and energy of the Exercises consists in practice and activity, as their very name makes clear; and yet I did not find myself able to refuse your request. However, if possible, the book should be given only after the Exercises have been made." Letter of Ignatius to Alexis Fontana, 8 October 1555, as quoted in David Lonsdale, *Eyes to See, Ears to Hear: An Introduction to Ignatian Spirituality* (London: Darton, Longman and Todd, 2000), p. 126.

3. Jules Toner, *Love and Friendship* (Milwaukee: Marquette University Press, 2003). Although Toner doesn't often apply his analysis of love to the Christian's love of God and God's love of the Christian, we have found it especially illuminating to do so.

4. Jules Toner's description of personal love is helpful here. "For in this mode I apprehend the inconceptualizable, radically lovable personal self, unique and unrepeatable, revealed but never fully revealed in any of its acts or in any of the traits which constitute his or her personality. . . .

Knowledge of others in the third mode is possible only by a non-discursive, non-conceptual, direct awareness—direct but, as experience shows, mediated. For we have no direct awareness of personal selves except as they show themselves in and through their acts (including words and gestures) and their qualities, which appear in those acts. While personal selves reveal themselves in and through their acts and qualities, unique persons exceed any and all of their acts and actual qualities . . ." (Toner, *Love and Friendship*, pp. 207-8).

Toner goes on to say, "The intuition by which the beloved's personal self is apprehended is mysterious, never fully explainable" (p. 208). When this "intuition" occurs, "the reality of the personal self is revealed . . . in and through the person's words, acts, and gestures. However, it is not revealed only or mainly in and through the meaning of the words spoken or the kind of acts performed or the kind of personality traits shown in them; it is revealed also and even more so by the indescribable way in which the words are spoken or the style in which the deeds are done. It can be the tone of voice in which the words are said, the fleeting compassionate smile or glance, the gracious gesture, the gloriously innocent laughter, the delicate tender touch which more than anything else carries the revelation. By reason of such an encounter one who would otherwise be to me a kind person, wise, gentle, brave, witty and so on, is now also an inexpressible lovable mystery" (p. 209).

5. For example, St. Gregory Nazianzen writes of his friendship with St. Basil: "When, in the course of time we acknowledged our friendship and recognized that our ambition was a life of true wisdom, we became everything to each other: we shared the same lodging, the same table, the same desires, the same goal. Our love for each other grew daily warmer and deeper. The same hope inspired us: the pursuit of learning. This is an ambition especially subject to envy. Yet between us there was no envy. On the contrary we made capital out of our rivalry. Our rivalry consisted, not in seeking the first place for oneself but in yielding it to the other, for we each looked on the other's success as his own. We seemed to be two bodies with a single spirit. Though we cannot believe those who claim that 'everything is contained in everything,' yet you must believe that in our case each of us was in the other and with the other." Gregory Nazianzen,

Liturgy of the Hours: According to the Roman Rite I, Advent Season-Christmas Season, trans. The International Commission on English in the Liturgy (New York: Catholic Book Publishing Co., 1975), p. 286.

6. As translated by H. Clay Trumbull in his *Friendship the Master-Passion; or The Nature and History of Friendship, and its Place as a Force in the World* (Philadelphia: John D. Wattles & Co., 1891), pp. 94-95.

7. 2 Corinthians 5:17 (RSV). Unless otherwise noted, all future scriptural references will be to this translation.

8. Cyril of Alexandria, *The Liturgy of the Hours: According to the Roman Rite II, Lenten Season-Easter Season*, trans. International Commission on English in the Liturgy (New York: Catholic Book Publishing Co., 1976), p. 891.

9. Basil the Great, *Liturgy of the Hours II*, p. 976.

10. Leo the Great, *Liturgy of the Hours II*, p. 660.

11. Cyril of Alexandria, *Liturgy of the Hours II*, p. 834.

12. Ignatius Iparraguirre, S.J., *How to Give a Retreat. Practical Notes*, trans. Angelo Benedetti, S.J. (Westminster, MD: Newman Press, 1959), p. 65. Iparraguirre also wrote *A Key to the Study of the Spiritual Exercises*, trans. J. Chianese, S.J., (Bombay: St. Paul Publications, 1959). This work is the best we've found on the Spiritual Exercises. Iparraguirre is a lifelong student of the history of the Spiritual Exercises. He compiled early (pre-1600) Jesuit manuscripts (called "directories") about how to give the Spiritual Exercises and wrote a history about how the early Jesuits gave them.

13. Elder Mullan, S.J., *The Spiritual Exercises of Saint Ignatius of Loyola: Translated from the Autograph* (New York: P.J. Kennedy & Sons, 1914), p. 15, paragraph 16. Mullan's translation does not use the now standard paragraph numbers present in Puhl's translation. All further references to this book will employ the translator's name and the now standard paragraph number.

14. Unfortunately, Iparraguirre drifts dangerously close to this, especially in his *How to Give a Retreat*.

15. Kevin F. Burke, *Pedro Arrupe: Essential Writings* (Maryknoll, NY: Orbis Books, 2004), p. 8.

16. Jules Toner has written a book on decision-making called *Discerning God's Will: Ignatius of Loyola's Teaching on Christian Decision Making* (St. Louis: Institute of Jesuit Sources,

1991). We'll refer to this book on occasion because it contains many helpful remarks about decision-making. However, Toner differs from us in that he often speaks as if decision-making entails discovering what God has in mind for an individual's particular situation.

17. Michael Ivens, S.J., *Understanding the Spiritual Exercises: Text and Commentary, a Handbook for Retreat Directors* (Trowbridge, Wiltshire: Cromwell Press, 1998), paragraph 231. Numbers in subsequent references to this book will be to the translator and paragraph, unless otherwise noted.

18. For His desire to save all men, see the meditation on the Incarnation. Ignatius says to consider "how the Three Divine Persons look down upon the whole expanse or circuit of all the earth, filled with human beings. Since They see that all are going down to hell, They decree in Their eternity that the Second Person should become man to save the human race" (102). For the desire to enlist men in His struggle to save the world, see the meditation on the Kingdom of Christ and the address the Lord makes to the whole world and each person in particular: "It is My will to conquer all the world and all enemies and so to enter into the glory of My Father; therefore, whoever would like to come with Me is to labor with Me, that following me in the pain, he may also follow Me in the glory" (95, Mullan).

19. Toner, *Love and Friendship*, p. 255.

20. See John 17.

21. See, for example, Juan de Polanco, S.J., *Year by Year with the Early Jesuits: Selections from the Chronicon of Juan de Polanco, S.J.*, trans. John Patrick Donnelly, S.J. (St. Louis: The Institute of Jesuit Sources, 2004).

22. Ignatius seems to have learned the practice of general confession from the Benedictine Abbot of Montserrat. After Ignatius's conversion, he set out from Loyola to the monastery of Montserrat, where he laid down his sword and dagger and took up a pilgrim's staff and beggar's clothes. Early in the century Abbot Garcia Jiménez de Cisneros had reformed the monastery and introduced the practice of having novices spend 10 or more days preparing for a general confession of all their sins. At that time this practice seems to have been little known or practiced, though it may have come about as the result of the Devotio Moderna. (See John W.

O'Malley, *The First Jesuits* (Cambridge, Mass.: Harvard University Press, 1993), p. 138.) This was a religious movement that emphasized the development of one's personal relationship with God. Ignatius, under the direction of the master of novices, followed a modified version of de Cisneros's practice by taking three days to write down his sins before making a similar confession.

23. "From a letter of Juan de Polanco, by commission of St. Ignatius, to Father Gaspar Loarte, June 5, 1556," in Martin E. Palmer, S.J., trans., *On Giving the Spiritual Exercises. The Early Jesuit Manuscript Directories and the Official Directory of 1599* (St. Louis: The Institute of Jesuit Sources, 1996), p. 25. Ignatius seems to have waited until people were ripe for making the Exercises. Xavier knew Ignatius for four years before making the Exercises and Pierre Favre knew Ignatius for about five years before making them. Ignatius by no means, however, always waited four or five years before giving the Exercises to someone.

24. "Directory Dictated to Father Juan Alfonso de Vitoria," in Palmer, *On Giving*, pp. 15-16.

25. Ibid.

26. "Second Directory of Father Diego Miró" in Palmer, *On Giving*, p. 177.

27. See ibid.; "Directory of Father Gil González Dávila," in Palmer, *On Giving*, p. 235; and "Directory of Father Juan Alfonso de Polanco," p. 135.

28. "Directory Dictated to Father Juan Alfonso de Vitoria," in Palmer, *On Giving*, p. 16.

29. Ibid., p. 22.

30. See "Reminders of St. Ignatius," p. 11, and "Second Directory of St. Ignatius," p. 12, in Palmer, *On Giving*; see also 72, Puhl.

31. When writing or talking about the Exercises, Ignatius might have said a lot of things, but he usually made sure to talk about food on the 30-day retreat. See, for example, "Reminders of St. Ignatius," "Second Directory of St. Ignatius," and "Directory Dictated to Juan Alfonso de Vitoria," all in Palmer, *On Giving*, pp. 11, 14 and 17. He says that as the table is being cleared from the noonday meal (dinner) the exercitant should be asked what he wants for the evening meal (supper) and when the table is being cleared from

supper the exercitant should be asked what he wants for dinner the next day. He should be given exactly what he asks for, whether it is a lot or very little.

32. "Counsels of Father Duarte Pereyra," in Palmer, *On Giving*, p. 55.

33. "Directory Dictated to Father Juan Alfonso de Vitoria," in Palmer, *On Giving*, p. 19.

34. George E. Ganss, S.J., Introduction to *The Constitutions of the Society of Jesus* (St. Louis: Institute of Jesuit Sources, 1970), p. 8.

35. Toner, *Discerning God's Will*, p. 17.

36. George Stormont, *Smith Wigglesworth, A Man Who Walked with God* (Tulsa, OK: Harrison House, 1989), p. 33.

37. "Directory Dictated to Juan Alfonso de Vitoria," in Palmer, *On Giving*, p. 21.

38. "Counsels of Father Duarte Pereyra," in Palmer, *On Giving*, p. 51.

39. "Directory of Father Gil González Dávila," in Palmer, *On Giving*, p. 244.

40. Ignatius says something similar in the first annotation: ". . . we call Spiritual Exercises every way of preparing and disposing the soul to rid itself of all inordinate attachments, and, after their removal, of seeking and finding the will of God in the disposition of our life for the salvation of our soul" (1). If the director chooses to begin the retreat with Annotation 1 or 21 and the exercitant is unfamiliar with the concept of inordinate attachments, the director should be aware that he will have to explain the Ignatian concepts of inordinate attachments and indifference. One can talk about indifference without talking about inordinate attachments, but it is more difficult to talk about inordinate attachments without also talking about indifference.

41. Joseph Rickaby, S.J., *The Spiritual Exercises of St. Ignatius of Loyola. Spanish and English With a Continuous Commentary* (London: Burns Oates & Washbourne LTD., 1923), p. 20.

42. *Gaudium et Spes*, 16.

43. Many students of the Exercises spend a lot of time discussing the difference between meditation and contemplation and studying each instance of the use of these words in the *Spiritual Exercises*. Ignatius calls the first and

second exercises "meditations," along with the exercises on hell, the Two Standards and the Three Classes of Men. He calls the exercises which center around an event in the life of Christ "contemplations." Generally speaking, one could say that a meditation is a more discursive reflection on revealed truths, while a contemplation is an imaginative participation in the life of the Lord. We are not, however, going to be too rigorous in our uses of these terms and may sometimes refer to exercises that Ignatius calls "contemplations" as "meditations."

44. The Kingdom of Christ and the Contemplation to Attain Love also have only two preludes.

45. In most of the exercises of the Second, Third and Fourth Weeks, the exercitant first calls to mind "the history of the subject I have to contemplate" (102) and then makes a mental representation of the place, followed by a petition for what he wants and desires. We'll discuss this additional prelude when we take up the meditations of the Second, Third and Fourth Weeks.

46. "Directory of Father Juan Alfonso de Polanco," in Palmer, *On Giving*, pp. 117-118.

47. "Notes on Meditation by Father Jerónimo Domènech," in Palmer, *On Giving*, p. 73.

48. "Counsels of Father Duarte Pereyra," in Palmer, *On Giving*, p. 55.

49. "Notes on Meditation by Father Jerónimo Domènech," in Palmer, *On Giving*, p. 74.

50. "Short Directory" in Palmer, *On Giving*, pp. 209-10.

51. Quoted in "*Actamiento*: Ignatian Reverence in History and Contemporary Culture," by Charles E. O'Neill, S.J., in *Studies in the Spirituality of the Jesuits* 8/1 (January, 1976): p. 7.

52. Polanco, *Selections from the Chronicon*, p. 10.

53. Gregory the Great, *Pastoral Care*, trans. Henry Davis, S.J. (New York: Newman Press, 1950) p. 89.

54. "Directory of Father Juan Alfonso de Polanco," in Palmer, *On Giving*, p. 118.

55. Ibid.

56. Toner, *Love and Friendship*, p. 241.

57. Mary Purcell, *The First Jesuit: St. Ignatius Loyola* (Garden City, NY: Image Books, 1956), p. 238.

58. Teresa of Avila, *Interior Castle*, trans. E. Allison Peers (New York: Image Books, 1961), p. 38.

59. "Directory of Father Gil González Dávila," in Palmer, *On Giving*, p. 247.

60. If the exercitant isn't Catholic, some directors simply have him make a twofold colloquy—one to Jesus and one to the Father. Other directors have the exercitant pray first to the Holy Spirit.

61. Ancient Homily on Holy Saturday, *Liturgy of the Hours II*, pp. 496-98.

62. "Directory of Father Antonio Cordeses," in Palmer, *On Giving*, pp. 273-274.

63. Ibid., p. 274.

64. Ignatius refers both to the activities of the "evil spirit" and of the "good spirit." The "evil spirit" refers to Satan or one of his demons. Technically speaking, "the good spirit" refers to an angel. Although Ignatius believed that God dealt directly with exercitants (15) he also believed that angels could mediate God's action. For simplicity's sake, we will simply refer to the action of God and the Enemy.

65. Ignatius to Sister Teresa Rejadell, 18 June 1536, in *Letters of St. Ignatius of Loyola*, ed. and trans. William J. Young, S.J. (Chicago: Loyola University Press, 1959), p. 19. In this letter Ignatius comments on the discernment of spirits. It's so helpful that we include it as an appendix. See also Annotation 9.

66. *St. Ignatius' Own Story: As Told to Luis Gonzalez De Camara*, trans. William J. Young, S.J. (Chicago: Loyola University Press, 1980), paragraph 20. Hereafter, *Autobiography*. All subsequent references will be to the paragraph number.

67. Ignatius to Sister Teresa Rejadell, 18 June 1536, in *Letters*, p. 19.

68. Ibid., p. 21.

69. Ibid.

70. *Autobiography*, 21

71. John Cassian, "Conference of Abbot Daniel: On the Lust of the Flesh and of the Spirit" in *A Select Library of Nicene and Post-Nicene Fathers of the Christian Church* (Grand Rapids: Eerdmans Publishing Company, 1964), Conference IV.2, vol. 11, p. 331.

72. *Autobiography*, 21.

73. Ignatius to Sister Teresa Rejadell, 18 June 1536, in *Letters*, p. 23.

74. In this chapter we are talking about consolations which are encounters with God. Exercitants can also experience consolations which arise out of an encounter with the Enemy. We will discuss consolations caused by the Enemy in Chapter 10.

75. In the first set of rules, when Ignatius describes consolation as an interior movement "aroused in the soul, by which it is inflamed with love of its Creator and Lord, and as a consequence, can love no creature on the face of the earth for its own sake, but only in the Creator of them all" (316), he is describing the results of an experience of personal love for the Lord. The rest of his description applies to experiences of semipersonal love.

76. The term "integral love" is Toner's. He discusses integral love in *Love and Friendship* on pages 195 and 209, making the distinction between the affective act of love and affective feelings of love. "While feelings of love are not essential for love, they are so for what I shall name integral love, the full response of human love" (p. 195).

77. Ignatius to Sister Teresa Rejadell, 18 June 1536, in *Letters*, pp. 21-22.

78. *Autobiography*, 11.

79. "Official Directory of 1599," in Palmer, *On Giving*, p. 302.

80. Ivens points out that "build a nest in a thing not ours," or, as he translates it, "build our nest where we do not belong" means "settle down in and regard as our own, what is God's property, not ours" (p. 223). He notes how the nest image is used in *The Imitation of Christ* (Book 3, Chapter 6), a text Ignatius loved: "'These souls who aspired to build their nests in heaven, became needy and wretched outcasts, in order that, through humiliation and poverty, they might learn not to fly with their own wings but to trust themselves under my wings' (trans. L. Sherley-Price, Penguin Classics, 1952)."

81. Ignatius to Sister Teresa Rejadell, 18 June 1536, in *Letters*, p. 22.

82. "Official Directory of 1599," in Palmer, *On Giving*, p. 302.

83. Ignatius to Sister Teresa Rejadell, 18 June 1536, in *Letters*, p. 22.

84. Some commentators on Ignatius propose using the rules for discernment to get in touch with one's thoughts, affective acts and affective feelings rather than discerning the action of personal spiritual realities in one's life. They do so by arguing that one discerns movements of one's soul, rather than spirits. As far as we can tell, Hervé Coathalem, S.J. introduced this interpretation into the English language literature on the Spiritual Exercises in 1961. Since then it has become quite common. Jules Toner, in *A Commentary on Saint Ignatius' Rules for Discernment of Spirits: A Guide to the Principles and Practice* (St. Louis: The Institute of Jesuit Sources, 1982), tries to distance himself from this interpretation, but in our opinion ultimately falls prey to it by arguing that it is possible to "leave Satan and demons out of the picture when discerning spirits" (35). Unfortunately, his discussion of the rules radically depersonalizes them and ultimately turns them into an ethical manual.

85. Ganss, Introduction to *The Constitutions of the Society of Jesus*, pp. 20-21.

86. Ignatius of Loyola, *The Constitutions of the Society of Jesus*, trans. George E. Ganss, S.J., (St. Louis: The Institute of Jesuit Sources, 1970), pp. 107-108.

87. Ignatius to Peter Contarini, 2 December 1538, in *Letters*, p. 37.

88. The manuscript called the "Autograph" is not actually in Ignatius's hand. It does, however, have a fair number of corrections in his hand and was used by him in giving the Exercises.

89. See *The Rule of St. Benedict*, Chapter 5, and Bernard of Clairvaux, "The Twelve Degrees of Humility and Pride."

90. See Iparraguirre, *A Key to the Study*, p. 82.

91. *Ignatius of Loyola: The Spiritual Exercises and Selected Works*, ed. George E. Ganss, S.J. (New York: Paulist Press, 1991), p. 408.

92. "Official Directory of 1599," in Palmer, *On Giving*, pp. 320-21.

93. See, for example, ibid., p. 321.

94. "The Spiritual Exercises: Text and Commentary," in *The Spiritual Exercises of Saint Ignatius of Loyola*, trans. W.H. Longridge, (London: A.R. Mowbray & Co., 1919), p. 2.

95. Iparraguirre, *A Key to the Study*, p. 71.

96. Jules Toner could say that the exercitant is asking for the grace to experience the Lord's life "as mine in him." The precision with which he describes the experience of friendship is a big help in describing the grace of the Third Week. The sorrow the exercitant experiences isn't the sorrow of an outsider or a spectator. One might be tempted to say that the exercitant is asking for the grace to experience the Lord's life "as mine," but it turns out that this isn't precise enough. If he is just experiencing the Lord's life "as mine," he could be experiencing a relationship of empathy, where he's projecting himself into him. Or it could even be a relationship of domination, where he's making him an extension of himself. It's important that he not only experience his life "as mine" but that he also experience his life "as his" or "as my life in him." However, if he is just experiencing his life as his, without any experience of "my life in him," it's probably a relationship of sympathy. In that case he has little or no experience of his own in the relationship. It can sometimes be as if he is invisible or nonexistent. In Toner's precise language, the exercitant is asking for and then experiencing the Lord's life "as my life in him." See *Love and Friendship*, p. 246.

97. Ivens says this is "a suffering which is ours but in and through which Christ makes us sharers in his own," *Understanding the Spiritual Exercises*, p. 147.

98. Richard B. Hays's translation. See his *The Faith of Jesus Christ: The Narrative Substructure of Galatians 3:1-4:11* (Grand Rapids, MI: Eerdmans, 2002).

99. At the Jordan Jesus invites them to come and see where he is staying. Next we see them at Capernaum. They still own fishing boats and Jesus asks to use their possessions. For example, he preaches from their boat. Finally he calls them to leave everything and follow him (275).

100. For example, in the supper at Bethany, Ignatius references Matthew 26, but the detail about Lazarus being there comes from John 12, which isn't mentioned. It looks like Ignatius adds the detail about Lazarus to the essentially

Matthean story of the anointing at Bethany because the exercitant has just finished meditating on the raising of Lazarus.

101. "Official Directory of 1599," in Palmer, *On Giving*, pp. 302-03.

102. Ignatius to Sister Teresa Rejadell, 18 June 1536, in *Letters*, June 18, 1536, p. 22.

103. Ivens, *Understanding*, p. 230.

104. Ibid.

105. Ignatius to Fathers Salmeron and Broet, September 1541, in *Letters*, pp. 51-52.

106. *Autobiography*, 54-55.

107. Ibid., p. 26.

108. This example is Thomas Green's, taken from *Weeds among the Wheat* (Notre Dame, IN: Ave Maria Press, 1984), p. 131. We use it, but come to a different conclusion than Green does.

109. Ignatius to Sister Teresa Rejadell, 18 June 1536, in *Letters*, pp. 22-23.

110. Some commentators on Ignatius's rules for discernment think that one has to see how a consolation unfolds over time and where it takes a person in order to discern whether it was from God or not. However, such a position makes it impossible to use most consolations as evidence in the process of making a choice. Ignatius thought otherwise. As we'll see in the next chapter, consolations play a key role in Ignatian decision-making.

111. "Directory Dictated to Father Juan Alfonso de Vitoria," in Palmer, *On Giving*, p. 20.

112. See, for example, Matthew 5:3, 40, 42; 6:2-4, 12, 19-34; 13:22, 44-46; 18:23-35; 19:16-30; 20:1-16; 22:15-22; 25:14-30; Mark 12:41-44; Luke 3:10-14; 12:13-21; 14:12-24; 16:1-13; 19:1-10. One can also look at Acts 4:32-37; 8:14-24; Romans 13:7; 2 Corinthians 8:1-9:15; 1 Timothy 6:17 and James 1:9-11, 2:1-9; 5:1-6.

113. See M.F. Sparrow, "Toward a Theology of Ordinary Life," *Pro Ecclesia. A Journal of Catholic and Evangelical Theology*, 2000, 9/1: 57-72.

114. Ivens, *Understanding*, p. 144.

115. In these directions, Ignatius speaks of "reforming and amending" one's life in contradistinction to "election."

Likewise, in the early directories, "reforming and amending" one's life is not always called an election (see, for example, "The Official Directory of 1599," in Palmer, *On Giving*, p. 340). Sometimes, though, the early Jesuits spoke of making an election on reforming one's life (see, for example, "Second Directory of Father Diego Miró," in Palmer, *On Giving*, p. 177).

116. "The Official Directory of 1599," in Palmer, *On Giving*, p. 319.

117. Instead of "benefices," we usually substitute "career."

118. An exercitant may decide to advise someone to do something, but what the person actually does is up to that person.

119. As translated by Toner in *Discerning God's Will*, p. 48. See also Ignatius to Father Francis Borgia, 5 June 1552, in *Letters*, pp. 257-58.

120. Toner, *Discerning God's Will*, p. 49.

121. Ibid.

122. "The Official Directory of 1599," in Palmer, *On Giving*, p. 326.

123. Gilles Cusson, *Biblical Theology and the Spiritual Exercises* (St. Louis: The Institute of Jesuit Sources, 1988), pp. 264-5.

124. *The Spiritual Exercises of Saint Ignatius*, trans. Pierre Wolff (Liguori, MO: Triumph, 1997), p. 168.

125. "Autograph Directory of St. Ignatius," in Palmer, *On Giving*, pp. 9-10.

126. "Directory of Father Juan Alfonso de Polanco," in Palmer, *On Giving*, p. 136. "The Philosopher" is Aristotle.

127. "Official Directory of 1599," in Palmer, *On Giving*, p. 319.

128. Ibid., p. 336.

129. *Autobiography*, 27.

130. Ibid.

131. Toner, *Love and Friendship*, p. 195.

132. *Inigo: Discernment Log-Book: The Spiritual Diary of Saint Ignatius of Loyola*, ed. and trans. Joseph A. Munitiz, S.J. (Inigo Enterprises, London, 1987). All subsequent references will be to the paragraph number.

133. "Autograph Directory of St. Ignatius," in Palmer, *On Giving*, p. 9.

134. There is no paragraph number because this is from the crossed-out paragraph.

135. Munitiz, the editor, notes, "Words in pointed brackets are supplied to clarify the sense," *Discernment Log-Book*, p. 25.

136. Ignatius to Father Francis Borgia, 5 June 1552, in *Letters*, p. 257.

137. *Discernment Log-Book*, 152.

138. Toner, *Love and Friendship*, p. 235.

139. Ibid., p. 255.

140. We've taken this phrase from Toner's description of a communion of personal love in *Love and Friendship* (p. 215). As we've noted before, Toner's descriptions of love and friendship illumine not only the love that men have for one another but also the love between God and man.

141. See Toner, *Love and Friendship*, pp. 113-17.

142. Iparraguirre, *A Key*, p. 104.

143. See Toner, *Love and Friendship*, p. 246.

INDEX

Affective response, 15, 18, 32, 94, 95, 96, 102, 103, 104, 125, 131, 132, 136, 138, 141, 142, 144, 147, 150, 166, 204, 208, 209, 212, 221, 222, 243, 274, 275, 281, 299, 305, 309, 315, 327, 328

Afterglow, 235, 236, 287

Agere contra, 27, 28, 29, 30, 31, 53, 70, 167, 190, 204, 207, 294

Amend and Reform (Puhl 189), 45, 249

Anima Christi prayer, 126

Annotations, 8, 70, 114, 324, 326

Application of the senses, 50, 51, 52, 55, 56, 57, 58, 202, 204, 272

Arrupe, Pedro, 32, 321

Borgia, Francis, 259, 300, 331, 332

Brébeuf, Jean de, 39

Cassian, John, 139, 326

Catechism of the Catholic Church, 20, 113, 120

Choose to intend, 257, 258, 259, 260, 284

Command and obey model, 35

Confirmation, 276, 282, 293, 296, 297

Confusion, 49, 60, 93, 111, 116, 117, 118

Consolations, 52, 62, 69, 115, 125, 128, 132, 133, 137, 140, 141, 142, 143, 144, 145, 146, 148, 149, 150, 151, 155, 201, 205, 207, 221, 222, 223, 225, 226, 227, 231, 232, 233, 234, 235, 236, 237, 282, 284, 285, 286, 287, 288, 290, 291, 294, 296, 297, 314, 316, 317, 327, 330

Contemplation to Attain the Love of God (Puhl 230), 37

Decision-making. (See also Election.), 23, 30, 31, 32, 33, 34, 35, 36, 38, 39, 54, 58, 87, 170, 174, 243, 244, 245, 246, 249, 250, 251, 253, 254, 256, 260, 261, 262, 269, 271, 272, 273, 275, 276, 281, 287, 289, 290, 291, 297, 301, 302, 303, 321, 330

Decisions, command-and-obey model, 35, 36

Decisions, first-time (Puhl 175), 272, 273, 274, 284, 285

Decisions, second-time (Puhl 176), 274, 275, 283, 284, 285, 286, 288, 289, 290, 291, 293, 297, 302, 303

Decisions, third-time (Puhl 177), 274, 275, 276, 277, 278, 279, 280, 281, 288, 297, 301

Desolation, 52, 56, 69, 70, 115, 128, 139, 146, 147, 148, 149, 150, 151, 155, 156, 157, 201, 222, 237, 286, 288, 293, 296

Detachment. (See also Indifference.), 26, 58, 81, 167, 174, 245, 265

Director, role of, 46, 68

Discernment, 5, 46, 59, 109, 110, 138, 140, 141, 147, 152, 155, 158, 197, 215, 222, 227, 237, 238, 239, 251, 256, 257, 258, 274, 283, 284, 290, 294, 297, 299, 326, 328, 331, 332

Discernment logbook, 290, 291, 292, 293, 295, 297

Disordered love. (See also Inordinate attachments.), 75, 79, 80, 81, 104, 127, 190

Election, command-and-obey model, 35

333

Election, introduction, 244, 272
Election, when to make, 257
Election. (See also Decision-making.), 23, 32, 36, 37, 45, 54, 55, 75, 81, 196, 251, 254, 256, 260, 261, 262, 266, 268, 270, 271, 272, 276, 277, 280, 282, 283, 290, 291, 293, 294, 296, 300, 301, 330
Enemy, 46, 59, 65, 68, 69, 70, 89, 105, 115, 125, 132, 134, 137, 138, 140, 145, 146, 147, 148, 149, 150, 152, 153, 154, 156, 157, 162, 170, 171, 175, 178, 193, 215, 222, 223, 226, 227, 229, 231, 232, 233, 234, 235, 236, 237, 238, 239, 246, 269, 271, 283, 284, 286, 287, 288, 289, 290, 291, 293, 294, 295, 296, 297, 299, 314, 315, 316, 317, 318, 326, 327
Examination of conscience, 41, 47, 62, 83, 84, 86, 123
False humility, 267, 309, 314, 316
Fasting, 62
First Prelude, 90, 91, 186, 199, 200, 214
First Week, schedule, 47
Fourth Meditation (Puhl 64), 49, 52, 128
Fourth Week, schedule, 57
Friendship, 11, 12, 17, 18, 19, 20, 21, 24, 26, 30, 32, 36, 37, 39, 97, 100, 107, 108, 120, 164, 166, 254, 256, 266, 302, 303, 304, 311, 319, 320, 321, 322, 325, 327, 329, 331, 332
Friendship with God, 12, 17, 19, 20, 21, 24, 26, 30, 100, 107, 120, 256, 311
Goës, Benedict, 39
Grace of the meditation, 93, 102, 201, 206
Gregory the Great, 104, 320, 325
Heart, 11, 32, 67, 91, 94, 95, 96, 97, 102, 103, 105, 106, 107, 109, 111, 113, 118, 119, 120, 122, 124, 125, 127, 128, 135, 139, 140, 141, 142, 147, 155, 166, 193, 201, 204, 205, 207, 209, 219, 224, 229, 232, 259, 264, 265, 278, 282, 283, 287, 288, 297, 301, 302, 306, 307, 312
Hell (Puhl 65), 48, 49, 90, 113, 118, 131, 202
Humiliation, 31, 327
Humility, 11, 17, 29, 33, 54, 58, 60, 98, 114, 165, 172, 175, 179, 180, 181, 182, 183, 185, 222, 256, 261, 262, 267, 269, 309, 314, 315, 316, 317, 319, 328
Humility, three kinds of (See also Love, three kinds of.), 11, 262, 267
Incarnation (Puhl 101), 50, 61, 112, 118, 170, 198, 202, 204, 226, 244, 249, 322
Indifference, 25, 27, 28, 55, 74, 75, 77, 79, 244, 263, 271, 278, 324
Inordinate attachments, 26, 27, 28, 30, 31, 34, 65, 75, 76, 79, 80, 135, 162, 163, 170, 185, 187, 188, 190, 204, 221, 244, 245, 260, 261, 262, 264, 268, 269, 271, 278, 280, 286, 290, 294, 301, 304, 311, 324
Insults and contempt, 7, 17, 29, 30, 31, 172, 173, 178, 180, 181, 183, 184, 208, 245, 247, 256, 265, 319
Intellect. (See also Understanding.), 52, 93, 95, 96, 98, 106, 125, 146, 205, 207, 310
Ivens, S.J., Michael, 45, 126, 128, 162, 243, 253, 255, 260, 322, 327, 329, 330
Laynez, 98
Lectio divina, 93
Love, carnal, 166
Love, implemental, 12, 13, 14, 15, 17, 19, 109, 144, 196, 243, 262

Love, personal, 12, 14, 15, 16, 17, 19, 37, 73, 103, 141, 144, 165, 196, 212, 223, 225, 235, 237, 243, 262, 264, 269, 302, 311, 319, 327, 332
Love, semipersonal, 12, 14, 15, 17, 19, 141, 143, 144, 196, 203, 223, 225, 237, 243, 262, 264, 301, 327
Love, three kinds of. (See also Humility, three kinds of.), 11, 262, 267
Matta, Father, 181
Meditation
  on the Conversion of Mary Magdalene (Puhl 282), 198
  on the Kingdom of Christ (Puhl 91), 31, 49, 50, 58, 161, 193, 246, 266, 322, 325
  on the Last Supper (Puhl 190, 289), 199
  on the Nativity (Puhl 110), 50, 61, 98, 198, 199, 200, 217
  on the Temptation of Christ (Puhl 274), 51, 198
  on the Three Classes of Men (Puhl 149), 51, 53, 58, 170, 184, 185, 190, 193, 204, 244, 245, 246, 325
  on the Three Kinds of Love (Puhl 165), 266, 267, 269
  on the Two Standards (Puhl 136), 29, 40, 50, 53, 58, 152, 170, 182, 183, 184, 190, 193, 204, 207, 244, 245, 246, 260, 262, 266, 319, 325
Memory, 93, 94, 96, 106, 118, 121, 122, 128, 130, 151, 200, 306, 307
Money, 24, 26, 45, 72, 75, 76, 77, 79, 126, 142, 157, 170, 175, 176, 177, 178, 179, 181, 184, 186, 187, 188, 189, 190, 232, 233, 247, 248, 249, 250, 251, 252, 255, 256, 258, 276, 307
Montoya, Antonio Ruiz de, 39, 75

Normal Christian life, 248, 249, 250, 255, 256
Obedience, 11, 35, 44, 45, 50, 53, 77, 119, 163, 182, 184, 198, 262, 317
Penance, 62, 102, 107, 135, 137, 142, 143, 150, 211, 256, 275, 290, 314, 316
Petitions, 125, 207
Polanco, S.J., Juan de, 271, 322, 323, 325, 331
Poverty, actual, 7, 29, 45, 53, 167, 172, 174, 179, 184, 185, 188, 190, 248, 249, 250, 256, 266, 286, 287, 288, 319
Poverty, chastity and obedience, 44, 45, 77
Poverty, insults and contempt, 29, 30, 58, 165, 172, 173, 174, 178, 181, 183, 184, 245, 265
Poverty, spiritual, 7, 29, 53, 167, 172, 174, 179, 184, 190, 266, 319
Preludes, description, 90
Preparatory Prayer, 90, 93, 99, 116, 122, 130, 161, 199, 201, 209, 305
Principle and Foundation (Puhl 23), 11, 41, 47, 71, 72, 73, 74, 75, 77, 78, 79, 81, 86, 89, 90, 98, 99, 111, 123, 126, 169, 174, 199, 254, 255, 256, 264, 265, 267, 269, 275, 288, 305
Reading, 7, 61, 78, 93, 101, 131, 137, 139, 199, 200, 203, 226, 239, 289, 291, 313
Reform life (Puhl 189). (See also Amend and Reform.), 45, 54, 249, 250
Rejadell, Sister Teresa, 4, 5, 137, 140, 142, 146, 326, 327, 328, 330
Reverence, acts of, 60, 98
Satan. (See also Enemy.), 29, 118, 140, 152, 155, 156, 172, 175, 177, 178, 179, 180, 204, 222,

225, 226, 227, 229, 231, 236, 237, 245, 246, 283, 286, 287, 304, 326, 328
Scripture reading, 93, 119, 200, 217, 218, 219
Scruples, 85, 222
Second Week, schedule, 50
Self-abnegation, 18, 80, 168
Senses, application of, 50, 51, 52, 55, 56, 57, 58, 202, 204, 272
Service, 11, 25, 28, 30, 53, 72, 73, 78, 90, 99, 124, 126, 129, 135, 143, 150, 156, 166, 167, 169, 189, 190, 228, 237, 252, 253, 255, 269, 275, 280, 289, 305, 313, 314, 315
Shame and confusion, 49, 60, 93, 111, 116, 117, 118
Silence, 67, 71, 98, 135
Sorrow, 49, 56, 59, 60, 61, 83, 91, 95, 102, 107, 111, 115, 122, 124, 131, 133, 135, 161, 196, 209, 210, 211, 212, 213, 224, 243, 304, 306, 329
Spiritual Exercises, 30-day retreat, 8, 40, 42, 46, 47, 49, 58, 91, 193, 207, 218, 323
Spiritual poverty, 7, 29, 53, 167, 172, 174, 179, 184, 190, 266, 319
State in life decision, 44
Take, Lord, and Receive prayer, 306
Taylor, Hudson, 31, 45
Third Week, schedule, 55
Threefold colloquy, 54, 58, 127, 128, 172, 184, 190, 211, 246, 260, 262, 266
Toner, Jules, 11, 17, 319, 320, 321, 322, 324, 325, 327, 328, 329, 331, 332
Understanding, 8, 23, 46, 69, 93, 94, 95, 105, 115, 118, 121, 125, 128, 130, 145, 175, 180, 183, 201, 205, 207, 225, 254, 274, 283, 299, 306, 307, 316, 318, 322, 329, 330
Union with God, 11, 116, 254, 261, 303
Unruly desires. (See also Inordinate attachments.), 75, 79, 80, 81, 104, 127, 136
Vitoria, Juan Alfonso de, 43, 48, 323, 324, 330
Wandering thoughts, 101, 104
Way of perfection, 44
Way of the Commandments, 44, 45
Way of the counsels. (See also Poverty, chastity and obedience.), 44, 45, 53
Wigglesworth, Smith, 324
Will, 11, 25, 35, 36, 37, 59, 70, 93, 94, 95, 125, 134, 136, 152, 186, 189, 207, 221, 222, 248, 272, 273, 284, 302, 310, 311, 312, 313, 324
Xavier, Francis, 31, 39, 323

Printed in Great Britain
by Amazon